Knowledge as a Feeling

Knowledge as a Feeling

How Neuroscience and Psychology Impact Human Information Behavior

Troy A. Swanson

ROWMAN & LITTLEFIELD
Lanham • Boulder • New York • London

Published by Rowman & Littlefield
An imprint of The Rowman & Littlefield Publishing Group, Inc.
4501 Forbes Boulevard, Suite 200, Lanham, Maryland 20706
www.rowman.com

86-90 Paul Street, London EC2A 4NE

British Library Cataloguing in Publication Information Available

Library of Congress Cataloging-in-Publication Data Available

ISBN 978-1-5381-7892-8 (cloth)

ISBN 978-1-5381-7893-5 (electronic)

Dedication

For my parents, who taught me the love of learning and the value of belief.

Contents

Foreword

Troy is a teaching librarian (as well as a scholar). He faces the same struggles and questions that all of us experience as we stand in front of a classroom full of students getting ready to start their research projects. He feels the same curiosity and perhaps frustration when attempting to teach seemingly straightforward lessons about source evaluation or topic development or citation or any number of information literacy topics. And yet, deep down, we know that it's not really straightforward, because when asked to explain something like source evaluation with a simple set of rules, we cannot. Our field hasn't stood still, it has been growing and learning: critical information literacy, algorithms and artificial intelligence, the ACRL Framework, Project Information Literacy, and so on. But somehow, I still don't feel quite equipped to meet the current moment as a teaching librarian. Why?

Information has moved out of the library into the wild, and the ground is still shifting. To adapt a Neil Gaiman quote, looking for information used to be like finding a specific plant in the desert, with a guide, but now it's like finding a plant in the jungle, by yourself. Even with our best efforts, many of our beautiful, brilliant students still manage to dredge up the weirdest, mustiest sources imaginable. (I have a personal list of favorites that I've gathered directly from students over the years.) Our students are not stupid or lazy, I *know* they are smart and creative and curious. And yet they still drag the roadkill of the interwebs onto their bibliographies, poorly cited because who can cite something with no actual bibliographic information? And even if many of them manage to finish the traditional research paper with an adequate grade and adequate sources gleaned from the library website, what information literacy skills and understandings are they taking with them to other parts of their lives? Is their curiosity satisfied or stifled? Are they transformed by learning? As I chat with them during class and they make me laugh, I have to wonder—do I really know anything about information literacy at all? Is information literacy even a thing?

I've been a teaching librarian in academic libraries for almost eighteen years, from my first post-library-school job until today. In that time, I've seen the development and eventual dominance of search engines for information retrieval, the growth of the social media complex for online socializing and entertainment, and the beginnings of everyday artificial intelligence (AI). Most of us carry around mini-computers in our pockets, little distraction machines that rob us of our attention and diminish our ability to focus or even read deeply. In this information environment, we've also been recently confronted with a wave of disinformation, misinformation, fake news, and straight-up lies. Each new wave of technological advancement (or devolution) has permanently altered the information systems that we use to retrieve, store, and manipulate information—that we and our students use to *learn*. The information universe is messy and complex and annoyingly dynamic. We've been bought and sold, our privacy violated and our relationships altered, but have we changed along with these systems?

From the perspective of library and information science, we might first ask questions about the role of social media platforms in the spread of misinformation or the potential for AI to snowball the creation and dissemination of misinformation or how organizing systems replicate societal biases and inequities—topics that are fascinating and troubling. But from the perspective of a teacher, I'm curious about the individual humans, my students, tasked with making decisions about that information. What about the ordinary information tasks students face all the time? Like whether or how much to believe that Instagram influencer? Or which of these websites will my professor not hate? Or, and perhaps most importantly, should I believe this information?

Fortunately for all of us, Troy decided he would get into it on a deeper level. *It* being the basis for it all—the underlying questions. How do our minds actually work? How do we reason? What is knowledge? What is information? Why and how do we trust this but not that? To develop this book, he spent several years reading and thinking about the literature from neuroscience, psychology, philosophy, and more, while also revisiting the classics of information science, along with recent trends and theories in information literacy. Reading this book was mind-blowing. More than anything, it raised a whole new set of questions for me about what we teach and how we teach it. It reframed my current understandings, which tend to center around information literacy threshold concepts (that I have pieced together into my own personal Frankenstein's info-lit-monster). Troy has written a book that opens up information literacy anew: fresh questions and insights, a new frame for the ACRL Framework, potential avenues for the long-sought theoretical basis, and, yes, practical considerations for information literacy teachers. Go ahead, get started—you won't regret it.

Lori Townsend (Shoshone-Paiute)
Associate Professor and Learning Services Coordinator
University of New Mexico University Libraries

Acknowledgments

As with any way that we know the world, this book has been a group effort over many years. I want to acknowledge and thank all of those who have helped me along the way.

I am deeply grateful to Lori Townsend for inviting me to speak at the University of New Mexico Libraries in 2017 and for contributing the foreword to this book. Her work on threshold concepts has been an inspiration, and I am thankful for her guidance and friendship. She is truly one of the most brilliant people I know.

I would also like to thank Margy MacMillan for her invaluable feedback on the initial draft of this book. Her expertise and clarity of thought made this text stronger, and I am grateful for her input. I am also thankful to Tish Hayes for her review of the chapters on power structures and for being such a wonderful office neighbor and friend. I have made a career by stealing Tish's intelligence and insights any chance I get. I am also grateful to Merinda Hensley for her time reviewing this manuscript. Her kind words were most helpful when I wasn't so sure how this thing was going.

I would like to extend my thanks to the many faculty members who have partnered with me in the classroom over the past two decades, including Tom Dow, Krista Appelquist, Jason Dockter, Laura Lauzen-Collins, Jeremy Shermak, Panshula Ganeshan, and many others. Their trust and partnership over the years has meant so much.

Finally, I would like to express my appreciation to my family and friends for their love and support throughout the writing process. Thank you to my wife, Kim, and our children, Skylar, Parker, and Lainey, for putting up me working on this book over breaks, in parking lots at swim practices, and in between races at swim meets. Their encouragement and belief in me have meant the world to me.

Preface

I am writing this book because I cannot find anyone else to do it—and I've tried. Information science and information literacy literatures—and the education literature as well—have a black hole when it comes to understanding how the brain processes information. There are a few writers trying to crack into this area but they are few and far between. We evaluate sources. We organize sources. But after a source enters the brain, we don't seem to really know how to talk about it. In 2015, I coedited with Heather Jagman a collection called *Not Just Where to Click: Teaching Students How to Think About Information*.[1] This collection was well received, and our authors submitted thoughtful and important chapters, but it did not do everything that I had hoped. I could not find an author who could write how the brain actually processes information and how this could inform our work in education, in libraries, and in information management. Recently, I read Laura Saunders and Melissa A. Wong's monumental book *Instruction in Libraries and Information Centers*.[2] Their work is amazing, and I value this text, but they barely even mention what happens to information once it actually enters our eyes (or ears) and becomes part of our lives. Recently, Alison J. Head, Barbara Fister, Steven Geofrey, and Margy MacMillan issued their *Project Information Literacy Retrospective*.[3] For fourteen years, Project Information Literacy has been a guiding light offering empirical research, but in fourteen years, they have never delved deeply into what neuroscientists are telling us. To me, there are still the following unanswered questions:

- How does an information source interface with our worldview so that we can process that information and make meaning?
- How do cognition, feeling, and memory come together when we process information?
- How have evolutionary forces shaped the way that we process information?
- How does identity and the concept of the self shape our use of information?
- How do group connections shape knowing?
- How does knowledge connect with power dynamics found within culture and groups?
- How does neuroscience in psychology delineate between information and knowledge?

For many years, I have picked up texts within information science, librarianship, and education hoping to find answers to these questions, but I have yet to be satisfied. In 2015, I tried to find people who could do this for me but came up short. So, I decided that the only way these questions would find answers is for me to write the book myself. The book that you are reading is my best attempt to pull together answers from across neuroscience, psychology, philosophy, and other domains of knowledge. The one clear answer is that once information enters our mind, it is nothing like storing information on the shelves of a library. Knowledge is not neatly organized in neurons. Knowledge is not built on reason and logic. The thing that we never talk about is that *knowledge is a feeling.*

This book is an argument describing why this is so and how we may shift our views of information seeking, information literacy, and knowledge production. Now, I will leave it to you to judge how successful I am at building this argument. I am sure that I have not quite gotten it right, but I ultimately hope that this book opens up a line of discussion to help librarians and teachers have a broader view for what it means to know.

In a broader sense, this book is an argument about the "post-truth" era in which we find ourselves. Those of us in educational settings may be shocked at the degrees of dis- and misinformation that have infused our politics and our national debates, but I am not so sure that the neuroscientists and psychologists are all that shocked. They get it, and the rest of us need to catch up.

This book is organized in five parts. Part I, The Brain and the Mind, offers a broad understanding of how the mind processes the world around it. Starting with rudimentary anatomy—very rudimentary—this section of the book walks step by step from the roots of memory, how memories form schemas, and how these schemas come together as a mental model for how the world operates. Part I also looks at different ways that the mind processes the world focusing on cognition, affect, emotion, and ultimately delineating conscious and unconscious processing. It ends by looking at the relationship between the mind and the body. This section draws heavily from neuroscience countering some of the basic assumptions about the mind that arise in the information science and education literatures.

After the foundations of the mind are in place, Part II, The Feeling of Knowing, explores how knowing results from our mental networks. It starts with the social nature of knowing and the ways that culture provided an evolutionary advantage for humans. I then look at the theory of mind and how our ability to understand other minds enables many aspects of what we do, especially related to teaching and learning. Part II introduces two important metacognitive areas of psychology, source monitoring and conflict monitoring. The section also looks at heuristics and mental shortcuts along with how rationality and reason function. The section ends by considering social epistemology and standpoint theory as possible areas of philosophy offering perspectives on the feeling of knowing.

In Part III, Patterns of Reality, I review the information science literature that connects to neuroscience and psychology. I consider how we define information and related concepts, such as uncertainty and relevance. This section considers broad ideas, such as information behavior, and information seeking, in terms of what the research in neuroscience and psychology demonstrates. Additionally, this section thinks about information literacy and the perspective from this area of thought. There are many lines of thought that we can advance in new directions and others that we need to hold back and course correct.

Part IV, Kuhlthau, Dervin, Nahl, and Everyday Life Information Seeking, focuses on these specific writers, who have had broad impact within information science. Kuhlthau's Information Search Process redefined how we view searching. Dervin's Sense-Making looks at how we make meaning. It moved our conversation from that of sources to how individuals understand those sources. Nahl's Affective Load may be the information science theory that most aligns with what we are seeing in neuroscience and psychology. Her focus on feeling and how this shapes our actions is a strong foundation for our profession. This section ends with a conversation about other theorists, who have tried to build connections between information, science and neuroscience, and psychology.

Finally, Part V, Metacognition and the Feeling of Knowing, offers a summary of the key themes within this book. It considers how we can recast information seeking and our understanding of knowledge as a profession. This section spends some time considering the Association of College and Research Libraries (ACRL) *Framework for Information Literacy in Higher Education*, which is a particular interest to me, given that I am an instructional librarian.

Notes

1. Troy A. Swanson and Heather Jagman, *Not Just Where to Click: Teaching Students How to Think About Information* (Chicago: Association of College and Research Libraries, American Library Association, 2015).

2. Laura Saunders and Melissa A. Wong, *Instruction in Libraries and Information Centers: An Introduction* (Champaign, IL: Windsor and Downs Press, 2020).

3. Alison J. Head, Barbara Fister, Steven Geofrey, and Margy MacMillan, "The Project Information Literacy Retrospective: Insights from More Than a Decade of Information Literacy Research, 2008–2022," *Project Information Research Institute* (12 October 2022), https://projectinfolit.org/publications/retrospective (13 Jan 2023).

Introduction

We Assume Rationality

When I took my first job teaching information literacy skills to students in 2000, I had to teach lessons on credibility. *Credibility* was the term I would have used then. *Why did we judge one source as credible and another as not?* When I was helping students, it seemed quite clear to me that the sources provided by my library's research databases were much stronger than the sources found on the open web. At that time, most newspapers were just starting to put articles online. Academic publications were hardly accessible online except through research databases. Ebooks were really years away from being manageable. There were no smartphones, no YouTube, no *New York Times* app. Creative Commons and *Wikipedia* were just being started in 2001 but neither would have significant impact for several years. When I would work with students on research, I would see them relying upon web *pages* that were amateurish, of sketchy provenance, and many times clearly biased. To me, the sources from my library provided much stronger authority. It came down to *authority* and *credibility*.

Authority and *credibility*. How do we teach students to evaluate information? Over the following decades, I worked with composition, speech, and social science faculty members to think about this. We used checklists. We discussed *information need*. We looked at author credentials, citations, and publisher reputation. Our checklists felt comprehensive. We wrote outcomes for information literacy, digital literacy, and metaliteracy. But through all of this, one question remained: *why?* Why do you believe one thing, and I believe something else? What is it about your brain that causes you to process information differently from me? Our checklists didn't offer an answer to this. Even when we both use the same checklists, you show up with different sources and different views.

These are the origins of this book. I knew that we could not really teach information literacy skills if we did not know how the brain processed information. And the years that followed made this feel increasingly vital. Through 9/11 truthers, Andrew Wakefield anti-vaxxers, Donald Trump birthers, climate change deniers, Donald Trump January 6th big liars, and COVID-19 anti-vaxxers, I have thought about how we should teach people the skills required to accurately judge information.

Most of the time we assume rationality. In our classrooms and in our libraries, we assume that people make rational decisions. We think that we can give them evidence and credible information and they will calculate all using logic. As an instruction librarian, I often work with first- and second-year college students who are engaging in some of their first college research assignments, mostly papers and speeches. When I am in college classrooms, I see our rationality assumption at work. It is easy for us to assume. If students can just find some "good" articles, read them, and sprinkle on some logic, then they will find the truth. But what I mostly see is students cherry-picking articles to match their preexisting beliefs or students keeping their biases alive by not actively understanding them. It is not uncommon to see faculty members teach critical thinking that does not actually change how students think. Instructors and librarians put in hours and hours of work, but what kind of changes do we see?

Now, don't get me wrong. There are many well-intentioned efforts happening, and I recognize that developing critical thinking is a process that can take years and years, but I often feel that we are floating above the surface of really engaging students. We never really break through. More importantly, I am not sure that most educators—and especially most librarians—understand how we process and interact with new information, whether this information is encountered inside or beyond the classroom. For two decades I have been interested in why people find one source credible while discounting another source. We often teach strategies such as evaluating sources—evaluating author credentials, publication reputation, timeliness of the information, etc.—or reading strategies such as lateral reading—reviewing across other sources to get perspective in the trustworthiness of the original source—but these have not felt like they are enough. They do not engage student belief. They do not actually consider how the human mind processes information. They do not address how we interact with information. Again, the driving assumption seems to be that if students can just get the right sources—*good sources*—logic will take the wheel as if the process is on automatic pilot. But when we interact with an information source something more complex is happening. Screenwriter Charlie Kaufman captured this perfectly in an interview on *Fresh Air*.

> To me, when I relate to a piece of fiction, you know, or a novel or something, it isn't that it makes me step outside myself, although sometimes there are those kinds of books. *But I mean, the things that I really relate to is when I read something that has articulated something that I felt but haven't been able to articulate*. And I find that incredibly moving. And I find an incredible sense of community in that.[1] (italics added)

I know that Kaufman is not a psychologist, but when I heard this the truth of it hit me. He is talking about fiction, but this rings true for all pieces of information: "*when I read something that has articulated something that I felt but haven't been able to articulate*." Here, Kaufman sums up the entire point of this book. I am going to argue that knowledge is a feeling. To know that something is true is a feeling. It is not an act of rationality. I am not saying that rationality does not come into play. But I am saying that rationality is not enough, and if we are to better understand the ways that our students interact with information in our classrooms, then we need to move beyond our assumptions of rationality.

If you have taken the time to start reading this book, I am sure you would not be surprised by the idea that humans are not rational. My guess is that you recognize the erratic ways that we make decisions. You probably recognize this in others and, those of you who are especially reflective, probably recognize it in yourself. How often do we let emotions get in the way of decisions? When do we ignore data and valid information in order to justify a preexisting belief? How many times have we let our desires override our logical decision making?

Additionally, you probably would not be very surprised by the fact that our identities have a strong correlation with the beliefs we carry around with us. To get a stark but visual representation of this, just compare voting patterns, belief in climate change, and vaccination rates. They all line up pretty clearly. Again, I am sure you are not surprised that the political choices we make are indicators of other beliefs we might hold. If you tell me you're a Republican, Democrat, Green, or Libertarian, this is enough information for me to use in making a fair guess on your views on a number of issues from gun regulation to climate change to minimum wage, and so on. Each of us carries our own exceptions to the rules and varying degrees of nuance, but on the whole, our identities and our beliefs about the world are deeply entwined.

Of course, even if we acknowledge that we can be irrational, we think of our stances on most issues as perfectly rational, grounded in evidence and balanced logic. When we think of actual issues, we can back them up. We can offer justifications. Take a second and think about the minimum wage as an example. What are your feelings about the federal minimum wage? Should it go up? Stay the same? Should it be eliminated entirely and let the market decide? There may be a few of you who do not have strong feelings but more than likely, you can list off support for your views. The inability for the minimum wage to keep up with inflation, the need for a living wage, the pressures of business owners to keep up with competitors, cost pressures that impact everybody, the value of work—there are many data points and arguments for and against increasing the minimum wage. If you have ever worked a minimum wage job or managed a team of minimum wage employees, these firsthand experiences probably color your perspectives. The great thing with the minimum wage as an example is that there really is not one "correct" answer. Ultimately, our views on the minimum wage are a judgment, and how do we make this judgment? Do we sit and look at rational arguments and weigh the evidence?

As you think about this, let's get a bit more specific. Over the last decade there has been a great push to make $15 per hour a standard for the minimum wage. Some local and state governments have accepted this and a few have even pushed beyond it.[2] I would like you to make some comparisons in your own mind. What *feels* better for you? Does $7.25 per hour (the current federal minimum wage as of this writing) feel right? What feels better, $7.25 or $12? How does $12 feel when compared to $15? How does $15 feel compared to $17.30 (the minimum wage of Emeryville, California, which is the highest in the United States)? When you compare these numbers, does one feel better than another? Unless one is an economist, most of us do not have a strict process for setting an exact rate, but almost all of us can land on a number that feels right. $7, $10, $12, $15, $17, wherever we are, we land somewhere. Some number makes sense to us, but as we arrive at this number, we do not do so with cold calculations. We utilize a mixture of personal experience, knowledge on the subject, and judgments about how society should operate. We may think of an article we read about how minimum wage drives up (or down) wages across all economic sectors. We may think about what it takes to afford the necessities of life. We may think about what it takes to run a business today. We probably think about how much we earn in our own jobs or jobs we've held in the past. We may picture the people who hold these jobs. (Do you picture adults? Teenagers? People of particular ethnicities? People who are dressed in a particular way?) And, if we're honest with ourselves, we understand that there are probably many unconscious factors driving our feelings. Our own histories—the things that we can't quite put our fingers on—are hidden underneath our decision. Our own biases, our own irrationalities, are at work driving us to an answer that *feels* right. Something is working outside of our awareness. It influences our answers to the minimum wage questions just as it influences our answers for all of the decisions that we make.

Notice that I have used the word "feeling." What *feels right*. When we take a stand on an issue, we are relying on a feeling. We often ask, "what is our *gut feeling*?" as if the answers we seek will come to us directly out of our body. Answers do not arise from logic and rationality. They come from the gut—or at least they do most of the time. After the fact, we can come up with justifications and reasons. When we get into an argument with others, we may pretend that we are perfectly rational, laying out nicely formed arguments, but if we are honest, then we have to admit that things are a bit more complicated than this. In one instance we can admit that we are not always rational but then in the next instance (especially when arguing with others) we are ready to rationalize and justify gut feelings as if we came to them purely through Aristotelian logic, or we had run a methodologically rigorous study.

What is a *gut feeling*? Neurologist Robert Burton notes that we often use the term "gut feeling" but it is often not clear what that means.[3] Clearly, this is related to knowledge and decision making but we do not literally mean that it comes from our guts. This is not the pancreas or intestines making decisions. When we turn to our gut feelings, our thoughts turn inward in some way. It is not emotion or an altered sense of being. This is a feeling that comes to us and seems to be some sort of internal interaction. Our gut feelings emerge from a kind of dialog within ourselves. We look at a problem, consider a solution, and hold an internal deliberation that brings us to some sort of stance. In order to get to the stance, it is as if we have to pause our conscious line of thought. We are not following logic to get there. We are not weighing evidence. This is not a purely rational effort. Our conscious mind pauses and asks a question internally. *How does this feel?* Before we can answer, we have to consult some sort of hidden process that is mostly inaccessible to our conscious selves. Freud called this "unconscious intentionality," in which he saw a significant—but hidden—force driving our mental lives.[4]

Neuropsychologist Mark Solms observes that modern psychology has moved past much of Freud's work, especially most of his specific findings.[5] But after surviving the behaviorists of the early twentieth century, and the "cognitive revolution" of the later twentieth century, twenty-first-century psychology—being propelled by innovations in brain imaging—is coming back around to some of Freud's larger themes: First, the recognition that unconscious intentionality is a driving force in our decisions. Second, we often resist—or find ways to explain away—our unconscious intensions, because we do not want to acknowledge the feelings contained within them. Finally, these unconscious feelings are largely driven by our biology and our very natures. These are the hidden forces that underpin our decision making and seem to be the "guts" in our gut feelings when we look at a problem and just know that our answer *feels* right. Burton calls this the *feeling of knowing*, which is an innate sense of rightness or wrongness highlighting our thoughts.[6] Understanding this feeling of knowing is a central requirement for understanding how we process information.

Often, we assume rationality in our classrooms, in our libraries, and even in our own decision making. In fact, the assumption of rationality is at the heart of Western thought. Neuroscientist Lisa Feldman Barrett calls this the "origin myth" of the Western tradition: namely, rationality is the thing that separates humans from animals. We carry on a continuing myth that humans have a brain with an outer system wrapped around more primitive smaller systems. It is as if our lizard brain is "gift-wrapped" in rational thinking. The evidence does not bear this out. Our minds do not flip-flop between rationality and animal instincts. Our minds construct our world based on our experiences.[7] To study how our brains interact with information is to study these constructions and much more. We must understand not only how our conscious mind interacts with our unconscious mind but even more basic, we must try to understand conscious and unconscious decision making, the subjective nature of studying our own minds, the impossibility of understanding the minds of others, and the limitation of what we can know. These are some of the largest mysteries of Western thought. I am not sure that this book will solve these ancient puzzles, but I hope that this will propel us forward.

I am writing this as a librarian with the assumption that other librarians and educators will be my audience. I am hopeful that other siblings-in-arms may benefit from this text, especially instructors, trainers, curriculum designers, school administrators, and so many others. I have written this in a way that synthesizes the neuroscience and psychology first and then offers implications for library and information science at the end. My attempt here is to pull together ideas in a useful way to advance the discussion around how we know, what drives our information-seeking behaviors, and how we may become more information literate. I believe that the feeling of knowing can help us rethink the foundational theories of our profession. This is a new threshold concept that once we cross it can help us to better serve our students and larger communities.

Information scientist Paul Sturges directly connects information science and neuroscience. He notes that information seeking literature and "information theory" lacks a focus on the brain and what neuroscience knows about the brain. He writes,

> A brain-centered approach to information science requires quite a serious re-examination and rethinking of much of what has been written or typed in information science for more than half a century.[8]

In this reexamination, Sturges notes several areas where information science must catch up to neuroscience: First, the relationship between the conscious and unconscious mind. Second, the acknowledgment that the brain is not a unity, but is a collection of networks that are interrelated and at play around decision making. Finally, he emphasizes that there is too much at work in the mind for consciousness to handle all of it at one time. Sturges's discussion has been a valuable call to action for me in the development of this book. He signaled the direction, and I have tried to follow.

Notes

1. Charlie Kaufman, "Charlie Kaufman On Being—And Directing," *Fresh Air*, October 23, 2008, https://www.npr.org/transcripts/96023004 (13 Jan 2023).

2. Andrew Soergel, "24 U.S. States Will See a Minimum Wage Increase in 2020," *U.S. News—The Civic Report*, January 2020, C16–C19; "State Minimum Wages: Most States Have Raised Their Minimum Wage Above the Federal Level," *Supreme Court Debates* 24, no. 4 (2021): 14–15; Greg Depersio, "The Top 5 US Cities with the Highest Minimum Wage," *Investopedia*, 2022, https://www.investopedia.com/articles/investing/080515/top-5-us-cities-highest-minimum-wage.asp (12 Jan 2023).

3. Robert. A. Burton, *On Being Certain: Believing You Were Right Even When You're Not* (New York: St. Martin's Griffin, 2008).

4. Mark Solms, *The Hidden Spring: A Journey to the Source of Consciousness* (New York: Norton, 2021).

5. Solms, *Hidden Spring*.

6. Burton, *On Being Certain*.

7. Lisa Feldman Barrett, *How Emotions Are Made: The Secret Life of the Brain* (Boston: Mariner Books, 2017).

8. Paul Sturges, "The Brain at the Centre of the Information Universe: Lessons from Popular Neuroscience," *Libellarium* 7, no. 1 (2014): 3–15.

Disclaimers

At the outset I want to offer a few disclaimers with the hope that you will grant me some degree of understanding as we move forward. First, I am a librarian writing about neuroscience, psychology, and philosophy. Delving into outside disciplines is a dangerous game, and I am sure that I have made my fair share of errors and misunderstandings. I have done my best to understand these areas and to fairly represent their ideas. I hope that you grant me forgiveness and understanding where I have screwed up.

Second, for most of this book, I am talking about the *normative brain*, which, in reality, does not exist. There isn't such a thing as an "average brain," but this has been a necessary assumption along the way. As you read, I hope you understand that all brains are different and that no one is standard. Whether we talk about introverts versus extroverts, old versus young, or anxious versus calm, no two brains are identical. Additionally, some brains are more unique than others. This book does not delve into a whole range of neurodiversity including individuals on the autism spectrum, others with ADHD, others still with high levels of empathy, and a whole range of other unique ways that minds can process our world. I acknowledge this shortcoming. I hope that I may be able to explore this diversity in the future.

Third, I need to acknowledge that I also am assuming a healthy brain. Except for a few examples that illustrate important points within the book, I do not discuss damage from physical harm or disease. Managing this range of complexity would have meant that this text would never be complete.

Finally, anyone who has read about the mind understands that different theorists have different names for how the mind works. Processes, parts of the brain, and larger functions are divided up differently by researchers and disciplines. Our naming a thing does not actually make it a thing. The mind is a complicated network of networks. When we try to understand, we give out names. Sometimes this is just semantics and other times it is more than that. This is a wordy way to say that I have made my own decisions about what to emphasize and what to not. I have used the names for processes and parts of the brain that I have found compelling based on the theorists that I have read. When theorists conflict, I had to make choices. As you explore this book and other books, I hope you will do the same as you build your own understanding.

PART I

THE BRAIN AND THE MIND

What is the difference between the brain and the mind? How do neurons come together to form networks carrying out the functions of the body? This section offers answers to these questions as it lays out the basics of memory, schemas, cognition, and other functions that process the world around it. An important aspect of this information processing results from the interaction between conscious and unconscious processing. The feeling of knowing is one of the outcomes of this interaction.

CHAPTER ONE

The Networks in Our Heads

The students in our classrooms and the patrons in our libraries are life support systems for brains. These brains absorb information and make decisions. Before we can move too far in seeing how the brain processes information and understands its world, we must build our own understanding of the brain as an organ in the body. This book is definitely not a book on anatomy, but working through some rough ideas about anatomy is required as a foundational component to the larger ideas that we'll explore.[1] Most importantly, the underlying biology of the brain reveals that our brains are not an information storage mechanism. They are not recording devices capturing the world. The brain is a unique information processing organ that is a part of a physical system with goals and purposes defined by evolutionary history.[2] To put it another way, the brain is . . . mind boggling.

For this book, I am going to be focusing on *the mind* and less on *the brain*. In day-to-day usage, the distinction between mind and brain doesn't carry much meaning, but some psychologists and neuroscientists do make a distinction. The brain is an organ of the body. It is physical. Its operations are biological and deeply connected with the rest of the body, impacted by energy levels, diet, and numerous other factors. The mind arises from the brain, but the mind is not something physical. It is a result, an expression.[3] Studying the mind is akin to studying metabolism, which is a process carried out through interactions between different bodily components. A metabolism is not a physical part of the body but is a process.[4] The mind is not a physical thing but is the result of interactions largely in the brain but also throughout the rest of the body. The brain is the raw capacity of the physical structures, and the mind is the resulting expression of this capacity. In the words of biologist James Zull in his book *From Brain to Mind*,

> This journey from brain to mind depends greatly on experience. True, biology also plays a role. The brain is a biological organ of the body, and its functioning depends on a range of biological processes from the expression of genes to even the diet. But the underlying biological structure—the neurons, the organization, and the multiple other structures—is just a foundation. It is the capacity of the brain to organize and *change itself* through experience that leads to development of the mind. By sensing, recording, and reproducing our experiences, the brain gets the capacity to think, decide, and act. It makes itself into a mind.[5]

Jasanoff emphasizes that anyone studying the brain or the mind should take care to not fall into overly idealizing either one. He calls this trap the "cerebral mystique," where the mind is disconnected from the body or treated as if its complexity is impenetrable to study. Jasanoff emphasizes that this idealization makes the mind into an abstraction and, thus, disconnects findings in neuroscience and psychology from impacting behavior. Scientific findings may make interesting reading, but they rarely apply in daily life. He writes,

> For the most part, the function of the human brain therefore remains abstract, unfathomable, and remote. Like events in far-off countries, neurobiological discoveries make for engrossing reading or research but still leave us largely untouched. To be changed by neuroscience, we need to get more personal with the brain, and to get personal we need to lose some of the exaggerated sense of wonder that distances us from the organ of our minds.[6]

I find this point particularly important for those of us in education. Our challenge seems to be taking readings about the brain and turning them into action. Along these lines, Jasanoff calls for caution when using a computer and/or information processing metaphor for the mind. It has become common to refer to the memory as information storage, cognition as processing, or nerve fibers as circuits. There are clearly some benefits and parallels between the mind and a computer—and this metaphor will pop up from time to time in this book—but the brain-as-supercomputer makes the brain distant and unknowable. Importantly, the metaphor fails in that the brain is not preprogrammed to process information and perform specific tasks as a computer might be. Yes, the brain has innate predispositions, but as Zull emphasizes, the brain's ability to adapt to the world around it and change itself is a significant difference.[7]

When we think of the human brain, we may think of the things that differentiate us from other living organisms, things such as language or art. But for the most part, our brains are not largely different from average living brains of any animal from aardvark to zebra. The primary purpose of the brain is survival.[8] Brains, as the centers of the nervous system, play a role in all bodily activities. All organisms have four key functions—amongst many functions—that they carry out throughout their lifetimes. These are defense against threats, regulation of energy supplies (including managing wastes), balancing fluids, and reproducing.[9] The brain spends much energy and effort ensuring that these tasks are carried out. It does this by budgeting out resources. Psychologist Lisa Feldman Barrett says that managing the "body budget" is a primary focus of the brain. It must ensure resources such as glucose or salt get distributed across the body when needed. This may mean directing the flow of resources in one direction while stopping the flow in another.[10]

The challenge for the brain is that it must do this without direct interaction with the world around it. The brain is locked up in the black box of our heads. Locked away from the outside, the only way that it knows what is happening in the world around it is through the sensory inputs that come to it. A first step for young brains is learning to manage the sensory inputs that are coming to it and make meaning out of them.[11] Moreover, in making sense of the world, the brain must react to it. LeDoux emphasizes the importance of the brain's ability to coordinate action as it reacts to the environment around it. He calls the nervous system a "sensory-motor integration device." As nervous systems have evolved over hundreds of millions of years, LeDoux argues that the primary need fulfilled by early nervous systems—found in our invertebrate ancestors—was detecting the environment and carrying out actions in response to this environment. Over millennia, nervous systems have evolved in complexity but all of them still complete this task.[12]

How does the brain do this? To answer this question, we must start with the neuron, which is the basic type of cell in our brain and nervous system. There are roughly one hundred billion neurons forming networks within the brain. Neurons are unique when contrasted with "typical" cells. For instance, red blood cells are discrete units with a distinctive shape that are amazingly small, visible only with a microscope. This is what we typically think about when we think about cells in our body, distinctly uniform. In contrast, neurons are something else entirely. A single neuron may have branches extending outward like a tree. They spread and branch, forming irregular structures of varying sizes. Some specialized neurons in the spine may each literally be a foot long. As neurons branch out in their tree-like formations, the axon of one neuron connects to a dendrite in another neuron. Dendrites function as a type of ear. One neuron connects to a neuron next to it. The dendrite receives a signal from the neuron next to it. The extending axon sends the signal onward. The neuron has an array of ions within it and the "flow of information" is actually an electrical charge that flows from one to the next. The average neuron has around *ten thousand* dendrites and roughly the same number of axons.[13]

In evolutionary terms, the neuron was a major step forward in how animals react to the world around them. The utilization of electric charges is significantly faster than other options such as releasing chemicals within cells. The neuron allowed for the development of a system of internal communication—the nervous system—where parts of the body can interact with the environment and send signals throughout the body calling for appropriate reactions. Over the evolutionary history of animals—especially vertebrates—the complexity of nervous systems increased and specialized. Vertebrate nervous systems are made up of two components: the central and peripheral nervous systems. The central nervous system consists of the brain and spinal cord. The peripheral nervous system is a network of nerves that connects the brain and spinal cord to the other tissues of the body. Information flows both ways, to and from.[14] The brain is at the center of managing resources and directing activity within the body. It is important to note that the brain is *embodied* so that things like self-concept, agency, and some aspects of cognition draw from the greater whole.[15] This will be explored in more detail later, but now it is enough to note that the brain is at the center of this bodily information apparatus.

Within the brain, neurons form complex patterns building layered connections. There are neurons that modulate the interactions of other neurons. Neurons can also form different types of feedback loops so the firing of one neuron can excite another neuron to act backward on the original neuron. Neurons can excite and silence each other in branching paths, turning on and turning off the root of circuits. For example, we can think about different kinds of pain. One kind of pain is a sharp stabbing pain that stops and another kind of pain is a throbbing pain that continues. This is based on two different neurons that connect to the same pain pathway in the body. The kind of pain that stops has an inhibitor that turns it off to communicate a short pain; the throbbing pain does not use that inhibitor and continues. All workings of our bodies, from breathing and other life support systems, to recognizing a person as a person and not a bird, to precisely differentiating the president of the United States from your first-grade music teacher are all made possible through connections of neurons.[16]

You may remember enough of your high school biology to know that groupings of neurons are organized into systems by neurobiologists. You can probably name some of them, such as the cortex or the amygdala. We can think of the brain as being made up of *core systems* that partner with each other to accomplish a wide variety of goals. One system may play a part in decision making, remembering, and experiencing different emotions. A core system is a "one-to-many" relationship where a single system contributes a portion of many different types of outcomes. This is in contrast to a "one-to-one" relationship, where one area of the brain has one job—area A for "sadness," area B handles facts, etc.—which is a common view of how the brain works. It is important to note that neurons do have specialties, and that neuronal systems also perform specific duties. But most neurons and neuronal systems are able to serve multiple functions.[17] As LeDoux writes,

> Functions are not, strictly speaking, carried out by areas, or even by neurons in areas. They come about by way of circuits that consist of ensembles of neurons in one area that are connected by nerve fibers or axons to ensembles in other areas, forming functional networks.[18]

Brain imaging technology has shown us that the brain is a *dynamic system* that is always working. Activity moves like traffic across a map for researchers to study and attempt to build understandings for how different areas connect to each other. As neurobiologist Rippon writes,

> Connectivity is the buzzword in brain imaging circles, and brain imagers are concerned with generating "roadmaps" of the brain by tracking the connections between different structures. We can now see how brain structures are linked together to form intricate "assemblies" that underpin all aspects of our behavior and allow us to experience and understand the world and (one hopes) each other.[19]

Neuroanatomists generally break down the brain into three broad zones or levels. In evolutionary terms, we can think of these levels developing from the "bottom up," which also reflect how they develop in utero.[20] Historically, the first area to evolve is the hindbrain or base of the brain. This area handles the body's life support systems, including circulatory and respiratory needs such as ensuring that our heart beats from birth to death. It handles digestion and waste disposal. It monitors the body's temperature and things like glucose levels in the blood and takes action to maintain needed balance. Next we have the midbrain, which handles sensory-motor behaviors and emotional reactions. This region handles some visual and auditory signals and is generally important in enabling the organism to react to the environment. Finally, the forebrain is the newest area of the brain in evolutionary terms. It is the upper surface of the brain. This area handles fine motor behaviors, but it is probably best known for being the center of decision making, memory, consciousness, and innate behaviors.[21]

Breaking down the brain in these three broad areas is an extreme simplification,[22] but it is true at a broad level. There are, however, a few things we should note. First, there is a great deal of inner connectivity between all three layers. Some parts of the brain are not clearly in the hindbrain or the midbrain but are in both. Second, the flow of ideas is not just top down but can go back and forth, up and down. Third, the aspects of behavior that are outside of consciousness—as we will explore later—are not just the purview of a single layer. Each section has unconscious behaviors, and it is difficult to pull apart the work of one area from another. Finally, evolution is not a process that just attaches one layer to the other without making changes. As the brain evolved, the hindbrain changed as did the midbrain and so on. Areas of the brain—or any part of the body—are not frozen in place once they developed in the first species to utilize them. They continue to be molded by forces of selection.[23] As noted earlier, Barrett emphasizes that this misconception of the lizard brain wrapped in rationality is one of the oversimplifications that has plagued Western thought.[24]

Solms emphasizes that most decisions are made drawing on all areas of the brain, transferring information between systems, allowing each area to contribute, before a choice is made. For example, he notes that it may not be correct to assume that final decisions are made in the forebrain by structures like the neocortex. Information can be sent up from midbrain to the forebrain, but the forebrain may take this and send it back down to the midbrain for a decision. We will explore this a bit later, but for now, it is enough to acknowledge that there is not a one-way flow of information from the bottom up.[25]

Those of us in education or in libraries do not need to be neuroscientists. But understanding these basics helps us to see the mind's information processing in a new way. From a neuroscientist's point of view, *learning* is a physical change in the brain. In new situations, the dendrites—the treelike structures on the neuron—branch out and build new connections to other neurons. As Doyle and Zakrajsek put it,

> Neuroscientist researchers have shown that when you learn something new, there is a physical change in your brain. . . . Our brains are adapting all the time, with unused connections fading away and new connections and networks being formed when new information is learned. When frequently activated and practiced, these new networks have the potential to form long-term memories. In fact, every time you use or practice newly learned information or skills the connections between the brain cells get stronger and your ability to recall the information also becomes easier and faster. Establishing new connections is like blazing a trail through thick forest, which is a great deal of work. But every time the trail is used it becomes more established and easier to follow.[26]

The establishment of these neural pathways and the strengthening of them is known as *long-term potentiation*. The result is that something that was new and awkward can become second nature and can be accessed without effort. The more that pathways are accessed, the more permanent they will become. The important thing in terms of learning is that new skills and new knowledge take effort and a time investment. Conversely, when neural pathways are not used, they constrict. Memories become foggy and skills that were once sharp become blunted.[27]

Neuroscience and psychology have long recognized that *mastery* of a subject or a skill is not something that is completed and achieved. Mastery is maintained through ongoing practice over extended periods of time. Real learning is not cramming. It is not absorbing in a short time. Meaningful learning takes time to build neural pathways and then ongoing work to keep these pathways strong. When it comes to learning a new skill or subject, the brain learns through connections. Connections to existing pathways help build new pathways. When you are working in an area where you have existing knowledge, it is easier to expand that knowledge, which anyone who has spent time in the classroom can also tell you. When you are in a new domain of learning, it can be very difficult. Many times there is a need to work through foundational knowledge that might be missing in order to really move toward mastery.[28] When neuroscientists have studied individuals who have mastered their crafts, they can observe structural differences in the brain:

> The left-hand motor control area was larger in string players, the right-hand one in keyboard players; the part of the brain concerned with hand-eye coordination and correction of errors was larger in elite mountain climbers; networks linking motor planning and execution areas to working memory were larger in elite judo players. Functional differences were evident as well; there were

> higher levels of activation in the action observation networks of expert ballet dancers; in archery specialists networks subserving visuospatial attention and working memory were more active.[29]

We reach mastery by practicing, and through practicing our neural pathways become more defined and readily activated. We practice so many times that it becomes automatic and we can do it without thinking about it. Simple mechanical tests are the things that we master first. Grasping moving fingers. Moving arms. Turning the head. Of course, mastery eventually becomes more complicated with more complex tasks. Think about driving a car. When we are learning, monitoring the road, the car's speed, the car's direction, and the rules we need to follow is very overwhelming. But, with time, driving becomes automatic and effortless.[30]

For babies it is difficult to pick up a pencil with the fingers, a very simple action for most of us. To do this requires the firing of thousands of neurons in their brains, and as time goes on they are able to focus those neurons. The challenge is not just the gross movement but in regulating the fine motor movement that is required.[31] Baby brains grow at an astounding pace. From conception on baby brains grow very fast. They are growing at about 250,000 nerve cells a minute and seven hundred new cell connections a second. By the age of six, the brain is at about 98 percent of the size of an adult brain. The brain will continue to grow throughout life but will have major development up until the early to mid-twenties.[32]

Again, this view of neural pathways and their relationship to learning is a gross simplification. This story leaves out a plethora of factors that shape brain development. For instance, hormones such as dopamine—instrumental in reward, happiness, and the reward of pursuing happiness—or hormones like oxytocin and vasopressin—prosocial and bonding influencers. These hormones, along with external factors such as stress, diet, or social influences, direct the development of our brains and, therefore, impact our thoughts and behaviors.[33]

Over the last three decades of research, it has been shown that our brains are much more plastic and malleable than anticipated. Forty years ago, the attitude was that the brain predicted a kind of unavoidable destiny. The common thinking held that our brains formed and then were locked in place throughout our lives. Today, we know that brains continue to change all the way through adulthood.[34] *Neuroplasticity* is an important feature of the brain. Pathways are changing over our lifespans in order for us to adapt to the world around us. But the malleability of the brain is finite. The brain has been shown to adapt and overcome damage, but only to a point. Additionally, for most of us, there are limits to the neural pathways we can build. Hours and hours of practice at any skill or study at any subject will make us better at those things. But hours of work are not going to transform us into a world chess champion or an Olympic-level swimmer.[35] For all of us, our genetic makeup will help us succeed in some directions but also limit us in other directions, including the functioning of our brains.

> Genes have plenty to do with behavior. Even more appropriately, all behavioral traits are affected to some degree by genetic variability. They have to be, given that they specify the structure of all the proteins pertinent to every neurotransmitter, hormone, receptor etc. that there is. And they have plenty to do with individual differences in behavior, given the large percentage of genes that are polymorphic, coming in different flavors. But their effects are supremely context dependent. Ask not what a gene does. Ask what it does in a particular environment and when expressed in a particular network of other genes. . . . Thus, for our purposes, genes aren't about inevitability. Instead they're about context-dependent tendencies, propensities, potential, and vulnerabilities. All embedded in the fabric of the other factors, biological and otherwise.[36]

In discussing the plasticity of the brain, we should not lose sight of LeDoux's key point that the brain's primary goal is survival.[37] The brain is malleable, but that does not mean that we are *consciously* molding neural networks. Much of the brain's activity is unconscious, which goes beyond life-support functions to include behaviors. LeDoux calls these "survival circuits" that are hardwired, instinctive reactions. These can impact perception, cognition, and arousal systems. The results of defensive reactions are an "organism-wide psychological state." The state is a method to coordinate the brain and body systems to cope with challenges that are coming at the organism. The fight-or-flight reflex is a classic example of such a hardwired reaction.

> The idea of survival circuits is in a way traditional—it simply refers to the circuits that control hardwired (instinctive) behaviors. Its advantage is that it isolates the objective function (response control) from presumed mental states (feelings).[38]

The amygdala's influence and activity is a commonly used example of a hardwired region of the brain that unconsciously influences behaviors. The amygdala is part of the forebrain. It is central in anxiety, fear, and aggression. It plays an important role in social uncertainty, including things like emotional decision making. The amygdala is active in learned fear and innate fears. It is a kind of defensive circuit detecting threats and preparing the body for action. Sensory inputs such as a visual stimulus will enter the brain, eventually split down two pathways. The first pathway goes directly to the amygdala, and the second[39] pathway goes to the cortex, where logic and reason are thought to reside. The second path through the cortex then feeds back into the amygdala and then both paths send information to other parts of the brain. The important piece here is that sensory information directly bypasses conscious, deliberate consideration flowing directly to the amygdala so that it can act quickly if needed.[40]

> The small amount of initial information that skips the cortex, reaching the amygdala directly, has a very rapid impact. It goes to the brainstem and the hypothalamus, both of which send direct signals to the body. The brainstem sends electrical signals through the spinal column to the muscles, producing almost instantaneous behavior such as the "startle reflex," which manifests itself in humans by jumping back, ducking, or freezing. The hypothalamus responds by secreting chemicals into the bloodstream, and those chemicals trigger more slowly developing yet powerful feelings throughout the body. We begin to feel fearful, sick, angry, embarrassed, or other powerful negative body responses to this brain activity.[41]

This amygdala circuit is a basic example of how brain systems interact, sometimes taking immediate action—even bypassing conscious awareness—other times intervening to stop action. Since the second pathway through the cortex flows back to the amygdala, this allows for the cortex to essentially override the initial reaction initiated by the amygdala. The upper pathway through the cortex allows for more positive experiences. It interprets what is happening and can override situations. During positive situations, the amygdala actually reduces its activity. Having feelings of joy might just mean the absence of fear. When the amygdala calms down and there is no fear, then we feel happy.[42]

In evolutionary terms, the human brain is the competitive advantage that we hold over other animals—as we will discuss throughout this book. But the uniqueness of the human brain isn't about size or even about density of brain cells. Humans do not have the largest brains. Generally, the biggest bodies have the biggest brains, so animals like whales and elephants win in size. Additionally, the ratio of the brain size to the body may be a predictor of success, but this breaks down in animals like ants, who have a much larger brain in comparison to the size of their bodies. The number of cells located in the brain don't seem to be the key indicators either. Some animals have more cells but are not smarter. There are neuroscientists seeking to understand if there are differences in neurons between species, and, importantly, how they function. Ultimately, it may not be a matter of size but a matter of how each works. But it is not entirely clear why our brains have allowed us to do things that other species have not.[43]

Before moving further, I want to pause for a brief mention of gender and the mind. This pause is warranted because many unsupported myths still float about. When looking at the differences between people who are biologically female and male or who identify as a woman, man, or another gender, the bottom line is that there are no differences in how the brain operates. Neurobiologist Gina Rippon's book, *Gender and Our Brains: How Neuroscience Explodes the Myths of the Male and Female Minds*,[44] goes into depth on the evidence exploring "gender differences" and the mind. It is also a nice general overview for how the brain and mind operate.[45]

Rippon notes that when it comes to gender, babies are set on different paths from the start. They are bombarded with stereotypes. Dressed in pink or blue. Given different opportunities. When studying behavior and trying to link it to brain data, there is also a big question about what is studied, what is dominant in terms of society, and how it is understood.

> It has always been assumed that the two distinct biological templates that produce different female and male bodies will also produce differences in the brain, which will underpin sex differences in cognitive skills, personalities and temperament. But the twenty-first century is not just challenging the old answers—it is challenging the question itself. One by one, we will see that past centuries are being dismantled. We will see what is happening to those well-known differences in masculinity and femininity, in fear of success, in nurturance and caring—even the very notion of female and male brains. Revisiting the evidence that supported these conclusions suggest that these characteristics do *not* neatly match the male/female labels they have been given.[46]

The inevitable question arises is, *what about hormones?* The research has shown that there are no clear-cut answers in terms of hormones. Androgens are often described as male hormones while estrogen and progestogens are called female hormones, but it is worth noting that these hormones are found in all of us. Yes, men have a higher range of testosterone, and women have a higher range of estrogen. But ferreting out the role that these higher rates might have and how these interact with cultural norms has proven difficult. One thing that is clear is that hormones are intertwined with culture and environmental interactions just like all biological functions that result in different behaviors. Attributing behaviors due to hormones based on gender is very difficult and studies of these differences have not offered clear answers.

> Hormones appear to have become yet another biological process coopted in the hunt for evidence that women's biology is not only different and generally inferior but periodically extremely deficient. The chemicals that were linked to women's capacity for motherhood became linked to their maladaptive emotionally, irrationality and, via the effects these chemicals had on the developing brain, lack of certain key cognitive skills. On the other hand, extra doses of testosterone were not only linked to men's capacity for fatherhood, but also to the necessary forceful personality characteristics and leadership skills allegedly essential for success in social, political and military circles and, again via particular effects on the developing brain, to the required cognitive capacity to be great thinkers and creative scientists.[47]

It is not that our bodies and our biological processes do not impact our minds, because they do. Sleep, exercise, diet, hydration, and a multitude of factors impact how we think and how our minds function. Our sense of self, our embodied mind, is deeply connected to biology. But ultimately, there seems to be no meaningful distinction between gender and the mind that can't be accounted for by social and cultural norms. For many of us, this may seem obvious, but it probably goes without saying that it is not obvious to everyone.

The picture of the brain that emerges is one of constant change and growth as individuals are shaped by the environment while also having hardwired systems that have been handed down to us through natural selection over millennia. For those of us in the classroom or in libraries, there are a few key takeaways that we should keep in focus as we move from talking about the brain to talking about the mind. First, at the most basic level, learning is about building circuits. This takes time and practice. New experiences connect to the existing structures that are in place, which can help or hinder the development of new neural pathways. Second, much of the work of the brain is done behind the scenes. We are not aware of most of what the brain does, and some behaviors are hardwired to ensure our survival. Third, the brain relies on one-to-many relationships where each area collaborates with other areas to create many outcomes. Information is passed between areas, allowing each to make contributions. Thus, we should not think of the brain as a rational center that has irrational tendencies, but, more accurately, as being made up of components that work in combination to create pathways that represent learning. This modular nature of the brain will come up again and again throughout this book with significant implications for how we create knowledge.

Notes

1. For those interested in a more complete—and authoritative—perspective on brain anatomy, read LeDoux's *The Deep History of Ourselves: The Four-Billion-Year Story of How We Got Conscious Brains*, Sapolsky's *Behave: The Biology of Humans at Our Best and Worst*, and Zull's *From Brain to Mind: Using Neuroscience to Guide Change in Education*, all of which offer accessible works for those of us who missed biology class in college.

2. Joseph LeDoux, *The Deep History of Ourselves: The Four-Billion-Year Story of How We Got Conscious Brains* (New York: Viking, 2019).

3. James E. Zull, *From Brain to Mind: Using Neuroscience to Change in Education* (Sterling, VA: Stylus Publishing, 2011); Virginia Campbell, *Are You Sure?: The Unconscious Origins of Certainty* (Hartford, CT: PYP Academy Press, 2020).

4. M. Peters, "Metabolism," *British Medical Association A-Z Family Medical Encyclopedia* (London: Dorling Kindersley, 2004).

5. Zull, *From Brain to Mind*, 10.

6. Alan Jasanoff, *The Biological Mind: How Brain, Body, and Environment Collaborate to Make Us Who We Are* (New York: Basic Books, 2018), 22.

7. Zull, *From Brain to Mind*. Advances in artificial intelligence may erode this difference over time but we are not there yet.

8. Bessel A. Van der Kolk, *The Body Keeps the Score: The Brain, Mind, and Body in the Healing of Trauma* (New York: Viking Press, 2014).

9. LeDoux, *Deep History of Ourselves*.

10. Lisa Feldman Barrett, *How Emotions Are Made: The Secret Life of the Brain* (Boston: Mariner Books, 2017).

11. Zull, *From Brain to Mind*; Barrett, *How Emotions Are Made*.

12. LeDoux, *Deep History of Ourselves*.

13. Robert M. Sapolsky, *Behave: The Biology of Humans at Our Best and Worst* (New York: Penguin Books, 2017).

14. LeDoux, *Deep History of Ourselves*.

15. Jasanoff, *The Biological Mind*.

16. Sapolsky, *Behave*.

17. Feldman Barrett, *How Emotions Are Made*.

18. LeDoux, *Deep History of Ourselves*.

19. Gina Rippon, *Gender and Our Brains: How Neuroscience Explodes the Myths of the Male and Female Minds* (New York: Pantheon Books, 2019).

20. Van der Kolk, *Body Keeps the Score*.

21. LeDoux, *Deep History of Ourselves*.

22. These three areas of the brain are gross generalizations but are useful for the discussions in this text. Some anatomists may break down the brain into six

areas. As a kind of elementary example, the *Wikipedia* entry for the brain notes, "Neuroanatomists usually divide the vertebrate brain into six main regions: the telencephalon (cerebral hemispheres), diencephalon (thalamus and hypothalamus), mesencephalon (midbrain), cerebellum, pons, and medulla oblongata." ("Brain" Wikipedia, https://en.wikipedia.org/wiki/Brain#Anatomy). In this discussion, I am heavily leaning on the broad overviews of LeDoux, *Deep History of Ourselves* and Sapolsky, *Behave*. They each use slightly different terminology and approaches, which I have tried to understand together.

23. Sapolsky, *Behave*.

24. Feldman Barrett, *How Emotions Are Made*.

25. Sapolsky, *Behave*.

26. Terry Doyle and Todd Zakrajsek, *The New Science of Learning: How to Learn in Harmony with Your Brain* (Sterling, VA: Stylus Publishing, 2019), 8–9.

27. Doyle and Zakrajsek, *New Science of Learning*; LeDoux, *Deep History of Ourselves*; Sapolsky, *Behave*; Rippon, *Gender and Our Brains*.

28. Doyle and Zakrajsek, *New Science of Learning*; Rippon, *Gender and Our Brains*.

29. Rippon, *Gender and Our Brains*, 111.

30. Zull, *From Brain to Mind*.

31. Zull, *From Brain to Mind*.

32. Rippon, *Gender and Our Brains*.

33. Sapolsky, *Behave*.

34. Rippon, *Gender and Our Brains*.

35. Sapolsky, *Behave*.

36. Sapolsky, *Behave*, 264–65.

37. LeDoux, *Deep History of Ourselves*.

38. LeDoux, *Deep History of Ourselves*, 345.

39. The use of "first" and "second" here does not denote an order or superior relationship between these two paths. I am using these terms to help keep these two paths separated.

40. Sapolsky, *Behave*; LeDoux, *Deep History of Ourselves*; Van der Kolk, *Body Keeps the Score*; Zull, *From Brain to Mind*.

41. Zull, *From Brain to Mind*, 60.

42. Zull, *From Brain to Mind*.

43. Jasanoff, *The Biological Mind*.

44. Rippon, *Gender and Our Brains*.

45. As evidenced by the number of times I have referenced Rippon's text in the preceding overview of the brain and mind.

46. Rippon, *Gender and Our Brains*, xix.

47. Rippon, *Gender and Our Brains*, 43–44.

CHAPTER TWO

The Future, Not the Past

Neuroscientists do not talk about *information* as librarians do. Often, librarians (and other educators) talk about information as a thing that gets put in our heads and filed away for us to access later. Neuroscientists talk about *memory* and *remembering*. In our minds, there really is no such thing as information, only memory. Most of the time, the difference between *information* and *memory* does not matter all that much. We describe memories as if they are physical objects. Fernyhough calls this the "conventional possession view of memory."[1] This holds that we file memories away in a type of internal storage system to be recalled later. We act as if our brains are recording devices capturing visual and audio recordings that we can access when needed. We are capturing a kind of objective history of our lives. It is as if memories are just books stored away on the shelves in our head.

Most of us still believe this even though we have our own evidence that memory is not perfect. We forget things. We disagree with friends over details of shared moments and events. Memories hit us at strange times out of nowhere. There is a randomness to all of it. But, despite this, we most often stand by our memories as a kind of truth that we carry around. We *believe* our memories and rely upon them. Burton puts it this way when talking about the fragility of memory:

> None of us have an instinctual belief that our memories are this fragile. Despite the proliferation of psychological studies questioning the accuracy of episodic memory recall, we cling to the belief that our pasts approximately correspond to our memories. Sometimes we sense that the details are a bit faded, but we

rarely doubt the essence of a memory. We rely upon the notion that, at the very least, the memories of our past reflect fundamental truths.[2]

Memory can be a fuzzy term. In a physiological sense, memory is the building of neuronal pathways. When a baby is first building the pathways that will enable the hand to pick up a toy, these pathways are a type of memory. Remembering allows the child to take that action again. Zull makes the claim that "mind is all about memory."[3] Everything we do, everything we think, everything is built on neuronal pathways that are the essence of memory. LeDoux differentiates between explicit memory—memories that can be drawn into consciousness—and implicit memory—memories working at a subconscious level.[4] We will discuss consciousness in more depth in later chapters, but at this point, we must acknowledge that there is a significant unconscious quality to much of our "memory." The sound of a wolf howling is a memory. It is learned. The ability to walk is another type of memory. If I ask you to think of your first pet or the first name of your father, these are memories that were not actively in your mind a moment ago until you read this sentence and, more than likely, you easily accessed these memories and made them active. Most of our memories—including learned behaviors—are part of our unconscious. Memories live somewhere outside of awareness until they are—voluntarily or involuntarily—called forth. For most of this chapter, I will be focusing on episodic or biographical memory, leaving unconscious processing for later chapters.

It may seem counterintuitive, but the purpose of memory is actually not about the past. Evolutionarily speaking, memory is about the present and future. Species that can learn from the past and recognize how the current situation reflects past situations will be more likely to survive. Individuals who learn that the rustling in the grass could be a tiger are less likely to be eaten by the tiger and more likely to contribute their genes to future generations. Memory is a tool for prediction applying past lessons to the present with the goal of anticipating the future. Memory is not documentation. Memory is preparation.[5]

This evolutionary view of memory has a number of important implications. First, when a memory is made, the ideas from the moment are abstracted and stored away while other possible ideas are ignored. Again, memory is not a recording. It is a *value proposition*. The more emotionally charged a moment, the more unique or more heightened the situation, the more likely that moment will be stored away, but, also, the more that the emotion will shape the memory itself. Often, it is more important to capture the emotional element of the situation than the details around it. It is more important to know if your last encounter with a relative or friend ended in an argument, so that the next time you see this person, you are prepared.[6]

Second, when a memory is recalled, there is a kind of assembly process that takes place. The primary goal of memory is to help us in the present moment, and, therefore, the present moment has a great deal of influence over how a memory is recalled. The current context around us will cause us to emphasize some parts of memories while neglecting other parts. Often, when we note failures of memory, it is really a failure of recall. We may know something but may not be able to access it. A memory does not exist in a vacuum. When we have failure of recall, it is often a failure of context and moment. The correct trigger to access the full memory may be absent.[7]

Finally, memory builds throughout life. Memory is never frozen in place but is changing and evolving as our understanding changes and evolves. Over time, the self grows and unfolds. When we think about ourselves and describe our lives, we inherently create a narrative structure to our lives. Even young children when describing their own lives build a narrative. So, when we think about past events, we add new details as we gain them. When we picture ourselves, we often inject our current views into the past. When we remember, we are literally changing our memories. The more often that we remember a moment, the more likely we will hold onto that moment into the future, but also the more likely we will update and change that memory.[8]

A kind of paradox around memory is that memory is actually not good with "temporal information." If you are given a date in the past, there is almost no ability to recall what actually happened to you on that day. The calendar has little to do with helping your memory. There are a few individuals with photographic memories who can connect events and dates, but they tend to be anomalies among the general population. When we think of our early memories or really any memories from our past, we have to use different kinds of markers to determine how old we were, where we lived, what year we entered or graduated from a school, when a child was born, etc., and then to try to work backward.[9] What were you doing in 2009? Well, if you graduated in 2008, and you just moved into a new apartment in 2010, then you can figure out what was happening in 2009.

Moreover, memory is not built consistently over our lifespans. Most of us have no biographical memories before the age of four to five years old. If we do, they are very rare. The memories that we do have from our earliest years are most often constructions from looking at pictures and hearing stories from parents, family members, or friends. Clearly, the physical apparatus for making memories is in place from infants onward. Infants and young children recognize faces and beloved toys. They learn to recognize foods they like (and dislike). Memory plays a key role in this development, and the evidence suggests that there is memory at work throughout our entire life. But we do not build biographical memories before the age of four or five. It is not exactly clear why, but part of the reason seems to be related to systems that come together to create consciousness and self-identity. An important part of this is language, which provides a tool to label and encode experiences. Language is about more than communication. It is about mentally organizing the world. The period where "childhood amnesia" ends directly corresponds to the point where most humans become "verbal beings." Researchers use the term *autonoetic consciousness* to describe the feeling that life is happening to you, that you are at the center of your own memories, which helps us organize our thoughts into a narrative. Of course, part of this delay in creating memories is biological. The brain is rapidly developing and key parts of the brain that connect to language are not developed. But when it comes to biographical memories, it's not so much that toddlers are unable to make biographical memories. It is more that they do not possess the ability to organize their biographical knowledge. There is a social dimension missing. Without language, children are not able to engage into social discourse with others that creates interpretation of events and replays recent activities to build stronger and stronger memories.[10]

Another example of uneven consistency of memory is the centrality of the memories created in adolescent and early adulthood—ages around fourteen years to twenty-five years. Researchers have identified a "reminiscence bump" from this time period in older adults who can vividly recall memories between fourteen and twenty-five. The general explanation for this is that the memories we develop during these time periods are vital in shaping us into who we are going to become. The brain is developing from that of a child into an adult. Our social understandings are becoming complex and our recognition of how the world operates is becoming more nuanced.[11]

As noted above,[12] there are two broad types of memory, *explicit* and *implicit* memory.[13] Explicit memory can be drawn into consciousness while implicit memory works at a subconscious level. If we remain focused on explicit memory, we can categorize this further into *episodic memory* and *semantic memory*. Episodic memories are linked to specific events and are generally personal experiences. Semantic memories, in contrast, are descriptions or abstractions about the world.[14]

> Semantic memories concern facts—things you know about the world. They are often acquired as the result of repeated experiences that form abstract representations of objects. Although not all apples are identical, over the

> course of many experiences with them you learn in a general sense what apples are—they are a roundish, often reddish, fruit about the size of a fist. But you also learn what they are not—they are similar to cherries in that they both are round, reddish fruits, but they differ in size and taste; both also differ from round red balls and marbles. Such semantic knowledge enables you to act appropriately when you encounter one of them. . . . Semantic memories of objects' names allow us to label objects verbally, but semantic memories are first and foremost about providing object information independent of verbal labels . . . semantic memories are acquired through specific experiences, but they are not tied to those experiences in any defining way. Episodic memories, by contrast, are linked to specific episodes from which they arise. Because an episode consists of a set of facts about a given event, episodic memories are often said to be defined by composite "what-where-when" representations. In addition, episodic memories include the experiencer in the experience, and are thus personal.[15]

Autobiographical memories are a form of episodic memories. In fact, these terms may often be used interchangeably, but generally, autobiographical memories are episodic but also place the rememberer into a time and place context. They are not just a remembered episode but a remembered episode with a time and place narrative around it. It is the remembered life story.[16]

Another way to understand memory is to look at *working memory* versus *long-term memory*. This is more of an operational perspective. Working memory is short-term information temporarily held in memory, often to complete a specific task. Working memory requires neurons to fire continuously for a short time to hold onto a thought or an issue that is directly at hand.[17]

> Working memory involves the transient storage of task-relevant representations for use in mental work. It is through working memory, and its so-called executive control functions, that information can be held in mind temporarily in the process of deliberating.[18]

Psychologists have long studied the limits of working memory. We generally can only remember four to seven concepts at a time. The common test is to hold a set of numbers in mind while working on other tasks and then give participants some sort of recall test at different time intervals.[19]

Long-term memory, on the other hand, is the storage of experiences and information over an extended period of time. Long-term memory is by definition a part of the unconscious mind in that we cannot possibly hold all of our memories in consciousness at one time. Most long-term memories are stored away and not present until called upon. When they are called upon, they are often shaped by the current context or need. Long-term memories have more stable physical requirements to hold onto them when compared to working memory, but due to this requirement, they take longer to capture. This does not happen instantly. There is an actual change that takes place.[20]

> Why different memories last longer than others turns out to be straightforward and not at all mysterious. Short-term memories are the result of rapid changes in the activity of enzymes already present at the synapse. Those enzymes are activated quickly and remain active for a short time. The synapse changes they produce also come quickly but last only a short time. However, long-term memory requires a second, slower process of assembly and cell change. Such memories alter the actual structure of the cell, and the alteration can last a long time.[21]

In a broad sense, there are three stages of memory processing: encoding, storage, and retrieval. The more deeply something is experienced, the more likely it is to be remembered, which has a major impact on encoding. There seems to be evidence that different types of components of an experience are stored in different areas of the brain. For instance, areas that deal with space may handle location information. The hippocampus deals with relationships between bits of knowledge. When there is something new or novel, the hippocampus really lights up. Your first experience at a special life event like your first day at school or your first visit to a particular city will be more vivid in your mind than the twenty-fifth day of school or your fourteenth visit to that city. Retrieval of a memory may be the most important part because if you cannot access a memory then it does not matter. Many times retrieval is outside of our conscious control. The brain is able to recognize familiar objects, situations, and places more readily than we are to consciously be able to recall or remember those things. So something may seem familiar but we are not able to quite place it. The brain can recognize information that it has deeply processed even if we are not able to actively recall it at will. Thus, we can make a distinction between two types of processes: a feeling of familiarity emerging from the unconscious and actively *remembering*. Remembering requires the activity of multiple cognitive functions spread across several regions of the brain. When a memory is recalled, a core idea of the experience is constructed even as additional information gathered over the intervening years can be tacked on.[22]

> It is important to recognize that memory is not a unitary brain function. We break it into fundamental elements: forming memories and recalling them. The challenge is to record the things that will make up our memories, and

> then, to recall them when needed. As implied previously, we are all given the machinery needed to form memories—the neurons that grow branches and form networks—but establishing the networks is one thing and putting them to use is another.[23]

At any moment, the brain is engaged in various processes all at once. The short-term memory systems hold new experiences in place even as previous experiences are fading away. As this is happening, long-term memory systems are being activated by contextual cues pulling memories into consciousness. This can recall pieces of some memories to strengthen them. At the same time, new connections between memories are being formed.[24]

Unfortunately, age has a negative effect on memory. The older we get, the more challenges we face at creating new memories or even holding items in short-term memory. Dodson, Powers, and Lytell found that not only were older adults more likely to misremember over time, but they were more likely to be confident in their memories than younger adults.[25]

As we can see, memory is in a constant restructuring process, with the emphasis on the present. This restructuring leads to potential fragility of and recontextualization of memories. Psychologists have documented *the misinformation effect* that demonstrates ways that memories can be altered. Memories are open to suggestions from people around us. The ways that questions are asked can lead to desired answers. Misleading information can be suggested and be combined with existing memories to alter those memories as they are recalled.[26]

As mentioned above, a great deal of memory is out of our direct control. Context cues activate different aspects of memories whether we want them to or not. This is true for explicit memories such as episodic or autobiographical memory, but it is also true for implicit memory as well. Reactions caused by trauma, as an example, can be beyond conscious control, existing between implicit and explicit memory largely activated unconsciously. Most of the time, our minds are creating a narrative structure to our lives through memories that are roughly situated in time and place. But during traumatic experiences this narrative essentially shuts down and the strong emotional reactions leave imprints that are disorganized outside of coherent narratives. Trauma leaves behind largely fragmented sensory impressions. This is why many times people do not have clear memories of trauma or in other cases memories reemerge later without warning. Post-traumatic stress reactions can be triggered by contextual cues that remind the brain of the traumatic event whether it is abuse, combat experiences, car accidents, or any number of other events. The context cues bring forth physical reactions such as panic attacks. Sometimes the memories of the traumatic event come into consciousness and sometimes they do not. One of the goals of talk therapy is to work against this *dissociation* that occurs when the memories of traumatic experiences exist as isolated imprints surfacing unexpectedly. The goal of talk therapy is to associate these emotional segments with a narrative element in autobiographical memory, which will allow the mind to move the event into the past.[27]

Memory is one of the places where we can experience the interaction between conscious and unconscious processing. Our consciousness receives memories and can play an active role in calling forth memories, but it does not play a role in organizing them. Not only could the conscious mind not manage all our memories, but if it did, it would be a slow, lumbering process. This is why the unconscious mind is actively working in the background, recognizing context cues and connecting the many processes related to memory to the present moment.[28] Given that the unconscious is the keeper of long-term memory, essentially all complex thinking must connect with the unconscious. In fact, most of our complex thinking entirely occurs in the unconscious.[29] At the same time, the concept of the *self* is built upon the narrative of autobiographical memory, which assumes our consciousness is the protagonist of the story.[30]

A vital aspect of a healthy mind is differentiating between things that we have lived and things that we have not lived. Our minds can engage in *deliberate imagining* where we can imagine actions, events, situations, and many other aspects of our world that do not exist. We can imagine actions that we might take while shutting down our motor responses and not following through on those actions. We may remember our dream of quitting our job or winning the lottery, but we still go work and we do not buy a mansion because we recognize dreams as dreams. In order for these things to happen, we must recognize memories we have actually lived and memories that we have imagined.[31]

The *source monitoring framework* is an area of study in psychology that examines the connections between memories and the ability of individuals to recognize the sources of those memories. If you hold a memory—semantic or episodic—are you able to remember the origins of that memory? I can remember the birthplace of my father but, obviously, I was not present at his birth. I remember this because he told me. Part of source monitoring is recognizing the difference between different external sources and internally generated sources, for example recognizing the difference between what you thought at the time and what you said at the time. This framework focuses on memory characteristics, most importantly perceptual information, contextual information, semantic detail, affective information (such as emotional reactions), and cognitive operations (identifying, elaborating, retrieving knowledge). All of these characteristics are important in the formation of the memory. Many memories enable us to identify the source just through the remembering itself. I know that the Chicago Bears lost to the Green Bay Packers in the NFC Championship game in January of 2011 because I was at the game. A painful memory! Decisions on sources are often made quickly and are non-deliberative. The sources for memories can be very obvious. However, there are times when memories cause a deliberative process where one must actively consider the source. This takes more time as we engage an internal discussion such as "does this seem plausible?" We are employing our own judgment to make an evaluation of the quality of our own memories. Emotion, stress, and the context of the moment can interfere with this evaluation.[32] Source monitoring is an idea we will explore in more depth later in this book.

From all of this, we can recognize a broader view of memory. The brain doesn't work in terms of *information* where a record is made, remains intact, and can be accessed in the future. Memories are constructed based on the needs of the present and future. They are changeable and susceptible to outside influences. But, with this being said, memory is the entire foundation for the formation and functioning of the mind. As Zull stated, "mind is all about memory."[33] Memory forms the self and how we see ourselves in that world. It is deeply entwined with our unconscious as the mind works to make connections between past and present as it anticipates the future.

For educators and librarians, understanding memory is important. This has implications for what we expect from students. Just because I mentioned some fact three weeks ago, that does not mean that all students—even those who were paying attention—will have perfect recall. Hearing a key idea, watching a video, or reading a book does not necessarily store away information for later use. But that input mixes and mingles and is pulled apart as it is stored away. It is important for those of us in libraries, who deal in the world of information, to understand that memory is different from information. Memories are filed away with a focus on the future. Memories are not quite the same thing as knowledge, but they are a first step in understanding what knowledge might be.

Notes

1. Charles Fernyhough, *Pieces of Light: The New Science of Memory* (London: Profile Books, 2013).

2. Robert A. Burton, *On Being Certain: Believing You Were Right Even When You're Not* (New York: St. Martin's Griffin, 2008), 83.

3. James E. Zull, *From Brain to Mind: Using Neuroscience to Guide Change in Education* (Sterling, VA: Stylus Publishing, 2011); Virginia Campbell, *Are You Sure?: The Unconscious Origins of Certainty* (Hartford, CT: PYP Academy Press, 2020), 202.

4. Joseph LeDoux, *The Deep History of Ourselves: The Four-Billion-Year Story of How We Got Conscious Brains* (New York: Viking, 2019).

5. Mark Solms, *The Hidden Spring: A Journey to the Source of Consciousness* (New York: Norton, 2021); Fernyhough, *Pieces of Light*; Zull, *From Brain to Mind*; Terry Doyle and Todd Zakrajsek, *The New Science of Learning: How to Learn in Harmony with Your Brain* (Sterling, VA: Stylus Publishing, 2019).

6. Solms, *Hidden Spring*; Fernyhough, *Pieces of Light*; Zull, *From Brain to Mind*.

7. Solms, *Hidden Spring*; Fernyhough, *Pieces of Light*; Zull, *From Brain to Mind*.

8. Solms, *Hidden Spring*; Fernyhough, *Pieces of Light*; Zull, *From Brain to Mind*.

9. Fernyhough, *Pieces of Light*.

10. Fernyhough, *Pieces of Light*.

11. Fernyhough, *Pieces of Light*.

12. LeDoux, *Deep History of Ourselves*.

13. Solms, in *Hidden Spring*, uses the terms *declarative* and *non-declarative* memory.

14. LeDoux, *Deep History of Ourselves*; Fernyhough, *Pieces of Light*; Solms, *Hidden Spring*.

15. LeDoux, *Deep History of Ourselves*, 294–95.

16. Fernyhough, *Pieces of Light*.

17. LeDoux, *Deep History of Ourselves*; Fernyhough, *Pieces of Light*; Solms, *Hidden Spring*; Zull, *From Brain to Mind*.

18. LeDoux, *Deep History of Ourselves*, 228.

19. Campbell, *Are You Sure?*

20. LeDoux, *Deep History of Ourselves*; Zull, *From Brain to Mind*.

21. Zull, *From Brain to Mind*, 182.

22. Doyle and Zakrajsek, *New Science of Learning*; Fernyhough, *Pieces of Light*.

23. Zull, *From Brain to Mind*, 172.

24. Zull, *From Brain to Mind*.

25. Chad S. Dodson, Emma Powers, and Mariko Lytell, "Aging, Confidence, and Misinformation: Recalling Information with the Cognitive Interview," *Psychology and Aging* 30, no. 1 (2015): 46–61.

26. Fernyhough, *Pieces of Light*; Michelle M. Pena, J. Zoe Klemfuss, Elizabeth F. Loftus, and Amelia Mindthoff, "The Effects of Exposure to Differing Amounts of Misinformation and Source Credibility Perception on Source Monitoring and Memory Accuracy," *Psychology of Consciousness: Theory, Research, and Practice* 4, no. 4 (2017): 337–47; Dodson, Powers, and Lytell, "Aging, Confidence, and Misinformation."

27. Bessel A. Van der Kolk, *The Body Keeps the Score: The Brain, Mind, and Body in the Healing of Trauma* (New York: Viking Press, 2014); Solms, *Hidden Spring*.

28. Solms, *Hidden Spring*.

29. Cambell, *Are You Sure?*

30. LeDoux, *Deep History of Ourselves*.

31. Fernyhough, *Pieces of Light*; Solms, *Hidden Spring*.

32. Marcia K. Johnson, Shahin Hashtroudi, and D. Stephen Lindsay, "Source Monitoring," *Psychological Bulletin* 114, no. 1 (1993): 3–28; Fernyhough, *Pieces of Light*.

33. Zull, *From Brain to Mind*, 202.

CHAPTER THREE

Bundles of Memories

If I ask you to picture an apple in your mind, you can do so easily.[1] What are you picturing? A fruit. Round. Probably red. Maybe green? Maybe whole or maybe sliced? When you draw this image into your mind, you are more than likely not remembering an exact moment in your life when you held a specific apple. You are probably holding a more general picture in your mind that is a composite based on your past experience with apples. We hold thousands of such pictures in our minds: tree, car, computer, hand, ball, cloud, school, and so many more. In addition to these pictures, we can conjure up a range of abstractions such as family, economy, gender, government, religion, and so many more. All of these are based on our experiences for how the world works.

LeDoux calls these generalizations *schemas*, which are a tool used by the mind to understand the world. Schemas are bundles of memories drawing on relationships within and between memories.[2] We can think of them as a type of mental model held by the brain. Lisa Barrett refers to schemas as *concepts*.

> Using your concepts, your brain groups some things together and separates others. You can look at three mounds of dirt and perceive two of them as "Hills" and one as a "Mountain," based on your concepts. Construction treats the world like a sheet of pastry, and your concepts are cookie cutters that carve boundaries, not because the boundaries are natural, but because they're useful or desirable. These boundaries have physical limitations of course; you never perceive a mountain as a lake. Not everything is relative.

> Your concepts are a primary tool for your brain to guess the meaning of incoming sensory inputs. For example, concepts give meaning to changes in sound pressure so you hear them as words or music instead of random noise.[3]

Barrett indicates that while our schemas—*concepts* to use her term—help us to organize our world, they also can lead to what she terms *experiential blindness*. Our experiences guide us to see the present moment in the light of the past.[4] Once we know the shape of a bird, a heart, or even an elephant, we can see these shapes all around us. This is why we see faces, animals, and other things in clouds. Rippon expands this idea saying that the brain relies upon a type of stereotyping. We use stereotypes—schemas—to make quick judgments based on the situation drawing deeply on the past.[5] Of course, there are many instances where the stereotypes are incorrect, but, nonetheless, the brain builds expectations for the world and leans heavily on what is familiar. Our schemas are part of the building blocks of cognition. They allow for new inputs to be abstracted or conceptualized, connected with expectations, and built into long-term memory efficiently. Schemas are important in the relationship between working memory and long-term memory. Without schemas, we do not have the abstractions that are important to the survival of our species.[6]

Unsurprisingly, schemas build upon themselves. New mental representations result from the existing mental representations. Past experiences—or more accurately, the schemas we build based upon past experiences—help us understand how future experiences may unfold. Psychologists call this *inference*, or "the production of new mental representations on the basis of previously held representations."[7] Importantly, inference occurs both consciously and unconsciously. In fact, it can be argued that inference may be largely due to unconscious processing.

> A *process of inference* is a process, the representational output of which necessarily or probabilistically follows from its representational input. The function of an inferential process is to augment and correct the information available to cognitive systems. An evolutionary approach suggests that inferential processes, rather than being based on a single inferential mechanism or constituting a single integrated system, are much more likely to be performed by a variety of domain-specific mechanisms, each attuned to the specific demands and affordances of its domain. The inferential processes carried out by these mechanisms are unconscious: they are not mental acts that individuals decide to perform, but processes that take place inside their brain, at a "sub-personal" level. People may be aware of having reached a certain conclusion—be aware,

> that is, of the output of an influential process—but we claim that they are never aware of the process itself.[8]

This processing outside of awareness sifts through schemas comparing the present to what we've seen before. Barrett calls this the *intrinsic activity* of the brain.[9] It is processing based upon the mental constructs we've built over our lives. The brain learns about the world through sensory inputs. It has learned to associate different sensory inputs with different meanings. Barrett uses the example of hearing a loud band. The ears capture this vibration through the air and immediately offer an interpretation. The brain understands that there must be some kind of cause such as a door being slammed or a gunshot. The brain is always constructing meaning from the sensory inputs it receives. Tastes, smells, colors, movements, shapes area all constructed into meaning. Many processes that we assume are hardwired into are actually constructed and learned. Music, as an example, feels as if it should be universal to all listeners but there are many variations around the world. Western music is built upon a structure of 12 pitches while the Indonesian gamelan music has 7 pitches per octave. Our expectations for what we count as "normal" are derived from our schemas.[10]

A further example is that of color. Physicists can break down the visible light spectrum and help us understand the rainbow based on wavelength but how your mind views color is largely dictated by your schemas for color. The range of cultural interpretations of color is very broad, and the number of colors people see in a rainbow is not universal by any means. In fact, some people—cultures—do not have a word for color at all.[11] The mind is highly social and relies upon the minds of others from the very start. We inherit the culture of the society into which we are born and that society hands us mental models—schemas—to help us neatly connect the sensory inputs coming at us.[12] Bourdieu uses the term *habitus* to refer to the dispositions that guide how we see the world and how we feel about that world. Our ability to make judgments rests upon a type of programming that a culture wires into our mind. This cultural transfer happens through observation but, importantly, it also happens through words.[13] The power of words is not just in communicating with others but in making abstractions within the mind. Language helps to move ideas into awareness. Words build context. Words capture schemas.[14]

LeDoux reminds us that schemas do not stop with understanding the external world, but we also use our *self-schema* to understand the internal world as well.

> When you are aware of who you are, you are drawing from your self-schema, which is what underlies your self-concept. Your self-schema includes your skills and abilities; your foibles; your social roles; your psychological attributes; your self-worth; how you look; how you feel and act; how your body responds in certain situations; what you expect your future to hold; how you feel about your family, friends, enemies, colleagues, acquaintances, and even your possessions, and un-possessed but desired things of either natural or man-made world.[15]

Our self-schema helps us to organize information about ourselves including our behaviors.[16]

Overall, our schemas are behind the scenes when we hold *beliefs* about how the world works. A belief is a kind of generalization that something exists or that a certain outcome will result. The next chapter will go deeper into how the mind builds predictions but for now, focusing on schemas, I want to note that schemas are important to the beliefs we hold. Mercier and Sperber make a distinction between *reflective beliefs* and *intuitive beliefs*.[17] Reflective beliefs are held in consciousness and are connected to reason and reasoning. Ultimately, we understand how we arrived at a reflective belief, and we can explain it. Intuitive beliefs, on the other hand, are not held in consciousness, so we are not aware that we even hold them. They are built on schemas. We may be aware of the outcome of an intuitive belief, but we may not be able to delineate the process behind that belief. I will explore this more later, but for now, it is important to note that schemas are foundational for intuitive beliefs.

As we interact with the world, not only is the unconscious using our schemas outside of our awareness, but it is, at the same time, updating and changing them based on new information. Obviously, our mind arrives at a pivotal moment when it encounters inconsistencies between the information it is receiving and the schemas it already holds. This happens when we try a new food that we didn't think that we liked and discover that, in fact, this new food tastes pretty good. It also happens when we assume that all librarians are quiet and meek, but when we meet a few of them we update our schemas about librarians. When the outside world matches our schemas, we tend not to take notice, but when we discover an inconsistency, we take note. This could involve updating schemas at the unconscious level, but it also may mean that the inconsistency is drawn into consciousness for us to address. When we hit moments of conflict, we are more likely to examine the source of the conflict. For example, if we are reading an article, we may examine the credibility of the source to see if this is someone we trust. If we discover a visual conflict, we may stop and take a second look at the thing that caught our eye. If we think that we saw bigfoot in the woods out of the corner of our eye, we may pause and take a second look. When we examine the sources of conflict, we are more likely to remember the sources of our schemas and beliefs into the future. But it is important to note that updating schemas is not always easy. Preexisting schemas do not simply vanish when conflicting situations arise. Schemas can be fragmented and stored away even if they are in conflict with updated schemas. Different contexts may activate different beliefs. Again, we will take this further in future chapters.[18]

Schemas are vital to our minds. They allow us to make generalizations about the world so that we do not need to sift through countless memories all at the same time. But, as you may guess, our schemas also contain biases and inaccuracies. When you take implicit bias tests,[19] you may be surprised at the biases they may reveal, as these biases rest on schemas tucked away in the mind. Some schemas can be directly updated and changed by the conscious mind but many cannot.

For librarians and educators, recognizing the value of schemas is an important step in seeing how the mind processes information. Here, we see the foundations of our beliefs, including our beliefs about who we are. Any information that our students encounter in our libraries or classrooms take the Pepsi challenge against the schemas our students hold.

Notes

1. As I noted at the outset of this book, I am assuming a normative brain for much of this book. I do want to note individuals with aphantasia, who are unable to produce mental images. Exploring this disorder is beyond the scope of this text but I do want to make this acknowledgement.

2. Joseph LeDoux, *The Deep History of Ourselves: The Four-Billion-Year Story of How We Got Conscious Brains* (New York: Viking, 2019).

3. Lisa Feldman Barrett, *How Emotions Are Made: The Secret Life of the Brain* (Boston: Mariner Books, 2017), 28.

4. Feldman Barrett, *How Emotions Are Made.*

5. Gina Rippon, *Gender and Our Brains: How Neuroscience Explodes the Myths of the Male and Female Minds* (New York: Pantheon Books, 2019).

6. LeDoux, *Deep History of Ourselves.*

7. Hugo Mercier and Dan Sperber, "Why Do Humans Reason? Arguments for an Argumentative Theory," *Behavioral and Brain Sciences*, 34, no. 2 (2011): 57.

8. Mercier and Sperber, "Why Do Humans Reason?," 58.

9. Feldman Barrett, *How Emotions Are Made.*

10. Feldman Barrett, *How Emotions Are Made.*

11. E. O. Wilson, *The Social Conquest of Earth* (New York: Liveright, 2012).

12. Rippon, *Gender and Our Brains*.

13. Pierre Bourdieu, *Distinction: A Social Critique of the Judgment of Taste* (London: Routledge, 1984).

14. Mark Solms, *The Hidden Spring: A Journey to the Source of Consciousness* (New York: Norton, 2021); Charles Fernyhough, *Pieces of Light: The New Science of Memory* (London: Profile Books, 2013); James E. Zull, *From Brain to Mind: Using Neuroscience to Guide Change in Education* (Sterling, VA: Stylus Publishing, 2011); Terry Doyle and Todd Zakrajsek, *The New Science of Learning: How to Learn in Harmony with Your Brain* (Sterling, VA: Stylus Publishing, 2019).

15. LeDoux, *Deep History of Ourselves*, 298–99.

16. I will talk more about the self and the embodied mind in later chapters.

17. Mercier and Sperber, "Why Do Humans Reason?"

18. Jason L. G. Braasch, Jean-François Rouet, Nicolas Vibert, and M. Anne Britt, "Readers' Use of Source Information and Text Comprehension," *Memory Cognition* 40, no. 3 (2012): 450–65.

19. To learn more about implicit bias, visit Harvard's Project Implicit at https://implicit.harvard.edu/implicit/.

CHAPTER FOUR

Constructing the World

For most of us, looking around and seeing objects doesn't feel that novel. Except for those of us with some sort of visual impairment, it is easy to take our vision for granted. We use it to navigate the world, enjoy a sunset, complete work, and read a book. We assume that our eyes present us with a degree of fidelity to the outside world. Our eyes focus on an object. We recognize the object, or, maybe, we do not recognize the object. We know that light hits our retina, it is transformed into electronic signals, and when these signals enter our brain, we see. But neuroscientists and psychologists are teaching us that seeing is more than pure visual processing. The truth of the matter is that often "seeing" is as much a mental construction as it is a matter of biological mechanics.

It is easy to assume that we see everything with a high degree of precision. If we would measure our visual field, we would find that our vision extends 200° horizontally and 100° vertically, *but* we only have high resolution in the 2° that surround the center of our gaze. We have photoreceptors compacted in the middle of our eye and fewer cells on the edges. These cells are not distributed across the eye evenly. We fool ourselves into thinking that we see clearly, because our eyes jump and focus all around. Even when we are not focusing on an item, our mind is constructing it and holding on to an image of what should be there when we are not looking directly at it. We have two types of specialized visual cells: cones and rods. Cones see color. In actuality, they only see types of color based on long (red), medium (green), and short (blue) wavelengths. They combine these three colors in order for the brain to interpret the multitude of hues in between. In addition to the cones, the rods see shades of gray, especially in dim light. In order for us to see, the mind must stitch together limited information based on the physical limitations of the eye itself. The eye detects a small portion of the electromagnetic spectrum—what we call visible light. It compresses this information to three colors and degrees of shading. Moreover, it can only focus on a minuscule portion of its overall visual field. The mind takes this limited input and constructs images that can feel quite intense and entirely complete. Yet, when we see, we do not feel as though we are sticking together limited data at all.[1]

But this is not the end point of the mind's construction that allows us to see. Seeing is not just an act of combining imperfect inputs. It is also an act of accessing schemas and memories. After light hits our rods and cones, it is transformed into an electric signal through the subcortical visual pathways to the primary visual cortex, located in the occipital lobe. The primary visual cortex utilizes specific brain circuits for handling different elemental features such as shape, color, depth, texture, motion, and others. These are a type of lower-level circuits that send information to secondary areas of the visual cortex. This sends to two different processing streams that connect to what the mind has experienced in the past. The ventral stream focuses on processing objects. The second pathway, called the dorsal stream, handles spatial action. Both of these streams connect to different areas of the brain for different purposes.[2] LeDoux notes,

> The identities and meanings of most objects in the world are not innately wired into the human nervous system. To recognize an object, its features have to be matched with stored templates that have been acquired via experiences with objects of that type. Therefore, in the process of building up perceptual representations of the objects that we "see" and interact with in our lives, the visual system partners with memory systems.[3]

There is a type of top-down interaction from cognitive areas such as the prefrontal cortex and bottom-up interaction from areas involved with storing long-term memory. The interaction acts almost like a kind of filter or prioritization when it comes to processing visual inputs. The mind is actively deciding how to process the inputs that it is receiving.[4] When we are seeing, the mind is working from expectations based on memories and schemas. *What the mind expects to see is part of the process of seeing.* We do this with all sensory inputs—hearing, touching, tasting, and smelling.[5]

It is worth reminding ourselves that the brain does not directly interact with the world. It is essentially locked away in the skull. Receiving inputs, sifting them across regions of the brain, making recognitions, and acting only take fractions of a second. But, in survival terms, this delay can be life threatening. Therefore, one fitness advantage that has evolved in our minds is to not wait for the sensory input. We construct our world as a type of *simulation*. The mind does not directly interact with the world, but is actually running a simulated world and then comparing that simulated world to the sensory inputs it is receiving. As Barrett tells us,

> . . . and so, trapped in the skull, with only past experiences as a guide, your brain makes *predictions*. We usually think of predictions as statements about the future, like "it's going to rain tomorrow" or "the Red Sox will win the World Series" or "you will meet a tall, dark stranger." But here, I'm focusing on predictions at a microscopic scale as millions of neurons talk to one another. These neural conversations try to anticipate every fragment of sight, sound, smell, taste, and touch that you will experience, and every action that you will make. These predictions are your brain's best guesses of what's going on in the world around you, and how to deal with it to keep you alive and well.[6]

As the mind is running its simulation, it is testing its predictions. It is anticipating sensory input, interpreting them, ignoring some inputs, and emphasizing others. The mind constantly operates an error-detection algorithm to see if its predictions hold up. When errors are detected, the mind takes note. These errors catch our attention. This is where we examine our world and update our expectations. This is how we update schemas and build new beliefs and understandings. The important thing to notice is that the mind does not construct the simulation based on a direct, stimulus-response mechanism. The simulation comes about based on a combination of inputs but also in combination with past experiences built into schemas. This is a participatory process that is part data interpretation, part filter, and part hypothesis testing. The world we experience is based on the actual world around us but also on the world we *expect* to be around us. We do not have the capacity to focus on every minute detail around us, so we rely upon assumptions. Many times, our minute-to-minute experiences are very conceptual.[7]

The mind's simulation is not just limited to raw sensory input. It is situational and, importantly, social. We are not just anticipating the physical world as we move through it; we are also anticipating the social world between individuals and across the many groups of people to which we belong. We rely on the many schemas we build that help us understand how we connect into these groups. From very early ages, infants recognize faces and build bonds with caregivers. The developmental cycle of the mind expands on the social connections around us. When we view the world, we are interpreting and making meaning based on cultural norms—schemas—that are absorbed through interactions and socialization. When we look at ourselves, we make interpretations based on how we understand who we are. How do I interact within these cultural norms? When we feel social pain, the mind reacts in ways that are similar to that of physical pain. Our social simulation is very strong.[8]

It may seem clear that the simulation is not an entirely conscious experience. In fact, we may argue that it is a mostly unconscious construction. The *intrinsic brain activity* mentioned previously when discussing schemas plays an important role in maintaining the simulation. These intrinsic networks are constantly firing connecting schemas and memories to the present moment.[9] A foundational idea in psychology is that of *unconscious inferences*. Our intrinsic brain activity accesses our experiences in order to infer various aspects of our current moment. We may view an apple but our experience in the moment is a combination of the actual sensory input from the moment mixed with the conceptual experience of "apple." When philosophers make the proposition, "I see an apple," we assume that there is an active "I" in this process when many times there is not.[10] This is not to downplay the importance of consciousness. Consciousness dictates experience by focusing attention and interactions. In any moment, intrinsic reactions activate but these can be overridden by cortical intervention. Psychologists do studies by flashing pictures, and the brain immediately activates before consciousness can intervene. But consciousness *does* intervene and mediates initial reactions.[11]

And, of course, it also works the other way. Unconscious reactions can also intervene and mediate consciousness.[12] For instance, intense sensory inputs can result in intense reactions such as surprise, pain, or disgust. Accidentally drinking spoiled milk will result in an immediate response. Ramming your toe into a table leg will also produce a response that jumps into consciousness. These are rather intense reactions that are difficult for the conscious mind to ignore. Reactions that are subtler are interoceptive reactions. *Interoceptive reactions* result from a bodily need such as hunger or thirst.[13] We need to note that the mind does not just receive inputs from the external world but it is also constantly monitoring its internal state. This internal monitoring results in changes more focused on bodily resources.[14] One of the jobs of your brain is to budget out resources. There are regions of the brain that focus on what Barrett calls "body budgeting."[15] These regions ensure that resources such as glucose or salt get distributed across the body when needed. As the brain constructs a simulation of the world around it, it is not just anticipating how it will react to external needs, but it is also anticipating how it will react to internal needs. For instance, just before standing, the brain anticipates this motion and increases blood pressure just enough to ensure blood flow to the brain so that we do not pass out every time we try to stand up.[16] Later chapters will explore the role of body budget in generating affect and how this impacts mood, behavior, and interactions with information, but for now, it is enough to note that interoceptive responses based on internal states are a factor in how unconscious processing builds the simulation we experience.

The simulation our mind constructs rests upon the interplay between conscious and unconscious processing, but the degree of the interaction between these processes is a major topic in modern neuroscience and psychology and, by extension, is a significant theme of this book that will be explored in more depth in later chapters. For librarians and educators, we must reflect on how the mind's simulation dictates the experiences we have and the ways we process the world. Conscious and unconscious processing interact to build the present. We have to acknowledge the resulting relativity between people. Campbell emphasizes that we should not expect that other people will think like us or even that we can get them to believe as we do.[17] The ways our minds construct reality should push us to recognize that people will inherently think differently than we do, and, therefore, we should be more tolerant of their different beliefs. Zull emphasizes the importance of recognizing variance and the invariance in navigating "reality."[18] When we recognize objects, people, or even situations, we must use characteristics that do not change in order to know what they are but also be able to navigate the infinite amounts of variance around them. Zull explains,

> Knowing what is real has been essential for survival of our species. It allows us to predict events and outcomes, invent tools and other objects, and have confidence in our perceptions. The invariance is part of the truth about the perceived world. It allows us to plan, manipulate, and design, because it is true.
>
> At the same time, our individual personal experience leads to a somewhat different collection of invariant characteristics, and this collection becomes part of the uniqueness of each perceiver. This is one aspect of our diversity. Each of our minds develop differently, but we all still reach accurate and shared concepts of the nature of the real world.[19]

Using words like *true* and *realty* should be done with caution and care. Neuroscientists and psychologists mostly leave these for the philosophers. Hoffman uses the metaphor of a computer desktop to help describe our relationship between "reality" and our senses.[20] When we use a computer, we are utilizing icons in pixels to accomplish various tasks. The icons and the pixels do not reveal how computer processors actually work. They do not reveal microchips, motherboards, storage, or computer networks. The interface allows us to accomplish tasks without needing to understand the underlying components. Similarly, our senses do not have to reveal the reality of our physical universe in order for them to be useful in terms of evolutionary fitness—which is ultimately the force that has shaped our sensory experience. We need our senses to help us accomplish the primary task of survival such as finding food, communicating with others, managing our physical bodies, and similar tasks. The visible light spectrum is only a small portion of the overall electromagnetic spectrum. Other animals see different wavelengths. Our ears only hear a limited range while other animals can hear higher or lower pitches. This is true for all our senses. They are attuned enough for survival and not more. As our minds construct our simulation, our experience with *reality* is bounded by these limits as is our understanding of *truth*. As Hoffman explains,

> According to standard accounts of evolution, payoffs can vary widely while the true state of the world remains fixed. It follows that seeing truth and seeing fitness are two distinct strategies of perception, not one strategy seen in different lights. The two strategies can compete. One may dominate and the other go extinct. So it is a central question, not a conceptual mistake, to ask: does natural selection favor perceptions tuned to truth or to fitness?[21]

His unequivocal answer to this question is *fitness*.

As we think about the mind constructing the simulation, we start to build a picture of how the neural networks in our mind come together to help us survive. Not only must our mind use past experience and schemas to filter the overwhelming amount of inputs that it receives, but it uses them to anticipate the world around it. As it monitors the external world, it is also monitoring internal reactions and processes in order to efficiently allocate resources. When we view the mind through this lens, we not only recognize that the brain is not an external recording device but we also see *how* it is not an external recording device. Our relationship between *reality* and *truth* are buffered through the interface of the simulation.

Understanding the simulation is important for librarians and educators. The simulation that our mind constructs is in many ways that expression of our worldview. The simulation includes hidden assumptions that are built into our schemas. This is another step toward the feeling of knowing.

Notes

1. Donald Hoffman, *The Case Against Reality: Why Evolution Hid the Truth from Our Eyes* (New York: Norton, 2019).

2. Joseph LeDoux, *The Deep History of Ourselves: The Four-Billion-Year Story of How We Got Conscious Brains* (New York: Viking, 2019).

3. LeDoux, *Deep History of Ourselves*, 245.

4. For a demonstration as to how the mind constructs visual images, visit "Akiyoshi's illusion pages" from Akiyoshi Kitaoka, Professor, Psychology, Ritsumeikan University, Osaka, Japan, where he demonstrates "anomalous motion illusion," at http://www.ritsumei.ac.jp/~akitaoka/index-e.html.

5. LeDoux, *Deep History of Ourselves*.

6. Lisa Feldman Barrett, *How Emotions Are Made: The Secret Life of the Brain* (Boston: Mariner Books, 2017), 59.

7. Feldman Barrett, *How Emotions Are Made*; LeDoux, *Deep History of Ourselves*; Robert A. Burton, *A Skeptic's Guide to the Mind: What Neuroscience Can and Cannot Tell Us about Ourselves* (New York: St. Martin's Griffin, 2014); Mark Solms, *The Hidden Spring: A Journey to the Source of Consciousness* (New York: Norton, 2021); Robert M. Sapolsky, *Behave: The Biology of Humans at Our Best and Worst* (New York: Penguin Books, 2017); Gina Rippon, *Gender and Our Brains: How Neuroscience Explodes the Myths of the Male and Female Minds* (New York: Pantheon Books, 2019).

8. Mark D. Pagel, *Wired for Culture: Origins of the Human Social Mind* (New York: Norton, 2013); Virginia Campbell, *Are You Sure?: The Unconscious Origins of Certainty* (Hartford, CT: PYP Academy Press, 2020); LeDoux, *Deep History of Ourselves*; Sapolsky, *Behave*.

9. Feldman Barrett, *How Emotions Are Made*.

10. LeDoux, *Deep History of Ourselves*.

11. Sapolsky, *Behave*.

12. Solms notes this in *The Hidden Spring: A Journey to the Source of Consciousness* when he talks about neuroscience and psychologist Jaak Panksepp's breakdown of affect.

13. Solms, *Hidden Spring*.

14. Sapolsky, *Behave*.

15. Feldman Barrett, *How Emotions Are Made*.

16. Feldman Barrett, *How Emotions Are Made*.

17. Campbell, *Are You Sure?*

18. James E. Zull, *From Brain to Mind: Using Neuroscience to Guide Change in Education* (Sterling, VA: Stylus Publishing, 2011); Campbell, *Are You Sure?*

19. Zull, *From Brain to Mind*, 119.

20. Hoffman, *Case Against Reality*.

21. Hoffman, *Case Against Reality*, 55.

CHAPTER FIVE

Internal Representations of External Events

Recognizing that the mind constructs the simulation does not help us understand how we act—make decisions—within that simulation. Actively deciding and interacting is the domain of *cognition*. You are probably familiar with the term and can probably offer your own definition. Discussions of cognition arise commonly in the education and information science literatures. Generally, the term is used to refer to mental life. It is used for *thinking*. Historically, Descartes's famous recognition *Cogito, ergo sum* connected cognition with a type of inner awareness. For centuries to come, Western thinkers saw consciousness as a defining characteristic of being human while animals were unthinking biological machines programmed to fulfill basic survival and reproductive drives.[1]

Unsurprisingly, Western thinking has come a long way since Descartes's proclamation. Modern neuroscience and psychology provide a better definition of cognition. LeDoux offers that cognition includes

> processes that underlie the acquisition of knowledge by creating internal representations of external events and storing them as memories that can later be used in thinking, reminiscing, and musing, and when behaving. Its dependence on internal representations of things or events, in the absence of the external reference of the representation, is what makes cognition different from noncognitive forms of information processing. Given this definition, processes that allow behavioral responses to immediately present stimulus are not, strictly speaking, under cognitive control. Only responses that depend on internal representations are.[2]

So, for LeDoux, the ability to store, call forth, and hold internal representations, often but not exclusively into consciousness, are the defining characteristics of cognition. This is important to note because cognition overlaps with other mental—largely cortical—functions such as consciousness, working memory, and executive function. In many cases, these terms can be used interchangeably. It is easy for those of us outside of psychology and neuroscience to be a bit sloppy or imprecise with our terminology using cognition to generally mean any mental process, but there are times—especially in professional or disciplinary discourse—where precision matters. It is my hope that the distinctions between cognition, emotion, affect, and other terms from science can be utilized within information science and education.

An important step in understanding how cognition functions is seeing that cognition is not just the domain of humans. Deliberations based on internal representations seem to be prevalent at different capacities in animals, especially in mammals. They seem to be the most developed in primate species, and, of course, quite complex in humans.[3] Naturally, studying internal presentations in other species involves some degree of conjecture. Even studying internal representations in other humans with minds that are not our own takes conjecture. For all of these species, holding a representation of an object or situation in mind, comparing it to present objects or circumstances, or manipulating representations in imaginary mental space presented a significant fitness advantage but allowing animals to accomplish goals and being flexible in responding to ever-changing situations. Cognition offers a more sophisticated problem-solving approach than that of reflex, chemical reaction, or conditioned response.[4]

Deliberative cognition differentiates human cognition from that of other animals. Deliberation uses mental models and runs experiments with them. Many animals such as bees, birds, and mammals use mental models especially when searching for food. They build models of the environment, but with deliberation it is more complicated than just using a model. The model allows an operation or imagined model to run. This is a mental experiment predicting possible outcomes before they happen.

> Deliberation allows one to envision possible response options and to use practical knowledge stored in memory to evaluate and choose the one that seems most likely to produce a useful outcome. Additionally, through deliberation, disparate pieces of information can be combined across multiple steps of reasoning to rapidly reach a decision. What would take many repetitions of trial-and-error behavior for a new response to be learned via outcome-based

> reinforcement can be compressed into a moment of internal simulation of the potential outcomes of possible choices.[5]

For those of us in the classroom, when we consider how learning takes place, we are thinking about deliberative cognition. Teachers provide content, discussion points, or assignments that engage the mental models of students. Students ponder this and respond.

We need to take care and recognize that not all cognition equates to deliberation. Most of the brain's processing and connections between ideas happens outside of conscious awareness. Delineating the point where *unconscious cognition* begins and other types of unconscious processing end is quite difficult. But there is increasing recognition among scientists that not all cognitive processes happen consciously. An often used, but also common example is when we are wrestling with a problem, seeking a solution, and we step away from the problem or even "sleep on" the problem, and, after a short break, the answer seemingly appears out of nowhere. A solution hits us and we are unquestionably able to recognize that this solution is a thing we have been seeking. All of us are familiar with this. Even though we are not consciously at work, our cognitive processes continue behind the scenes, seeking solutions that we were not able to achieve consciously.[6]

The frontal cortex is generally thought to be the home of cognition. It uses great amounts of energy. This energy is expensive; this is the origin of *cognitive load*. There is a limit to the number of tasks or amount of information we can hold at one time. If we are asked to do too much we will start to fail at specific tasks.

> Importantly, increased cognitive load on the frontal cortex, and afterward subjects become less prosocial—less charitable or helpful, more likely to lie. Or increase cognitive load with a task requiring difficult emotional regulation, and subjects cheat more on their diets afterward.[7]

Cognitive load is one way to measure the limits of conscious and unconscious processing.

Images are an important piece of cognition. To be able to see images and think in images is key to our thought process. Images are highly memorable and help capture situations. Images in our mind are *visual*. Even when we're imagining an image, and not actually seeing it, the visual parts of our cortex light up. Our other senses can produce "images." Our sense of touch is very important in creating our body image and recognizing how we interact with the world. Smell, hearing, and taste can generate images in our mind based on our memories that might be associated with them. When we smell a tulip, we do not actually see the tulip, but the smell might be associated with an image. We must recognize that images are electrical patterns on the surface of our brain. They are inputs generated by our senses.[8]

Similar to images, there is also a link between language and cognition. By language, it is not necessarily the physical ability to talk but the mental language and inner dialogue that comes with it.

> Language allows thoughts to wander in novel directions and yet stay connected as a "train." It provides words to label external objects and to characterize and recognize our perceptions, memories, concepts, thoughts, beliefs, desires, and feelings. The words individuals use reflect the things of significance in their culture. . . . But language does more than simply name and categorize objects and events and organize their underlying concepts. With language also comes syntax, or grammar, which structures our mental processes that engage their operation when we are thinking, planning, and deciding.[9]

Language's syntax connects to hierarchical reasoning. Many different animals use sounds to send signals and even share information. Everything from birds to apes can use sounds for various types of communication. But only humans can manipulate sounds and symbols to communicate information about the present, past, and future. Through language only humans are able to set events such as predator and prey interactions within a timeframe and location. They can indicate when and where. Language is a primary tool in pattern processing and in the development of schema.

Understanding the relationship between language, images, memory, and schemas is complicated to say the least. Cognition brings all of these together. Many activities, especially new activities, require intensive focus and a significant exertion of cognitive load. But with enough practice, they are transferred to other parts of the brain and become automatic. For example, learning a piece of music is very intensive at first, but over time, any piece becomes automatic. With practice, mechanics involved in performing the music move from the frontal cortex to more "reflexive brain regions" such as the cerebellum.[10] Thus, actions that require a heavy cognitive load at first become easier over time. For those of us in educational settings, this emphasizes the importance of practice. For students, juggling new terminology, connecting this with meaning, and adjusting their own schemas can be overwhelming at first but with time, new ideas and new skills can become second nature.

The frontal cortex is the slowest part of the brain to mature. The brain's development in adolescence is very important in shaping the brain into adulthood. Basically, most other parts of the brain are close to maturity during adolescence but the frontal cortex is lagging. This results in a period of extremely high risk taking. Sometimes this results in very positive outcomes and novel experiences. Sometimes this is very detrimental to the long-term health of the individual. One of the interesting processes that happens in the adolescent brain is that the brain becomes more efficient. There is evidence that in early adolescence or right before adolescence starts the brain has more neurons or gray matter than the adult brain. In adolescence, we actually reduce connections and become more efficient with existing connections. Throughout adolescence the brain then continues to grow and cortical tasks become more complex. The ability to think abstractly grows in the ability to "reappraise" how we feel about situations.[11]

Additionally, the frontal cortex is important in social behavior. For instance, neuroscientists can see the activation in the frontal cortex in social situations. They can differentiate between "reward-driven" and "advice-driven" circuits in terms of behavior. These different networks activate based on whether there is an internal drive versus an external drive. Across primates, the larger the frontal cortex, the larger the primate social group. The different ways that groups form within primates seem to be driven by the size of the frontal cortex (making subgroups and then rejoining the larger group), and it is probably also true that groups push for the selection or a more complex frontal cortex. One plausible explanation for this relationship is that in social settings individuals need to put in check (inhibit) the base survival behaviors in order to compromise and cooperate. Stronger cognitive processes are important to intervening into instinctive processes.[12]

Given the resource intensity of cognition, there is a survival advantage to putting cognition on hold during times of quick decisions. We cannot suffer the illusion that cognition dictates all of behavior. As noted previously, we can react to external stimuli without cognitive or conscious intervention. The example of fear reactions in the amygdala is one demonstration, as are autonomic reactions based on physical sensation such as pain.[13] But beyond these examples, there are other noncognitive behaviors that we might classify as "learning." One example is *Pavlovian conditioning* where a response—usually an innate, survival response—is associated with an external, reoccurring stimulus. Another example is *instrumental conditioning* where a unique or novel response is reinforced through a positive outcome or reward.[14] Feeling hunger when walking into the kitchen is a Pavlovian response. Giving a child a time-out or even corporal punishment for inappropriate behavior is a type of instrumental conditioning. Both cases alter behavior through noncognitive means. LeDoux proposes that it is the combination of learning through instrumental conditioning along with the newly evolved ability to hold mental representations in mind—cognition—that is the source of the flexible thinking in mammals.[15] This is a revolutionary step in evolutionary terms, and this combination of mental capacities makes deliberative cognition especially useful. LeDoux's view also demonstrates the *modularity* of the brain. When the brain processes information, it does not do so as a unified whole but acts with different modules that have evolved over time. These modules can work together, and they can also be in conflict. When conflict arises, we often evaluate the very nature of our thinking.

This brings us to the first mention of two ideas that we will return to repeatedly: the interrelated ideas of *metacognition* and *reflection*. Deliberative cognition not only allows humans to build mental models about situations and objects, *but it also allows us to build mental models about thinking itself.* Metacognition is classically defined as thinking about thinking.[16] Appropriately, there's a great deal of thinking about metacognition in the education literature.[17] *Reflection is a type of metacognition that draws on the feeling of knowing to make judgments about our beliefs*—ideas we'll explore more later. Metacognition and reflection both engender a type of internal awareness. Other people cannot do this for us. We must do this ourselves. "The goal is to become aware of what we assume, think, and believe, and how we use that awareness in our mental activities."[18]

As Hoffman argues, there are limits to what we can know, and, accordingly, there are limits to metacognition and reflection. The subjective nature of cognition makes it impossible for us to step away from our own minds in order to get the perspective of others.[19] Neuroscience and psychology have allowed us to take significant steps, but there are still many steps left ahead. One important limit that these fields still face is to *really* understand the mechanics of cognition itself.

> Though we have an excellent idea of the mechanics of how information is transmitted and a growing understanding of how it is physically stored in the brain, we are willfully ignorant of what information actually is at a physical level. The entire field of information theory struggles with this essential mystery.[20]

For librarians and educators, seeing reflection as a skill to teach is important in helping students evaluate their own cognitive processes. Reflection is how we judge our own beliefs. It is an avenue to seeing the schemas we hold.

Notes

1. Joseph LeDoux, *The Deep History of Ourselves: The Four-Billion-Year Story of How We Got Conscious Brains* (New York: Viking, 2019).

2. LeDoux, *Deep History of Ourselves*, 205–6.

3. LeDoux, *Deep History of Ourselves*.

4. LeDoux, *Deep History of Ourselves*.

5. LeDoux, *Deep History of Ourselves*, 226.

6. LeDoux, *Deep History of Ourselves*; Eugene T. Gendlin, *Experiencing and the Creation of Meaning: A Philosophical and Psychological Approach to the Subjective* (Evanston, IL: Northwestern University Press, 1997).

7. Robert M. Sapolsky, *Behave: The Biology of Humans at Our Best and Worst* (New York: Penguin Books, 2017), 50.

8. James E. Zull, *From Brain to Mind: Using Neuroscience to Guide Change in Education* (Sterling, VA: Stylus Publishing, 2011); Virginia Campbell, *Are You Sure?: The Unconscious Origins of Certainty* (Hartford, CT: PYP Academy Press, 2020), 202.

9. LeDoux, *Deep History of Ourselves*, 236.

10. Sapolsky, *Behave*.

11. Sapolsky, *Behave*.

12. Sapolsky, *Behave*.

13. LeDoux, *Deep History of Ourselves*; Sapolsky, *Behave*.

14. LeDoux, *Deep History of Ourselves*.

15. LeDoux, *Deep History of Ourselves*.

16. Zull, *From Brain to Mind*.

17. Jennifer Webb, *The Metacognition Handbook: A Practical Guide for Teachers and School Leaders* (Suffolk: John Catt Educational, 2021); Roger Azevedo and Vincent Aleven, ed., *International Handbook of Metacognition and Learning Technologies* (New York: Springer, 2013), https://link.springer.com/book/10.1007/978-1-4419-5546-3 (12 Jan 2023).

18. Zull, *From Brain to Mind*, 259.

19. Donald Hoffman, *The Case Against Reality: Why Evolution Hid the Truth from Our Eyes* (New York: Norton, 2019).

20. Robert A. Burton, *A Skeptic's Guide to the Mind: What Neuroscience Can and Cannot Tell Us about Ourselves* (New York: St. Martin's Griffin, 2014), 109.

CHAPTER SIX

Giving Meaning to the Moment

Even if you were not familiar with cognition at the start of the last chapter, you definitely are familiar with emotion. If I name them, you can easily feel them. Happiness, fear, anger, love—these are the markers of life. If you name your most vivid memories—the birth of a child, a major accident, the death of a family member—they are often connected to some of our most powerful emotions. The average, nondescript days of life that are not connected to strong emotional responses tend to blend together and get jumbled up in memory. Almost all of us feel that we have a strong understanding of emotions because they are interwoven into our lives. But, like most things with the mind, our common view does not hold up under scrutiny. And, for our purposes here, emotions offer insight to how the mind processes the inputs it receives.

The traditional view of emotional reactions holds that they are universal and hardwired into our brains. From birth, our brains arrive with built-in emotional responses that we must fight to control. Our experiences seem to confirm this. People scared of heights wish they could climb the ladder up to the roof of a home but we know that our fear response will paralyze us if we do. When we give the speech at the upcoming birthday party, we take deep breaths in an effort to not be overcome by tears of joy in front of gathered friends and family. We play a game with a sibling or friend and promise ourselves that we are not going to get angry if they do not play fairly, but we cannot help ourselves as rage overtakes us. The traditional, Western view of emotion sets up emotion as a force that interrupts our lives, and—importantly, when interacting with information—emotions gets in the way of rational decision making. This traditional view sees emotion as a residual evolutionary remnant wired into our brain competing with logic and intelligence. Maybe emotions were useful at some point in our evolutionary past, this view holds, but we have since moved on. Attaining enlightenment is to tame our emotional instincts. Emotions may be something that all humans share with other animals, but we'd be better off to leave them behind.[1]

> Emotions are thus thought to be a kind of brute reflex, very often at odds with our rationality. The primitive part of your brain wants you to tell your boss he's an idiot, but your deliberative side knows that doing so would get you fired, so you restrain yourself. This kind of internal battle between emotion and reason is one of the great narratives of Western civilization. It helps define you as human. Without rationality, you are merely an emotional beast.[2]

Barrett calls this *the classical view of emotion*, which has deep roots stretching back to Darwin, to Descartes, to ancient philosophy in traditions such as the stoics, and probably further than that.[3]

One of the many challenges to understanding emotion is that in common usage *emotion* is used to refer to a number of responses in humans and in animals. When breathing increases, muscles tense up, nostrils flare, and palms sweat, which emotion is this? We may have a sense for what an emotion feels like, but it is tough to recognize it. On top of this, the terms we use to refer to individual emotions are also used to cover a range of responses. What's the difference between *fear* and *anxiety*? How about *love* and *lust*? If you can define the differences, could you recognize them if you saw them in other people? What does *anxiety* look like if we ran into it in the world and how exactly is that different from general *fear*? Not only is the language murky, but trying to really connect the semantics to the observable world is also murky.[4]

So what are emotions? Neuroscientist and psychologists are definitely not in complete agreement but, generally, emotions are viewed as reactions or interpretations made by the mind to help explain or react to what is happening around the individual. They are not universal but are constructions learned over time. Emotions are not an uncontrollable reflex but are created by each individual based upon past experiences. Each emotion is a type of schema that the mind connects with reactions in the body. Emotions are not universal, and, in fact, different cultures have different emotional responses. Of course, similarities exist, but they are hardly shared by all people. For instance, the Micronesian people of Ifaluk view emotions as interactions between individuals and not representations of inner states. In cultures such as in Japan, some emotions are thought of as more actions that are taken. The Dutch have a term for an emotion that does not exist in English, *gezellig*, which refers to a type of "coziness" or "comfort" at being at home.[5]

> An emotion is your brain's *creation* of what your bodily sensations mean, in relation to what is going on around you in the world. Philosophers have long proposed that your mind makes sense of your body in the world, from René Descartes in the seventeenth century to William James (considered the father of American psychology) in the nineteenth . . . neuroscience now shows us how this process—and much more—occurs in the brain to make an emotion on the spot. I call this explanation the *theory of constructed emotion*.[6]

Within the brain, combinations of circuits activate to bring forth our emotions. As with all mental states, there is no one area for each emotion but connections of multiple areas result in different emotions. More than this, different combinations may result in reactions that have similar or the same result. This is the principle of *degeneracy*, which generally means "many to one." Many combinations of neuronal pathways can result in the same outcomes. This greatly complicates our understanding of emotion because we may see a smile and see someone laugh, but this may be caused by one set of neurons in one instance and another at a different time. The behavior may be the same but internal responses in the mind may be markedly different.

LeDoux's view of emotion is one that is not shared by all neuroscientists, but it is worth highlighting because it forces us to really step away from our intuitive understandings of emotion. He directly states that emotions are part of cognition. They are part of a mental model for how we should behave in a given situation.

> [Emotions] are not hardwired states programmed into sub cortical circuits by natural selection, but rather cognitive evaluations of situations that affect personal well-being. They thus require complex cognitive processes and self-awareness.[7]

In this way, emotions help bring unity or understanding to the experience at hand. They are an interpretation or meaning to a particular moment. LeDoux takes this line of thought even further by removing *causation* from emotions. This runs against our intuitions, but he argues that emotions do not cause us to act. Our behavior is independent of emotion. Behavior and emotion may react to the same stimuli but they do not connect to each other. LeDoux points to experiments where threatening stimuli are presented subliminally—often flashed before the eye at speeds beyond what the brain can comprehend. Physical responses such as increased heartbeat or sweating palms can be detected—physical responses often associated with fear—but the individual does not report back a feeling of fear. When the same approach is used with individuals with amygdala damage, the individual reports back a feeling of fear but does not have the physical response. LeDoux argues that our behaviors are often driven by—or at least influenced by—survival circuits that are present in all animals—threat detection, seeking food, balancing internal resources, reproduction, and others. These survival mechanisms take action to keep the animal alive and do not need to rely on consciousness or emotions. The mind uses emotions to help make sense of the moment and infuses consciousness with this (often strong) interpretation. Emotions are different for each of us because our schemas are built up over our lives utilizing different memories and becoming more complex as time goes on.

I want to take note of some important distinctions in how I am conceptualizing emotion. I am following Barrett and LeDoux, who view emotion as a part of cognition—as noted above—but drawing a distinction between cognition and affect.[8] Thus, the major distinction I am making in this book is between cognition and affect, *and* I am including emotion *as a part* of cognition. Psychologists and neuroscientists have not reached consensus on this. There are researchers who separate cognition and affect but do so while including emotion as part of affect.[9] One traditional view that can be connected back to Darwin lumps all *feelings* into three layers. The first layer contains "universal expressions" of fear, anger, sorrow, disgust, surprise, and happiness. The second layer includes social feelings such as pride and envy. The final layer comprises background feelings within the body that offer states of feeling like excitement or lethargy. These different levels of feelings subsume all emotions and pretty much everything that is not pure cognitive processing.[10] As a further example, Pham offers a general review of the distinction between "emotion and rationality." He writes,

> In this review, the term "emotion" will be used somewhat broadly to refer to the presence of affect in general. It will be use not only in reference to emotions proper—that is, intense affective experiences such as anger, fear, joy, and love that I have clear emotional referents—but also in relation to milder affective responses, feelings, and states, including moods that do not have clear referents. This wide-ranging use of the term "emotion" is intentional. If one wants to have a full appreciation of the rationality or irrationality of emotional

phenomenon, it is important not to restrict one's analysis to the most intense emotional experiences.[11]

This *emotion-as-affect* perspective is fairly common in the information science and education literatures where *emotion* and *affect* are often used interchangeably. In these literatures, any mental feeling, any mental sensation is equated to an emotion or labeled with the term affect. The feeling of knowing, fear, love, the feeling of causation, and anger are all lumped together as emotion and/or affect. Some of this is just tradition and common usage. No matter what we call them, the human brain will continue to function as it has for the last 250,000 years. But I see value in connecting emotion with cognition and separating them from affect, which is connected to body budget.[12] Affect plays a role in feelings connected to consciousness.[13] All of this will be explored in more details later, but as this discussion of emotion winds down, I want to challenge the traditional views of emotion you may hold. I do not consider tiredness or excitement to be emotions. Emotions are cognitive reactions to situations based on schemas we carry with us.

Emotions are important cognitively because they create a value reaction that highlights cognitive moments. This is why they matter. They are reactions that make one instance stand out from all the rest. LeDoux calls emotions "the mental center of gravity for the human brain."[14] *Emotions make basic survival circuits and unconscious behaviors have cognitive meaning. This allows them to be more easily stored away into memory for future access*. We interpret our experiences based on fear, happiness, lust, and other emotional interpretations that help build the narratives of our biographical memories. When our body reacts to protect itself by running away, we color this reaction with fear to better understand our own mind. When reproductive drives help us make poor decisions in the moment, we layer on lust and desire to explain these urges. When we act defensively and say something we shouldn't to a coworker or friend, we deeply feel the anger rush through our body. When our mind works to build connections with others and share in moments, we laugh together and experience humor. In all of these cases, emotions intensify the experience and offer cognition a handle for the moment.

From this perspective, we can start to gain some useful insights into the brain and behavior in terms of emotions. First, as the brain processes information, it is coloring reactions with emotion that will help it with future access. Emotions make moments distinct. This has implications for learning, engagement, and for the classroom in general. Second, many circuits drive behavior, and most of them are outside of our conscious experience. If we accept the idea that emotions do not cause behavior—a premise that seems to fly in the face of our intuitions—then we have to also accept that actions that we often blame on emotions must come from other mechanisms in the mind. If I did not punch my brother in the nose out of anger, then why did I punch him? If it was not the anger, what was it? Most importantly, we start to see that our conscious selves may not be in control of our behavior at the level we suppose. We *feel* in control. We *feel* like we are making self-aware decisions. But are we?

For librarians and educators, we can see that the ways our minds process information are quite distinct from the purely rational processing we often assume. Cognition is not pure critical thinking, but cognition is interwoven with emotion. Emotion helps us add meaning to cognition. Emotion marks value. From a survival perspective, this is vital. Emotions make memories stand out so that we are prepared for the next interaction. For educators, this could be useful in understanding engagement and a more meaningful type of learning.

Notes

1. Lisa Feldman Barrett, *How Emotions Are Made: The Secret Life of the Brain* (Boston: Mariner Books, 2017), 59; Joseph LeDoux, *The Deep History of Ourselves: The Four-Billion-Year Story of How We Got Conscious Brains* (New York: Viking, 2019).
2. Feldman Barrett, *How Emotions Are Made*, xi.
3. Feldman Barrett, *How Emotions Are Made*.
4. Feldman Barrett, *How Emotions Are Made*.
5. Feldman Barrett, *How Emotions Are Made*.
6. Feldman Barrett, *How Emotions Are Made*, 30.
7. LeDoux, *Deep History of Ourselves*, 200.
8. Affect will be explored in the next chapter.
9. Michel Tuan Pham, "Emotion and Rationality: A Critical Review and Interpretation of Empirical Evident," *Review of General Psychology* 11, no. 2 (2007): 155–78; Bessel A. Van der Kolk, *The Body Keeps the Score: The Brain, Mind, and Body in the Healing of Trauma* (New York: Viking Press, 2014); Mark Solms, *The Hidden Spring: A Journey to the Source of Consciousness* (New York: Norton, 2021); Robert M. Sapolsky, *Behave: The Biology of Humans at Our Best and Worst* (New York: Penguin Books, 2017); James E. Zull, *From Brain to Mind: Using Neuroscience to Guide Change in Education* (Sterling, VA: Stylus Publishing, 2011).
10. Zull, *From Brain to Mind*.
11. Pham, "Emotion and Rationality," 156.
12. Feldman Barrett, *How Emotions Are Made*.

13. Robert A. Burton, *A Skeptic's Guide to the Mind: What Neuroscience Can and Cannot Tell Us about Ourselves* (New York: St. Martin's Griffin, 2014); Solms, *Hidden Spring*.

14. LeDoux, *Deep History of Ourselves*, 368.

CHAPTER SEVEN

A Summary of the Moment

From birth to death, our brains are at work managing the wider range of functions required to keep us alive. Hydration, breathing, managing sugars, and managing salts are among many tasks under the brain's constant monitoring. As a self-organizing system—like all life—our bodies work to resist entropy. Self-organizing systems must separate themselves from the external world. If there is no difference between the system and the external world, then it is not a system anymore.[1] Following this line of thought, Barrett says that the primary job of our brain is to manage our "body budget."[2] Like all systems, our body has limited resources and evolution has equipped us with mechanisms to ensure the efficient use of these resources. If we had to consciously manage these resources, our conscious mind would be overwhelmed to the point where we could not function. Even if we did not consciously manage these resources but we were just *aware* of how these resources were being distributed, we would also be overwhelmed. It is to our benefit that these details are mostly walled off from awareness.[3] Yet our awareness cannot be entirely walled off. We benefit from awareness of the state of our body. Consciousness is not entirely separated from this process of resource management. This is where *affect* enters the picture.

Affect focuses on the different types of background feelings that are present with us all day. One way to think about affect is our current *mood* or feeling about our state of being. A multitude of mechanisms impact our affect; many of them connect with the idea of our body budget. Feeling run-down from lack of sleep, jittery from too much caffeine, or energized after eating a granola bar prior to a workout, all are examples of affect. Other factors such as social interactions also impact affect. Receiving high marks on a test, expressions of love or affection from a partner, or accomplishing an important task may push our mood in positive directions, and, of course, there are many examples of unfortunate circumstances that can equally push our mood into negative directions. Affect is a *feeling* that summarizes how the body is doing at any particular moment. Sometimes affect hangs around over a day while other times it may change multiple times within short periods.[4]

We can think of affect as having two components. First, the feelings that make up affect are *valenced*. They are pleasant or unpleasant, or, to put it simply, they are good or bad. Generally, affect isn't really neutral, since we don't feel neutrality. If we are feeling "okay," then we probably feel good overall. Second, affect contains a dimension of *arousal*. Are we calm or agitated? Are we moved to action or are we chilled out? Valence and arousal help us see the biological connections of affect. We may not always understand the root mechanisms behind our moods but this does not matter most of the time as our moods push us in directions to address the underlying causes.[5]

Solms makes a compelling point that by definition, feelings are conscious, and, thus, affect must be in consciousness.[6] It does not make sense to say that we have an unconscious feeling. The body may have various unaddressed needs that go unnoticed until they reach a tipping point where a feeling arises into consciousness, but unmet needs alone are not affect. The body does a good job of prioritizing needs and selecting the primary need to make into a feeling and enter consciousness. Zull, on the other hand, complicates things by arguing the opposite. He calls affect "background feelings" that are present but we may not be actively aware of them at each moment. They are present but can be ignored.[7] Debating whether an ignored feeling counts as a feeling is probably not especially fruitful for this text, but recognizing affect as feelings surrounding consciousness seems to be the primary importance. Isen emphasizes that affect is often context dependent. It enters consciousness based on the situation and the moment. Sometimes it is ignored, and sometimes it is very present.[8] For instance, everyone can think of times when they didn't get enough sleep and were dragging. There are times when we get pulled into an exciting project or a fun event and our tiredness leaves our mind, only to be rediscovered later. There are other times when we get more work dumped on us or we have to sit through meeting after meeting and our tiredness weighs heavier and heavier on us. The context of the moment impacts how our affect plays out.

I again want to make note that although I am separating affect from emotion, not all theorists do so. Many still follow the traditional view that affect and emotion are both types of feelings, and, therefore, are different—or at least related—components of the same processes. Solms calls moods "emotional affects" that impact consciousness.[9] Isen follows a very traditional view that classifies emotions and moods on a type of continuum of feelings. Affective states range from intensive emotions to mild moods.[10] Pham follows suit, calling moods "incidental emotional states."[11] I bring this up to acknowledge perspectives from neuroscience and psychology even though I am not following these traditional perspectives. By following Barrett and LeDoux in viewing emotion as part of cognition and separating them from affect, we see emotion as a constructed reaction—through schemas—and we view affect as a result of other unconscious, bodily resource management.

No matter where researchers and theorists view the relationship between cognition, emotion, and affect, they universally agree that affect impacts how we make decisions and influences our behaviors. They accept the idea that affect offers an evolutionary advantage by allowing bodily needs to enter consciousness, which moves animals beyond mere instinct to address needs.[12] Moreover, affect permeates consciousness. When I discussed the mind creating a simulation of the world around it and that simulation's reaction to *interoceptive* reactions[13]—reactions to internal states within the body—this is largely connected to affect. Researchers have documented many ways that affect impacts decision making. Positive affect is known to increase flexibility and creative thinking. Negative affect can close our minds to opportunities. Affect can encourage or interfere with rationality and reasoning. It can push or hinder risk taking depending on the situation. The background feelings we have push us in different directions all depending on the context of the situation. Affect acts as a mitigating factor and rarely a factor on its own.

> When your budget is unbalanced, your affect doesn't instruct you how to act in any specific way, but it prompts your brain to search for explanations. Your brain constantly uses past experience to predict which objects and events will impact your body budget, changing your affect. These objects and events are collectively called your *affective niche*. Intuitively, your affective niche includes everything that has any relevance to your body budget in the present moment. Right now, this book is within your affective niche, as are the letters of the alphabet, the ideas you're reading about, any memories that my words bring to mind, the air temperature around you, and any objects, people, and events from your past that impacted your body budget in a similar situation.[14]

Anything outside of your affective niche is just ignored by the brain. It is just noise. This is important for how your mind processes the world. As we generate the simulation around us, our bodies are reacting and preparing for things to come, amping up energy if we anticipate stressful situations or calming down if we recognize safety and support. Our minds offer us a kind of summary of the moment, and we experience this summary as part of affect. So, affect is a feeling based on bodily needs but also a feeling anticipating what we may need to do within the moment. It draws on unconscious processing, making a best guess for what is needed.

Through affect we start to get a broader view of what it means to *know* something. Knowledge does not just reside within cognitive decision making. The mind draws from the affective niche around it and generates a summary feeling that we experience as part of affect. This summary colors cognitive processes and is the background for all that we do. This is a first glimpse of the feeling of knowledge. For librarians and educators, we also must recognize that affect colors the learning within our students. Raw cognition does not exist. It is all colored by the feeling of the moment.

Notes

1. Mark Solms, *The Hidden Spring: A Journey to the Source of Consciousness* (New York: Norton, 2021).
2. Lisa Feldman Barrett, *How Emotions Are Made: The Secret Life of the Brain* (Boston: Mariner Books, 2017), 59.
3. Robert. A. Burton, *On Being Certain: Believing You Were Right Even When You're Not* (New York: St. Martin's Griffin, 2008); Joseph LeDoux, *The Deep History of Ourselves: The Four-Billion-Year Story of How We Got Conscious Brains* (New York: Viking, 2019).
4. James E. Zull, *From Brain to Mind: Using Neuroscience to Guide Change in Education* (Sterling, VA: Stylus Publishing, 2011); Barrett, *How Emotions Are Made*; Alice M. Isen, "Positive Affect and Decision Making," in *Handbook of Emotion*, second edition, ed. Michael Lewis and Jeannette M. Haviland (New York: Guilford Press, 2000), 417–35; Solms, *Hidden Spring*.
5. Feldman Barrett, *How Emotions Are Made*; Isen, "Positive Affect and Decision Making." Solms, *Hidden Spring*.
6. Solms, *Hidden Spring*.
7. Zull, *From Brain to Mind*.
8. Isen, "Positive Affect and Decision Making."
9. Solms, *Hidden Spring*.
10. Isen, "Positive Affect and Decision Making."
11. Michel Tuan Pham, "Emotion and Rationality: A Critical Review and Interpretation of Empirical Evident," *Review of General Psychology* 11, no. 2 (2007): 155–78.

12. Solms, *Hidden Spring.*
13. See chapter 4 on the simulation.
14. Feldman Barret, *How Emotions Are Made*, 73.

CHAPTER EIGHT

The Orgy of Utter Chaos

When we think about learning or we think about how we process information, we often assume that this takes place in conscious awareness. I search for an article, I read it, and I actively acquire knowledge. This takes place in consciousness. We are consciously learning. When talking about cognition, we noted conscious and unconscious processing. In the previous chapter, we noted that affect arises from unconscious processing, and it enters *consciousness*. I have referenced consciousness several times, but what is it? Like with many aspects of the mind, neuroscientists and psychologists do not have a consensus on what consciousness is. It is one of the most hotly debated areas of research. But for educators, understanding consciousness is so very important because consciousness is the source of the self and is pivotal to learning.

The challenge of comprehending consciousness is that it is difficult to escape subjectivity. How do we step outside of it and see things as they *really* are? Or, to put it another way, how do we see things as they really are as opposed to how they *appear to us*? Ultimately, how does the physical matter of the brain generate the qualitative experience of our moment-to-moment living? This is called the *hard problem of consciousness*. Mapping brain activity and understanding neurons and dendrites does not help us make the jump to the phenomenal experiences of the mind. We cannot isolate and study consciousness cells, because consciousness cells do not exist. Physicists can predict black holes and geneticists can sequence the human genome, but neuroscientists are just beginning to scratch the surface of consciousness. It cannot be easily captured by a formula or mathematical model.[1]

In fact, the scientific study of consciousness is fairly recent. For the first half of the twentieth century, behaviorists dominated the study of the mind. The behaviorists believed that our psychology was solely shaped through interactions with the environment. They acknowledged no inner experience but, instead, focused on inputs and outputs. By the 1960s, the *cognitive revolution* gained prominence as researchers focused on brain structure and information processing, utilizing the computer as a metaphor for the mind. The cognitive revolution moved away from the behaviorists, but consciousness remained largely ignored. It was Francis Crick of DNA fame who in the 1990s had the standing, or just the freedom, to step forward and define consciousness as an aspect of the mind to be studied. Now, consciousness is a major area of study that can be mind-bendingly meta. How can one mind that is totally immersed in its own subjective experience attempt to study another mind that is equally as immersed in its own subjective experience? This *problem of other minds* is a correlate of the hard problem of consciousness.[2]

Offering a definition of consciousness is a bit slippery. Since you are reading this, I am going to assume that you have experienced human consciousness. At least, I am assuming that you are not a dolphin or a bird. Your own experience of consciousness is some sort of guide. Consciousness is the "perception of meaning," to use LeDoux's phrase,[3] that utilizes memory in order to have awareness of the present, past, and future. Consciousness allows us to hold a thought, recognize our thoughts based on our past experiences, project these thoughts into the past or future, and, perhaps most importantly for consciousness, set ourselves in the present.

Researchers use the term *consciousness* in two different ways: the first as a waking state and the second as experience. Consciousness as a waking state focuses on awareness or alertness and is contrasted with sleepiness or being in a coma. The second is consciousness as experience, which is often called *phenomenal consciousness*. Consciousness as phenomenon tries to capture the idea of the subjective, qualitative experience of what it *feels* like to be conscious. This is the willful, directed feeling of awareness. The difference between the two uses of the term can be seen in the difference between *being conscious* versus *having consciousness*.[4] Consciousness is not information processing or, in common parlance, *intelligence*, which is more the realm of cognition—as noted previously, cognition can be conscious and unconscious.[5] LeDoux says that consciousness

> requires not only non-conscious deliberation using mental models and perspective cognition, which some animals can do, but also requires the ability to

> be reflectively aware of oneself as the agent of the forecast, and also as part of the subject matter. This may well be a human specialty.[6]

In this book, when I refer to consciousness I am generally referring to *phenomenal consciousness*—the subjective experience of the human mind.

Researchers tend to view generated consciousness as existing on levels. There are higher and lower levels of consciousness. Lower-order processes connect with higher-order processes in the generation of consciousness. Neuroscientists report examples where patients suffer cortical damage or damage due to disorders such as hydranencephaly in children. In these cases, individuals show responsiveness and behavioral reactions. They are awake, but, to use Solm's description, "their experience is contentless."[7] It is as if pieces of consciousness exist, but the processing required to interpret experience cannot completely pull consciousness together. Are these individuals conscious? It is difficult to say they are not. These examples emphasize that we should not view the generation of consciousness as an all-or-nothing state but yet another phenomenon generated by brain components.[8]

A primary facet of consciousness is the *feeling* of being conscious. Understanding the feelings related to consciousness is central to the arguments of this book. Solms states that "Feelings are fluctuating, existentially valued, subjective states with differentiated qualities and degrees of confidence. That is the stuff of consciousness."[9] Feelings related to consciousness are different from emotions. The *mental sensations* of consciousness are not the same as thoughts. But they surround and give meaning to thoughts. We do not have control over mental sensations. They are involuntarily generated in the unconscious but sent into consciousness. Examples of these mental sensations, include things like the *feeling of agency* where we feel in control over our actions, *the feeling of knowing* where we recognize truth in a thought, or *feeling of mental effort* such as working hard to complete a math problem. It is as if the mind, through these feelings, has evolved a type of *internal sensory system* that helps us determine *how* we experience thoughts. In this way, our mental life is given a qualitative dimension. Cognition becomes more than pure logic and reason, because it is embedded within mental sensations.[10]

It is important to remember that as the brain creates the simulation of the world around us it is our consciousness that experiences this simulation. Our conscious mind does not interact directly with the outside world. But the simulation is almost entirely generated by unconscious processing. Our conscious mind does not have access to mechanisms that generate the simulation. Even the management of our most basic memories occurs outside of consciousness. We can draw memories into our mind, but how they are stored and their specific aspects that are stored away are outside of consciousness.[11]

Those of us within the realm of education can start to see the significance of this conversation. In terms of learning, it is not just that we are processing information cognitively—creating mental models marked by emotion that connect with memory and schemas—but this cognitive process is interlaced with mental sensations (feelings). We are thinking, but we are also feeling. Feelings of control. Feelings of knowing. Feelings of how the self connects with ideas. Learning is encased in these feelings.

This, then, brings us to the unconscious. Exploring consciousness is impossible without contrasting it with the unconscious work that our mind carries out every second we are alive. Outlining consciousness is meaningless unless we can say what it is not. The idea of the unconscious is not new. It has been around for centuries, but, perhaps most famously, Freud shined the spotlight on *unconscious intentionality*. Freud emphasized that people were unaware or, if they were aware, avoided acknowledging the role that unconscious processing played in their decisions and mental life. They resisted the subjectivity of the mind, and their resistance centered on the feelings—biologically driven feelings—that unconsciousness revealed. Now, most of Freud's specific findings and theories have been rejected or greatly altered over the years, but his overarching view that our mental lives were driven by feelings derived from bodily functions aligns with the current thinking in the field.[12]

In seeking to define the unconscious, we must first acknowledge that the conscious and unconscious are deeply entwined and cannot be easily pulled apart. They influence each other and work off each other.[13] By definition, the unconscious mind would include all processes outside of awareness. Zull calls this the "default network,"[14] which seems to radiate in the background and is associated with feeling and behavior instincts. Stanovich calls the unconscious "algorithmic-level processing."[15] It makes recognitions based on probabilities generated by the past as it monitors the environment around it. This includes the networks that manage "survival circuits"[16] and the networks that manage the "body budget."[17] Once again, this discussion highlights the modular nature of the brain.

Think about all of the different mechanisms that operate outside of conscious control. If we had to consciously manage life support, resource allocation, waste disposal, and all of the other functions that the mind manages while also drawing recognitions from memory, interpreting language, and managing social interactions, our consciousness would quickly be overloaded. Given a specific stimulus, a specific mental mechanism goes to work. As an example, we can think about a giant chocolate shake (or any dessert of your choice). Most of the time when we see a chocolate shake, we have a desire to consume it. But in limited instances after we have just stuffed ourselves with some other kind of food, we may see the chocolate shake and have a revulsion to it. The desire to eat it and the revulsion from it are directed unconsciously. As another example, we can think about light entering the eye and going into the visual cortex. As noted earlier, even in cases where images are flashed too quickly for consciousness to recognize the image, the visual cortex still receives the stimulus and is activated. Unconscious reactions may take place, but those reactions are not fixed.[18] We can see that the unconscious mind is not one mechanism but really a grouping of disparate processes. In fact, these processes are grouped as "the unconscious" mostly because they operate outside of our awareness but not because they necessarily are related in function.

Our unconscious processing plays a vital part in decision making. Most choices we make arise from unconscious processes. Burton uses the metaphor of an immense committee meeting within the brain.[19] As a decision arises, the various networks fire into action, weighing our past experiences, our unconscious desires, our recognition of past experiences. The networks argue, coerce, and influence each other in order to shape the decision that must be made. This takes place below consciousness. The committee takes a vote and sends that vote into consciousness.

> To get an idea of the magnitude of this process, imagine billions of committee members, each with at least 10,000 hands reaching out to shake hands, prod, poke, seduce, or fend off the other members. Miraculously, this orgy of utter chaos is transformed into a relatively seamless and focused stream of consciousness. Even given the amount of potential information incoming at any instant, we can focus on a single aspect of consciousness and either not notice or ignore the enormous subconscious din.[20]

When we think about the committee metaphor, we start to get a glimpse as to why it is hard to change our beliefs and resist our biases. Before consciousness can step forward, the decision filters through the unconscious being shaped by the committee members—schemas—we have built over a lifetime.

This also means that when we make decisions or choices, we may not know why. All conscious thoughts have aspects of unconscious processes behind them. It follows, then, that all thoughts, whether conscious or unconscious, are probably connected to the same mechanisms. The circuits underlying our choices are probably the same, but the difference is that the results of the circuits may be conscious at times and remain unconscious at others. For some reason, a thought that becomes conscious has crossed a threshold from background processing into awareness. But our conscious minds cannot access the reasons that the scales tipped. We do not know why.[21]

As an example, name a random city on earth. Can you pull a city name into your consciousness? *Jakarta, London, Cairo, Tempe, Peoria*—I am sure you could easily bring up a city name into your mind, but more than likely, you do not know why. If you named the city where you are currently living or visiting, then maybe you can take a pretty good guess as to why you named that city, but if you truly thought of a random name, you have no way of knowing why you thought of that city. You just did it. We can take this further. Imagine two identical cars. Any model—a sedan, an SUV, compact car, pickup truck, etc. Now, imagine one is blue and one is red. They are identical in all aspects. They drive the same. Get the same miles per gallon. They only difference is the color. Because I am a pretty nice guy, I am going to magically gift you one of these cars. Which one would you refer? Blue? Red? Again, most of us can easily select one color over the other without much effort. But why? We make these kinds of arbitrary decisions every day. If we have to arbitrarily choose, such as choosing between right hand or left hand, selecting a number between 1 and 10, naming a city, or selecting one color over another, those choices come to us as a feeling. The reasons for our choices are not really conscious. They are made and then they enter consciousness. If we could not make these decisions, we could not function. We couldn't select the clothing to wear each day. We couldn't decide if we wanted a bowl of cereal or an omelet. In evolutionary terms, indecision is very costly. There seems to be a fitness advantage to easily choosing.[22] But why did we make those decisions? Why did we select the red car? We often cannot really know.

Unconscious processing protrudes into consciousness all the time. Any time that an idea, a thought, or a recognition hits us *out of nowhere*, it is not really out of nowhere. This is unconscious processing at work, dealing with a problem or successfully making a connection and then sending this recognition into consciousness. Sometimes we purposefully put the unconscious to work on a problem. We can do this by stepping away from a difficult problem. The psychology literature calls this approach *incubation*. This is when a person steps away from a problem, and a solution presents itself seemingly out of nowhere or the problem seemingly "solves itself" when we sit back down to reengage with it. Another type of incubation is when we "sleep on a problem," and in the morning, the answer has arrived in our sleep as if by magic. It is not exactly clear how incubation works. It seems that the unconscious mind continues to work on the problem even when the conscious mind is not. It could also be that stepping away allows all ideas to simmer and be forgotten a little bit. This means that distracting or incorrect approaches are reduced and have less impact, clearing the mind for conscious and unconscious processes to operate, making stronger and more accurate approaches more obvious.[23] It is fair to say that the creative process is reliant upon the interface between the conscious and unconscious, and perhaps the true skill of the thinker, the artist, or the creator is mastering this connection.

> The artist regresses consciously and voluntarily into his unconscious dimension, which is above all dynamic, and brings the force of unconscious drives and desires into the forefront of his images. Because the cognitive unconscious is mainly analogical, freely associative, characterized by concrete images, and guided by the pleasure principle, it explains the importance of the phenomenon of the wandering mind and of incubation in the development of creative solutions to problems. Stimulating the unconscious dimension facilitates the emergence of moments of creativity that promotes new combinations and permutations of ideas.[24]

But it is not just thoughts that are sent from unconscious into consciousness. It is the feelings associated with those thoughts: The feelings that are a part of consciousness itself. The *mental sensations* that accompany being self-aware and conscious. These feelings act as a way to summarize the work of the unconscious. They are an accumulation of the work of the brain.

> Feeling is a precious inheritance. It carries within it the wisdom of the ages: an inheritance that extends backwards over eons to the beginning of life itself. When homeostasis eventually gave rise to feelings, the crux of this new capacity was that it enabled us to know *how we are doing* within a biological scale of values. Feelings entrain predictions that are grounded in the accumulated experiences in situations of biological significance of literally all of our ancestors. Feelings enable us to do what is best for us, even as we do not know *why* we do so.[25]

If consciousness is built upon feelings, then one of the key aspects of a thought that makes it conscious must be the feelings that accompany it. A thought cannot be in awareness and also be entirely void of the mental feelings that embed it in consciousness.[26]

Imagine the adaptive advantage that conscious and unconscious processing can offer to a species. In new or unfamiliar situations, the unconscious offers feelings that it pulls from past experience while it works through the range of possible meanings and memories that might be useful. At the same time, conscious experience focuses attention and stabilizes intentionality. Consciousness enables active awareness of the moment. Both processes interact to address uncertainty and increase the odds of survival. Unconscious processing acts much quicker and requires fewer resources, which can be an advantage in times where quick action is needed. Yet there is also an advantage in survival terms to having a conscious system that can override automatic processes. As new situations become familiar, then consciousness fades to the background and unconsciousness transforms novelty into routine.[27]

The interactions between the conscious and unconscious processes offer us a new view of learning in the classroom. So often, teachers lament the lack of "critical thinking" within students, but we can see that our minds have evolved to avoid critical thinking when possible because it is resource heavy. We automatically fall back on routine and familiarity and only break up the routine when necessary. Additionally, our worldview, our biases, our assumptions exist in schemas operating outside of our awareness arising as feelings. Our decision making results from the modularity of the mind. Our conscious awareness is only part of the story.

From the ancient Greeks to the enlightenment, and even in the present, the conscious self has dominated our view of the mind. The Cartesian *cogito, ergo sum*—I think, therefore I am—has placed the *I think*—our self-awareness and our consciousness—at the center of mental life. Even as we have learned more about unconscious processing, and we recognize how much of our thinking is outside of awareness, we still have difficulty letting go of our assumption that the conscious mind is in control. LeDoux calls the conscious mind "vain,"[28] as it assumes that it calls the shots and makes the big decisions. And there is no doubt that this vanity is a further advantage of consciousness. When we live our lives, we feel as if we are the main character in our own dramas. Consciousness gives us center stage. Thanks to consciousness, we live our lives in a directed narrative starring a unified self. We take ownership of behaviors, we make explanations for decisions that we make, and we provide intention to the lives we live. Most of the time we feel a sense of mental order. The inaccessibility of our own neural networks is a defense mechanism against the cacophony of our mental processes. As quoted above from Burton, "Miraculously, this orgy of utter chaos is transformed into a relatively seamless and focused stream of consciousness."[29]

Burton offers a great example from Major League Baseball of how humans can construct experience and narrative.[30] Hitting an MLB pitcher's fastball is one of the most difficult feats in sports. The pitch itself moves faster than the eye can actually see. This means that batters are not physically able to watch the ball as it approaches the bat. Batters actually use their anticipation of the current state of the game, the positioning of the hand of the pitcher, guesses as to where the ball will appear, and a degree of luck to make contact with the ball. But when you hear batters talk about their hits, they say things like, "I was just seeing the ball well today" or "I could follow the ball right to my bat"—both of which are physically impossible. It's not that batters are lying in interviews but that their minds are constructing an experience to explain how the batter made contact with the ball. Consciousness builds a narrative.

Even as we have learned so much about consciousness and how it operates, locating consciousness in the brain remains a primary component of the hard problem of consciousness. Neuroscientists are far from agreement on this one, but there are some broad agreements that we can note. First, consciousness is *emergent*. The mind's outcomes emerge from groupings of neurons. These neurons are not devoted to one thing, but larger outcomes emerge from them—things like consciousness, intentionality, and meaning are examples.[31] Second, the cortex, which is thought to be the home of higher-order processing such as cognition and executive functions, seems to play an important role in consciousness and is traditionally called the home of consciousness, although this view is increasingly challenged.[32] Third, the recognition that consciousness requires feeling—*mental sensations*—has led neuroscientists to recognize the role of the brainstem—home of so called lower-order processing—in consciousness. The lower areas of the brain are thought to be the source of affect as well as feelings that surround awareness. As Solms argues,

> *The cortex becomes conscious only to the extent that it is aroused by the brain stem*. The relationship *between* the two is hierarchical; cortical consciousness depends upon brainstem arousal.[33]

Finally, there is broad agreement that consciousness arises from the interactions between higher and lower areas of the brain, but the central debate seems to be the role that these areas play and which area seems to be primary. For my discussion in this text, we do not really need to take a side in this debate or delve much deeper into the subregions of either the cortex or the brainstem. But it is enough to recognize that the components of consciousness are assembled from these different areas of the brain.

I also want to take a moment to note the differences in terminology between *consciousness*, *cognition*, *attention*, and *executive function*. These terms are closely related and often used interchangeably, but we are at a point where it may be useful to note that they do not refer to exactly the same things. Cognition is the ability to store, call forth, and hold internal representation either consciously or *unconsciously*. Cognition focuses on processing, or, to put it another way, thinking. It takes place as part of consciousness but also as part of unconscious processing. It utilizes schemas and memory. Executive function, on the other hand, is more attentional. It involves self-control and working memory. Executive function is more purposeful. Making a plan, remembering instructions, setting goals, and filtering out distractions are all part of executive function.[34] Executive function is not exactly the same as attention, although attention is part of the equation. There are different types of attention. *Focused attention* refers to an immediate need such as answering the phone or pouring a glass of milk. *Sustained attention* takes more effort, requiring longer focus. This may include activities such as reading a book or working on a project. *Effortless attention* is a type of focused attention that feels almost automatic, where self-awareness is turned off. This could be happening while competing in a sport or writing programming code. This is the kind of *flow* made famous by Mihaly Csikszentmihalyi in his 2009 book *Flow: The Psychology of Optimal Experience*.[35] Finally, there is *effortful attention*, which happens when engaging in an activity that you dislike or find difficult. This requires more effort to be in control of your attention.[36]

Setting consciousness in contrast to cognition, executive function, and attention helps us better understand consciousness. Burton's *involuntary mental sensations* are absent in cognition, executive function, and attention.[37] These feelings are the defining factor of consciousness. The feelings surrounding consciousness set it apart from the others. The feeling of knowing, the feeling of agency, and the feelings that make up the self are required. To be conscious is to *feel* conscious. This is quite different from cognition, attention, and executive function. Cognition can be conscious *and* unconscious. Executive function really centers on the functions absent any feelings. Attention can be conscious, but it can also turn into flow, which is less than fully conscious. Contrasting these pieces of the mind helps us better understand them all.

As we think about the relationship between consciousness and the unconscious, it is difficult to break away from the traditional, Western view that the mind is a unified, rational, decision-making machine. The perspective has been ground into our own worldview—especially those of us schooled in Western thinking—and it just feels right. Not only do we discount the interplay between the conscious and unconscious, but we overvalue or assume that conscious thought—typically assumed to be *rational thought*—is superior.[38] But once we see the importance that feeling has on consciousness, we see that our decisions are built on an interplay between the conscious and unconscious mind. It is the feelings—decisions generated by unconscious processing—that drive our thinking.

Consciousness seems to step in and weigh options that are identified by the unconscious. This is very much in line with philosopher and psychologist John Dewey's classic view of *reflective thinking*. As the mind surveys the world and finds what is expected, it ignores most things. But, when something is unexpected, the mind hesitates and must think reflectively. As Dewey wrote in the first decade of the twentieth century,

> Thinking begins in what may fairly enough be called a forked-road situation, the situation which is ambiguous, which presents a dilemma, which proposes alternatives. As long as our activity glides smoothly along from one thing to another, or as long as we permit our imagination to entertain fancy is a pleasure, there's no call for reflection. Difficulty or obstruction in the way of reaching a belief brings us, however, to a pause. In the suspense of uncertainty, we metaphorically climb a tree; we try to find some standpoint from which we may survey additional facts and, getting a more commanding view of the situation, may decide how the facts stand related to one another.[39]

Dewey was not a neuroscientist, but his description of reflective thinking neatly describes one role of the conscious mind. As the mind generates a simulation of the world, we tend to overlook what is expected. The things that fit the simulation blend away and are taken for granted. But when something doesn't fit, conscious and unconscious processing step in and take note.

Pagel notes that when the algorithmic processing of the unconscious mind finds something that it cannot process, then consciousness is there to weigh options and make determinations.[40] Beyond just weighing options, consciousness brings a degree of dexterity to our thinking that the unconscious mind alone could not. Applying ideas through language, helping us categorize experience and our place in it seems to play an important role of consciousness.

When we think we think in language, we build a framework for relationships between ideas.[41] It is as if consciousness has a type of veto power over the automatic processes operating in the background of the mind. We can identify and counteract our assumptions about the world through consciousness.[42] In cases of trauma such as post-traumatic stress syndrome, the unconscious mind takes over. It forces us to relive violent or traumatic moments as if they are happening in the present. One theory as to why talk therapy is effective is that this is a mechanism for the conscious mind to intercede using language and help the unconscious mind to reorganize traumatic memories, storing them in long-term memory.[43]

But we should be careful not to overstate the ability of the conscious mind to act. We cannot escape the fact that all conscious thought originates in the unconscious mind. Importantly, the *feeling of knowledge*—the mental sensation of certainty—originates in the unconscious. To *know* something, to see truth, is a feeling that is recognized by consciousness but arises outside of consciousness. This is one of the sensations that defines consciousness itself, but its origins are in the automatic processing happening outside of awareness.[44] Raoelison, Thompson, and de Neys tried to test reasoning ability by separating it from unconscious processing.[45] They tried to see if a greater cognitive capacity (i.e., being smarter) helped people intervene and correct errors. Their most interesting finding was that people with higher cognitive capacity were better at catching unconscious errors, but generally, people with higher cognitive capacity were more likely to have better unconscious decisions overall. "Smarter people do not necessarily reason more accurately because they are better at deliberately correcting erroneous intuition's but because they intuit better."[46] One of the advantages of the feeling of knowing is that it is a mechanism that summarizes unconscious processing. It provides a summary, a result, for the myriad of processing taking place outside of awareness.[47]

Yet, we cannot know when the feeling of knowing is accurate. It is not enough to just have that feeling. We need to test it.[48] There seems to be increasing evidence that the interaction between intuition and reasoning is optimal.

> When you've engaged in all those brain systems, when you've done the thought experiments and feeling experiments of how things might play out in the long run, and when you've prioritized the inputs—gut reactions are taken seriously, but they're sure not given veto power—you'll know exactly why something seems right or wrong."[49]

In chapter 3 when we discussed schemas, we looked at the idea of *inference*, or "the production of new mental representations on the basis of previously held representations."[50] We noted that inference can happen consciously and unconsciously. Inferential processes taking place at the unconscious level are often being carried out by multiple, domain-specific processes arriving at an *intuitive* outcome. Our intuitions represent a summary of our unconscious processes. Our *intuitive beliefs* can be strong and can lead us in various directions even if we are not able to identify the processes we used to reach those beliefs. This would stand in contrast to our *reflective beliefs*, where we are consciously aware of the *reasons* behind them. Our *reasoning* may be connected to the content of a belief, a process that took us to that belief, or sources of authority that support the belief. But ultimately, with reflective beliefs, we understand the origins of these beliefs. In practice, beliefs are never purely reflective or intuitive, but an interplay between both.[51] Jasanoff puts it well:

> The brain is special because it helps orchestrate our behavior *without* distilling us down to an essence. It is a transit point for myriad influences that work jointly on us and through us.[52]

This perspective challenges us to think differently about how the mind works. Burton uses the committee metaphor to describe the various mechanisms operating within the brain to come to a decision.[53] But I prefer to think of the brain as a democracy where different processes come together to debate and argue and vote. In the morning as we are getting ready to start our day and we step on the bathroom scale, our conscious reasoning makes a commitment to skip the hot fudge sundae or the frappuccino on the drive home from work. But as the day goes on, and we face the ups and downs, the stress, the dealings with others, other mental processes begin to go to work behind the scenes. Survival instincts desiring calories. Processes seeking to address low blood sugar and low energy levels. By the time we drive home and we are getting closer to that potential hot fudge sundae or frappuccino, our reasoning has competition for our decision. If we are going to maintain our self-control, our conscious mind must overcome these unconscious desires. In common parlance, our *willpower* must take over. As Stanovich convincingly states,

> Likewise, in self-control situations, people have no trouble at all realizing that they are made up of multiple minds and that an override of the autonomous mind is necessary. In fact, they are all too aware of it. The struggle between minds is, in fact, almost the defining feature of these situations. There are situations where we have to resist temptation: where we have to get up and make breakfast despite wanting to sleep; have to resist an extra $3 coffee in the afternoon because we know the budget tight this month; or are on a diet and know that our snack should be carrots and not chips. Here, the internal struggle is palpably real. It is only too apparent to us in these instances that there are parts of our brains at war with each other. Our natural language even has a term to designate these instances: *willpower*. Willpower is a folk term, but in the last two decades, cognitive researchers have begun to understand it scientifically.[54]

For librarians and educators, if we are to really understand how learning works, how the mind processes information, we have to recognize that consciousness is *only a part* of our processing, and a small one at that. The mind is made up of a myriad of processes, which enter our consciousness as intuitions and feelings—especially the feeling of knowing. This provides a more nuanced perspective on knowing. Conscious reasoning—actively weighing evidence and utilizing logic—is only one piece of the puzzle of knowing.

Notes

1. Robert A. Burton, *A Skeptic's Guide to the Mind: What Neuroscience Can and Cannot Tell Us about Ourselves* (New York: St. Martin's Griffin, 2014); Mark Solms, *The Hidden Spring: A Journey to the Source of Consciousness* (New York: Norton, 2021); Donald Hoffman, *The Case Against Reality: Why Evolution Hid the Truth from Our Eyes* (New York: Norton, 2019).

2. Solms, *Hidden Spring*.

3. Joseph LeDoux, *The Deep History of Ourselves: The Four-Billion-Year Story of How We Got Conscious Brains* (New York: Viking, 2019).

4. Robert A. Burton, *On Being Certain: Believing You Were Right Even When You're Not* (New York: St. Martin's Griffin, 2008); LeDoux, *Deep History of Ourselves*; Solms, *Hidden Spring*.

5. Solms, *Hidden Spring*.

6. LeDoux, *Deep History of Ourselves*, 264.

7. Solms, *Hidden Spring*, 58.

8. Burton, *Skeptic's Guide to the Mind*; LeDoux, *Deep History of Ourselves*; Solms, *Hidden Spring*.

9. Solms, *Hidden Spring*, 212.

10. Burton, *On Being Certain*; Burton, *Skeptic's Guide to the Mind*; LeDoux, *Deep History of Ourselves*; Virginia Campbell, *Are You Sure?: The Unconscious Origins of Certainty* (Hartford, CT: PYP Academy Press, 2020); Solms, *Hidden Spring*.

11. Solms, *Hidden Spring*.

12. Solms, *Hidden Spring*.

13. LeDoux, *Deep History of Ourselves*.

14. James E. Zull, *From Brain to Mind: Using Neuroscience to Guide Change in Education* (Sterling, VA: Stylus Publishing, 2011).

15. Keith E. Stanovich, *Rationality and the Reflective Mind* (Oxford, UK: Oxford University Press, 2011).

16. LeDoux, *Deep History of Ourselves*.

17. Lisa Feldman Barrett, *How Emotions Are Made: The Secret Life of the Brain* (Boston: Mariner Books, 2017).

18. Hugo Mercier, *Not Born Yesterday: The Science of Who We Trust and What We Believe* (Princeton: Princeton University Press, 2020).

19. Burton, *On Being Certain*; Burton, *Skeptic's Guide to the Mind*.

20. Burton, *On Being Certain*, 51.

21. Burton, *On Being Certain*; Burton, *Skeptic's Guide to the Mind*; LeDoux, *Deep History of Ourselves*; Campbell, *Are You Sure?*

22. Campbell, *Are You Sure?*

23. Burton, *Skeptic's Guide to the Mind*; Ken Gilhooly, "Incubation in Creative Thinking," in *Cognitive Unconscious and Human Rationality*, ed. Laura Macchi, Maria Bagassi, and Ricardo Viale (Cambridge, MA: MIT Press, 2016), 301–13; Campbell, *Are You Sure?*

24. Riccardo Viael, "Brain-Based Bounded Creativity," in *Cognitive Unconscious and Human Rationality*, ed. Laura Macchi, Maria Bagassi, and Ricardo Viale (Cambridge, MA: MIT Press, 2016), 323.

25. Solms, *Hidden Spring*, 299.

26. Campbell, *Are You Sure?*

27. Burton, *Skeptic's Guide to the Mind*; LeDoux, *Deep History of Ourselves*; Solms, *Hidden Spring.*

28. LeDoux, *Deep History of Ourselves.*

29. Burton, *On Being Certain*, 51.

30. Burton, *Skeptic's Guide to the Mind.*

31. Campbell, *Are You Sure?*

32. LeDoux, *Deep History of Ourselves.*

33. Solms, *Hidden Spring*, 128.

34. LeDoux, *Deep History of Ourselves.*

35. Mihaly Csikszentmihalyi, *Flow: The Psychology of Optimal Experience* (New York: Harper and Row, 2009).

36. Terry Doyle and Todd Zakrajsek, *The New Science of Learning: How to Learn in Harmony with Your Brain* (Sterling, VA: Stylus Publishing, 2019).

37. Burton, *Skeptic's Guide to the Mind.*

38. Burton, *Skeptic's Guide to the Mind*; Feldman Barrett, *How Emotions Are Made*; Campbell, *Are You Sure?*

39. John Dewey, *How We Think* (CreateSpace Independent Publishing, 2014), 11–12.

40. Mark D. Pagel, *Wired for Culture: Origins of the Human Social Mind* (New York: Norton, 2013).

41. Pagel, *Wired for Culture.*

42. Campbell, *Are You Sure?*

43. Bessel A. Van der Kolk, *The Body Keeps the Score: The Brain, Mind, and Body in the Healing of Trauma* (New York: Viking Press, 2014).

44. Burton, *On Being Certain*; Burton, *Skeptic's Guide to the Mind*; Campbell, *Are You Sure?*

45. Mattieu Raoelison, Valerie A. Thompson, and Wim de Neys, "The Smart Intuitor: Cognitive Capacity Predicts Intuitive Rather Than Deliberate Thinking," *Cognition* 204 (June 2020), https://www.sciencedirect.com/science/article/pii/S0010027720302006 (14 Jan 2023).

46. Raoelison, Thompson, and de Neys, "The Smart Intuitor," 33.
47. Solms, *Hidden Spring*.
48. Campbell, *Are You Sure?*
49. Robert M. Sapolsky, *Behave: The Biology of Humans at Our Best and Worst* (New York: Penguin Books, 2017), 507–8.
50. Hugo Mercier and Dan Sperber, "Why Do Humans Reason? Arguments for an Argumentative Theory," *Behavioral and Brain Sciences*, 34, no. 2 (2011), 57.
51. Mercier and Sperber, "Why Do Humans Reason?"
52. Alan Jasanoff, *The Biological Mind: How Brain, Body, and Environment Collaborate to Make Us Who We Are* (New York: Basic Books, 2018), 235.
53. Burton, *On Being Certain*; Burton, *Skeptic's Guide to the Mind*.
54. Keith E. Stanovich, *Rationality and the Reflective Mind* (Oxford, UK: Oxford University Press, 2011), 111.

CHAPTER NINE

The Wisdom of the Body

As the mind generates its simulation and our conscious and unconscious processes interact within that simulation, the mind places itself within the experience. The mind is not a member of the audience simply kicking back and watching the simulation play out. Despite the Western tradition of the *ghost in the machine* emphasizing the separation or dualism of the mind and body,[1] the mind is not just along for the ride within the body. In order to make sense of the world, the mind generates the concept of the self that is unified with a body. The self and the self-in-relation-to-the-body impacts how we think and what we think.

When we think about the *self*, we must start by acknowledging that the self, like anything else in the mind, is generated over time utilizing combinations of networks. The self can be a bit of an illusion that vanishes when we try to hold on to it. Like consciousness and the mind overall, there is no objective stance from which we can step away and view the self.[2] The self is a schema developed by the mind. We can recall that schemas are generalizations built on bundles of memories. Our self-schema rests upon all aspects of how the mind understands itself in the world. This may include physical traits, perceived psychological attributes, our history, assumptions about how we act within particular situations, skills, deficiencies, and a myriad of other attributes that we consciously hold or unconsciously process. Our self-schema constantly changes just like other schema presenting itself based on the moment and situational context. The moment-to-moment input shaping the self-schema helps to anticipate the unfolding present. Some researchers have called this the *working self* which is made up of cultural aspects defining how the self connects with other people.[3] One way to think about the self is to think about an internal identity that we use to separate "me" from "others." Recognizing *I/me/mine* from *you/they/them* is vital in understanding autobiographical memory and even what counts as "real" in the world. Mental health requires the mind to differentiate between imagination, reality, the self, and others keeping them all separate.[4]

An important aspect of self-schema is *the feeling of agency*. This is a *mental sensation*—a feeling—that is part of consciousness. The feeling of agency is wrapped up in the notion that we can make choices in our world. We feel that we have a choice and that we have control over those choices. A simplistic way to think about self-schema and agency is that self-schema is a high-order concept that we use in memory and within consciousness. Agency is also an aspect of consciousness, but it is generated at a lower part of the brain as part of the feelings that make up conscious awareness. The sense of agency is a sense of purpose and control around behavior. It gives us a sense that our actions are more than just pure reflex. The sense of agency is the sense that "you" are the one making decisions. If your friend grabs your arm and lifts it up into the air, you may still feel ownership over the arm, but you do not feel that you were the one who lifted it. You would not have a sense of agency in lifting your arm.[5]

A foundational part of the feeling of agency is the feeling that the body is mine. This feeling of "mineness" is the result of sensory perceptions. We can feel our bodies and see our bodies, and, from this, we build a portion of our agency. This includes the comfort level of our own personal space around us and our bodily self-image. In some cases such as amputees, the schema does not match the reality when they have feelings of ghost limbs that do not exist.

Significantly, our physical body and the feelings emanating from it build our mind. This is the concept of the *embodied mind*, where the mind is more than just an operator of the mechanistic body. The mind emanates not just from a brain locked up in the skull but from the entire body. There is increasing recognition that our bodies impact not only what we do but also how we think. The mind *feels* the body. It is a part of the body. Many of our thoughts are driven by *bottom-up mechanisms* where external stimuli push our thinking. Bottom-up attention puts the environment front and center. The environment is in the driver's seat. When the horn honks from an oncoming car, we immediately look and act. Or, maybe we are pondering our next vacation, and we wonder how this became a center of our attention? Then we realized that we saw the name of a river on a road sign. We remembered a boat trip we took down that river, and we thought about vacations. This led us to thinking about summer plans and our next vacation. Attentional cues from the environment push us to ideas that lead us to the next idea. These can be sensory inputs like the horn honking. These can be ideas from something we recognize that sends us down a path. Many times, these are *social stimuli* driven by other people or situations.[6]

> The relationship between brain and environment goes much further than the truisms that people are products of their time and place, that both nature and nurture are important, or that learning and memory arise from experience. When the boundary between the brain and environment is blurred, every thought and action, even at the moment it occurs, becomes a consequence of influences in the wider world. By examining these connections, we will again combat the mystique of the brain as controller and appreciate the extent to which our brains are natural entities subject to the universal laws of cause and effect.[7]

The view of the *biological mind* is the view of interconnected processing constantly processing and interacting with the world through the body. The mind functions, not as a computer compiling data, but as an extension of the world. Memory, feeling, reactions, and understandings come from the immersive experience of living.[8]

Extending these ideas, we can see how some have come to explore the *wisdom of the body*. They believe that if we are to find "truth," then we are not going to find it through antiseptic, intellectual analysis. We must move away from the trend in Western thinking for *disembodied intelligences* where the body is treated as a thing not to be trusted. In this line of thought, the body is disconnected from rationality obstructing our understanding of the world. In order to discover the wisdom of the body, we must use *embodied knowledge* as a means to bridge the gap between the conscious mind and unconscious processing. True knowing originates in fostering a *felt sense* where we ask questions of the body and listen to the bodily response.[9]

> To take embodiment seriously is to take seriously how one speaks and how one listens to the self and other. The recognition that one is an embodied being includes the acknowledgement that even in a situation of being an observer one is an involved observer—someone who is being affected by and is affecting what is taking place. Being a researcher or a therapist requires that one become fully and thoughtfully involved. It is as if one is engaged in a dance of moving forward and moving back; one steps closer and steps away, has an effect and is affected, all as an embodied being.[10]

We will explore the idea of the felt sense and how this connects to the feeling of knowing in later chapters. For now, the important piece of the discussion is to note that recognizing the embodied mind is to see the physical body as a path between the conscious and unconscious mind. In engaging the body as a part or knowing, we are opening a type of inner monologue. Meditation, various forms of therapy, psychedelic drugs, art, and many other avenues have tried to bridge this gap between conscious and unconscious knowing with varying degrees of success.

When thinking about how to bridge this gap, the work on addressing trauma and working to treat victims has been instrumental in increasing our understanding of embodied knowledge. When we face trauma, being a soldier, rape victim, victim of violence or catastrophe, etc., we often want to move on with life away from the trauma, but our brain does not move on. The slightest stimuli can activate trauma. When a triggering event takes place, the brain acts as if the trauma is happening within the present moment. Feelings of panic, rage, terror, and even shutting down flash across the mind. Trauma acts out in a multitude of ways depending on the individual and the moment. Individuals can lash out at others, damaging relationships. Sometimes the conscious mind is not even aware of the causes of the trauma as the unconscious mind activates. During moments of high stress, the unconscious brain takes over and partially shuts down higher brain functions, even shutting down consciousness entirely. The rest of the mind acts by running, hiding, fighting, or freezing. When awareness kicks in later, we may be in entirely different positions or places and not understand how we got there. The brain's primary goal is survival.[11] *Dissociation* is a common outcome of trauma where the overwhelming nature of trauma fragments experience by interrupting the mind's construction of the self.

One avenue of treatment is to create a bodily response to the trauma, helping the brain reclassify events in the past. Some people can do this through discussion, others do this with writing, and others can do it through drawing or art. A first step in dealing with trauma is noticing the body's reaction to triggering events. Noticing the reaction involves noticing the physical sensations and how they impact us. After we notice the physical reactions, we can notice our thoughts and how our thoughts connect to the physical sensations. There is a way that these register in our body. Noticing how the body stores memories and emotions and reactions to them is the first step to changing them and living with them.[12] Treating trauma is one example where the conscious mind uses the body to intervene to address activity within the unconscious mind.

> One of the clearest lessons from contemporary neuroscience is that our sense of ourselves is anchored in a vital connection with our bodies. We do not truly know ourselves unless we can feel and interpret our physical sensations; we need to register and act on these sensations to navigate safely through life. While numbing (or compensatory sensation seeking) may make life tolerable, the price you pay is that you lose awareness of what is going on inside your body and, with that, the sense of being fully, sensually alive.[13]

The embodied mind has several implications for our libraries and classrooms. First, the learning mind cannot be pulled away from the environment around it. Social interactions and environmental cues move the mind in different directions. Second, the mind doesn't just observe and compute but also interacts with and changes. The feelings that make us who we are are not just mental sensations but are physical. The brain is not just the ghost in the machine. It *is* the machine. Third, the self is a generated schema. When we think about how we learn, the self is part of our equation. That learner is built over time and experience. Finally, bodily knowing is one avenue to bridging the gap between conscious and unconscious processing. This is a very important idea that we will explore more as we delve into the feeling of knowing. The body is one potential interface with our unconscious processing because it connects to the feelings between consciousness and unconscious processing.

Notes

1. Gilbert Ryles, *The Concept of Mind* (London: Hutchinson, 1949); Alan Jasanoff, *The Biological Mind: How Brain, Body, and Environment Collaborate to Make Us Who We Are* (New York: Basic Books, 2018), 235; Virginia Campbell, *Are You Sure?: The Unconscious Origins of Certainty* (Hartford, CT: PYP Academy Press, 2020).

2. Campbell, *Are You Sure?*

3. Joseph LeDoux, *The Deep History of Ourselves: The Four-Billion-Year Story of How We Got Conscious Brains* (New York: Viking, 2019).

4. Bessel A. Van der Kolk, *The Body Keeps the Score: The Brain, Mind, and Body in the Healing of Trauma* (New York: Viking Press, 2014); Ledoux, *Deep History of Ourselves*.

5. Van der Kolk, *Body Keeps the Score*; Robert A. Burton, *A Skeptic's Guide to the Mind: What Neuroscience Can and Cannot Tell Us about Ourselves* (New York: St. Martin's Griffin, 2014); Campbell, *Are You Sure?*

6. Jasanoff, *Biological Mind.*

7. Jasanoff, *Biological Mind*, 120.

8. Jasanoff, *Biological Mind.*

9. Steen Halling and Mical Goldfarb, "Grounding Truth in the Body: Therapy and Research Renewed," *Humanistic Psychologist* 19, no. 3 (Autumn 1991): 313–30.

10. Halling and Goldfarb, "Grounding Truth in the Body," 328.

11. I have hesitated in including this section on trauma, but this discussion offers an important aspect of the relationship between consciousness and unconscious processing. This is a painful and difficult subject. If you are interested in a more authoritative treatment of the subject, please turn to Bessel A. Van der Kolk's excellent book, *The Body Keeps the Score: The Brain, Mind, and Body in the Healing of Trauma.*

12. Van der Kolk, *Body Keeps the Score.*

13. Van der Kolk, *Body Keeps the Score*, 272.

CHAPTER TEN

Our Deep Connections to Other Minds

If we look at our progress so far, we have the physical brain and built out the sections of the mind. But to really understand how we process information, we need much more than memory, cognition, affect, and the multitude of processes at work. We must also examine how minds connect to each other.

Our mind is very much connected to other minds—not physically connected, but imprinted with the connections so strong that we might as well be physically connected. Up to this point, I have said very little about the social nature of the mind. It is not possible to overemphasize the importance of the ways that humans connect with each other. I have not delved too deeply into it because it needed its own treatment. In order to understand the social mind, we must understand two competing realities. We have a great ability to help each other and cooperate, but at the same time form competing groups that are in conflict. In evolutionarily biological terms, society and culture are survival strategies where the group is an extension of the individual. The underlying aspects here are complex, extending back through our evolutionary history.

One rule that has remained consistent over the four-billion-year history of life is that a species' genetic inheritance predisposes that species to a specific environment and specific type of existence. Environmental factors shaped genetic fitness, which was handed down from generation to generation. Perhaps it could be argued that bacteria might be the exception to this, but when it comes to plants and animals, a species was locked into a place within an ecosystem—that is, of course, until our closest hominid ancestors arrived. Our genetic heritage was shaped on the savannas of Africa, but the species of *homo*, specifically *homo erectus* and *homo sapiens* (humans) escaped Africa—in the case of *homo sapiens*, literally spreading to every corner of the globe.[1] As Pagel writes about humans,

> Here was a single biological species using just a single coalition of genes that was nevertheless able to adopt different guises and forms in different places. In one place we could be like the heron able to pull fish from the sea, in another like a lion able to bring down large prey, and another like a camel able to survive in the desert, and in yet another we could float on the water like a duck or seagull.[2]

Humans, like few other species, have escaped the environment that shaped their genes. But within the human archeological record, there is a great mystery. Biologically modern humans with the genetics and anatomical structure shared by all of us today came into existence somewhere around two hundred thousand years ago. For most of our existence, humans lived within the plains of Africa, but around fifty thousand to eighty thousand years ago something changed. Around this time, humans left Africa, starting our spread around the world, and at the same time, the fossil record has explosive evidence for the existence of culture—not just the use of tools but the burying of the dead, the use of pigments for color, and artifacts suggesting symbolic use of art. Some of these changes, such as burying the dead, show up earlier in the archeological record but only in limited locations with inconsistency, not at all on the scale that would come. Somewhere around fifty thousand years ago, biologically modern humans became psychologically modern humans, leaving Africa, shaping the environment, and transforming all parts of the planet, so for three-quarters of our existence, we lived in our home ecosystem; but then something changed.[3]

It's important to emphasize that this "sudden" change fifty thousand years ago was a long time coming. First off, we are closely related to other primates such as chimpanzees that have not escaped their environment. Chimps live in groups and cooperate in hunting and other activities while being competitive with nonrelative groups. Our social inheritance is shared by our evolutionary cousins stretching back millions of years. In fact, *homo sapiens* were preceded out of Africa by *homo erectus*, who also used tools and fire over almost two million years ago. *Homo erectus* spread across Africa, Europe, and Asia. They disappeared around one hundred thousand years ago as human territory expanded, leading some to hypothesize that it was *homo sapiens* who ended *homo erectus*.[4] We may never know for sure, but what we can say is that humans were not the first species to demonstrate some of the characteristics that led to our dominance. However, in almost two million years, *homo erectus* never built cities, settled all of the islands of the Pacific, or established agriculture. *Homo erectus* and *homo sapiens* descended from the same genetic heritage, but only one had the right combination to spread across the globe.[5]

And what caused that genetic combination? What tipped the balance fifty thousand years ago to leave behind widespread evidence of culture? What allowed humans to take existing traits such as group living and the utilization of tools to the next level? Some have hypothesized that the anatomical changes such as walking on two legs allowed us to change physically and support our larger brains. Others have argued that the tools themselves pushed our brains to grow more complex. It is difficult to say precisely, but it seems very clear that the *social brain hypothesis* played a significant role. This theory states that living in close-knit groups pushed primates to evolve more complex brains. Living closely with other individuals is tricky business; threats can arise within the group as well as externally from other groups. Dealing with cultural rules, cooperation, internal disputes, and other social pressures shaped our brains. Many types of thinking that we assume are cognitive may actually be social in their development. For instance, let us consider the ability to use our imaginations around potential threats such as predators or other groups of humans who may hurt us. We have the unique ability to think through possible scenarios and anticipate things that have not yet occurred. This imagining could have a social nature based on the need to share ideas with others to coordinate actions. In order to understand other people or to communicate ideas to them, we may have developed an imagination that would aid us in these tasks. The reality is probably less simplistic than this example, but evolutionary psychologists believe that fitness pressures transformed our brains, emphasizing genes that allowed the social brain to become our greatest advantage over other species. The social brain hypothesis says that group existence changed the very structure of the brain.[6] In order for the social brain hypothesis to work, individuals must be bound together, and the glue that holds them together is culture.

The saying *knowledge is power* may seem overused in our technology-driven, hyper-connected world, but in evolutionary terms, it is quite accurate. The accumulation of knowledge, and vitally, the ability to pass that knowledge down to offspring so that they can build upon it, has become a human fitness advantage.[7] The system that underlies this accumulation and transfer is *culture*. It is not just the knowledge itself that is important but the underlying rules of interaction between individuals that matters most. Humans, as a species, do not just pass genes on to their offspring. We pass ideas and systems of interaction.[8]

At birth, human minds are "cultural blank slates," to use Pagel's terminology[9]—but not the kind of blank slates that philosopher John Locke proposed. Our minds come primed and ready for language, socialization, causation, to compute numerical quantities, and to mimic people around us. But they are not primed to automatically be part of any particular culture. We inherit the arbitrary culture that we are randomly assigned at birth. Just as some animals such as ducklings are imprinted to follow their parents at birth, we are almost equally imprinted by the culture around us. It is difficult to escape and shake it off. Culture defines how we relate to others, how we view ourselves within groups, and the perspective we use throughout our lives to understand how the world operates. Culture is an evolutionary strategy that has proven to be more effective than any other adaptation including wings, shells, poisons, deception, camouflage, odors, etc. People, especially anthropologists, often ask what makes us human and separates us from other animals. The clear answer is that we have culture. All of the typical answers to this question including gods, art, language, intelligence, are bound up and described by culture.[10]

The groups into which we are born become our "cultural survival vehicles,"[11] providing us with a kind of protective layer between us and the world. Just as our bodies provide a protective layer around our brains, culture protects us from the world around us by giving us a connection to the larger group through "language, cooperation, and a shared identity."[12]

When we enter a culture, the ideas within that culture occupy our minds and get us to transmit them to other people. Just as we can be infected by a virus, we can also be infected by ideas. It can be difficult to fend off some ideas. Ideas about relationships, drug taking, birth control, bravery, and others can enter our bodies and can be in direct conflict with our genes, often hampering our likelihood of survival and reproduction.

> With the advent of culture, another sphere of evolving entities arose that does not share the same route into the future as our genes. This new sphere of evolution was the world of ideas. They are cultural replicators that exist by inhabiting our minds, and their "purpose" is to get us to transmit them to other minds.[13]

Entire aspects of culture, including art, music, and religion, which we often consider important in giving life meaning, seem to perform the function of binding us together. These *cultural enhancers* do not bring about a specific product in survival terms such as food, shelter, or tools. They work behind the scenes to motivate and alter how we approach problems in life. They may connect us in ways that feel meaningful, giving us mechanisms to demonstrate commitments to each other. But this system of connection has a byproduct. Many ideas may lead to conflict.[14]

We must remember that the benefit of the cultural spread of ideas is to hold on to and share the best ideas within a group of people. But we must also note that the system does not singularly filter for truth and objectivity. It may seem obvious, but culture is not a scientific-like process seeking measurable outcomes. Group cohesion is primary. And, as we are well aware in our modern world, idea-to-idea warfare is a feature and a bug of the system.[15]

> If I can influence the consensus to move in a direction that favors me (whatever I'm doing is cool), then I'll probably benefit even if my objective understanding of the world is biased. For this reason, it makes sense that our cognitive machinery evolved to be only partially constrained by objective reality, as the social consequences of our beliefs are often just as important as the objective consequences. Indeed, some researchers have argued that our minds evolved the ability to process logical arguments not so we could discover the true state of the world, but so we could convince others of the accuracy of our own self-serving beliefs.[16]

Both true and false ideas compete for survival as if they were genes to be passed along to the next generation.

In previous chapters, we discussed unconscious processing and the mind acting on intuitive mechanisms, where the mind makes predictions for how the world works. Our expectations for the physical world may come from observations, but our predictions about the social world—our interactions with others—are built around cultural norms. From this perspective, we can think of a sociological theory like Bourdieu's *habitus* in a new light.[17] Habitus is an explanation for how people react within a set of expectations or rules but also how their reactions are not strictly governed by those rules. At various times, individuals react within the rules to get an advantage or react against the rules as a way to gain notoriety. This is a type of mental calculus where individuals assess the probabilities of certain outcomes based on experience and social understanding. Individuals are guessing how they should react and how others will react. Culture acts as an operating system written onto the mind. Decisions and choices are not simply conscious, rationally driven considerations, but often, unconscious processing weighing group dynamics and ingrained systems of interaction developed within the mind from birth.

Clearly, many animal species gather information about the environment around them and share it with other individuals of their species. From bees dancing in a hive to help others find nectar to whale song playing a part in mate selection to chimpanzees screeching about danger around them, humans do not have a monopoly on communication by any means. We can fairly say that many species share information in order for other individuals to *learn* and make choices. But only humans demonstrate *social learning*, which differentiates us from all other animals. For a perspective on this, we can think about humans compared to chimpanzees, which share a vast majority of our genetic makeup. Young children ages two to three years old perform similarly on many tests to chimpanzees. These include locating hidden objects and using sticks to reach items on shelves. But the same children show advanced skills compared to chimps when it comes to social tasks. They could learn faster by watching others, they recognized social cues, and they followed the gaze of others to find an object—all skills outside of the capacity of a chimpanzee.[18]

Social learning may be a slippery concept to define, but two factors are important. The first is a type of sophisticated copying without the reinforcement of rewards. Humans can recognize a novel approach to a problem simply by observing. The second is a type of conceptual understanding. It is not just that we are able to copy an action but that we understand *why* that action is important. Many animals, especially primates, can be trained in different tasks. A chimpanzee can be trained to wash dishes. The reason the chimpanzee does this is that it wants to get a reward such as a banana. It is just as happy to wash a clean dish as a dirty dish as long as it gets the reward. A chimpanzee cannot comprehend the idea of a *clean dish*. There's just an action that results in a reward. Biologists call animal learning *stimulus enhancement* where actions that already exist within an animal are rewarded and are emphasized. This is not social learning, where an action is improved upon or changed.[19]

In social learning, the individual understands motivation and goals and uses this to adjust actions aimed at particular outcomes. To do this, the individual must have a *theory of mind*, which no other animal species possesses. The theory of mind is the ability for an individual to recognize that other individuals have similar minds to theirs. This allows them to describe mental states of others and, therefore, understand motivations. In humans, the theory of mind emerges somewhere around the age of three or four.[20]

Given that you are reading this book, you are well aware that social learning does not just happen by observation but also through language, which makes social learning and culture possible. As noted previously, many animal species are able to communicate but only humans have language. Human language is unique from other forms of animal communication in its property of being *compositional.* Other forms of animal communication have *dimensionality* based in length and intensity. Grunting, chirping, roaring, beating of the chest, using orders, and other forms of communication may communicate differing levels of meaning beyond just yes/no, one-versus-another signals. But only human language has units of meaning—words—that follow rules defining subjects, objects, and verbs. Through language, we can communicate millions of ideas. We can observe and share information about the external world while also sharing information about our internal worlds to each other. We can define the past, present, and future as we make plans. Language is one of our key tools in pattern processing and in the development of schemas. Language is a mental framework for meaning.[21]

In the words of Pagel, language is a "neural-audio technology for rewiring other people's minds."[22] It's the ultimate *social technology* for sharing symbolic meaning. Through language, we can reach into the minds of others, planting ideas, gaining influence, or establishing connections. Even though I am mostly focusing on speech—verbal and signed—when I refer to language, the principles are similarly true with symbolic meanings in arts and systems of mathematics.[23]

If we focus on spoken language for a moment, we can note the ways that different areas of the brain must work together in order to have language. First, the auditory cortex detects sound. This does not necessarily have to be spoken sounds but, really, just any sound. We can attach meaning to all different kinds of sounds. The meaning making is connected to the integrative cortex. In this area, there are specialized components for understanding sounds as language. This is a type of pattern recognition that separates spoken words from other types of sounds. Beyond just understanding what we hear, we also must produce our own sounds. Speaking is a type of action that has significant impact on the brain. When we speak silently to ourselves, much of the brain activity is similar to when we are actually using our physical voice. There is a language processing that takes place whether we are just thinking words to ourselves or if we follow through and produce the sounds of words. Producing language works in the opposite direction of hearing someone speak. We must start with an idea or an image and translate that into sound and meaning. So, in one direction we are bringing in sound and recognizing the meaning, and in another direction, we start with the idea to produce the sound. The organization of ideas in preparation for and interpretation of language as it is received is centralized in the frontal cortex. To write the word *tree*, speak the word *tree*, see an actual *tree*, hear the word *tree*, and interpret the meaning of a *tree* requires different areas of the brain taking action together.[24]

The mix of culture, language, and social learning brought about our species' ability for coordination and cooperation, the essence of our dominance as a species. *Coordination* is the ability for individuals to align their individual behaviors and actions to compliment the work of others, generally to achieve a goal or outcome.[25] Coordinated systems involve rules, the ability for individuals to make decisions, and feedback mechanisms so that individuals can evaluate the success within the system. Driving a car with reasonable expectations of safety, the availability of apples at your local supermarket, and starlings flying in huge clouds of birds without plummeting to their death are all examples of coordinated systems at work. Coordinated systems can be large and quite complex, but at root, they are often a matter of assembling the systemic components to allow groups to operate.

Cooperation, on the other hand, is something different. It is often a prerequisite for coordination to be successful, and, crucially for human survival, it works against the self-interested tendencies that we sometimes assume are behind many of our decisions. Cooperation is the *willingness* of individuals to participate even when they may have justification to be distrustful.[26] Humans hardly have the corner on the market for cooperation. Plants and animals alike cooperate for survival. From pack animals to insect colonies, to algae and fungus living as a lichen, to millions of other examples, cooperation for survival is an important aspect of life. For many species, reproduction is a cooperative endeavor requiring the individual to overcome other violent, or at least distrustful, tendencies essential for survival.

Despite this widespread cooperation, it will probably come as no surprise that human cooperation is at a level unlike that of any other species. In fact, our common usage of the word *cooperation* probably undersells the meaning here. Devotion, commitment, and affection to the point of self-sacrifice seem more accurate. In almost no other species will individuals sacrifice their well-being for that of others, even for their own offspring. And the question is, "why?" We do not know exactly, but if the social brain hypothesis holds and we became smarter in order to manage social relationships, then the fitness advantage of cooperating outweighed other alternatives.[27] In order for our groups to be successful, all group members must be in concert with each other, seeing the same challenges and building a world together. Human cooperation is driven by a type of innate desire to share the contents of our mind with other people. We share mental sensations, with the goal of eliciting reactions in others. All of us can relate to the frustration of sharing an exciting or even a sad story with someone else who reacts with indifference.

When we tell a story and we exaggerate the outcome, we are sacrificing factual details in order to communicate the accurate emotional content we feel. When we caught that huge fish last weekend, it was not, in fact, a great white shark, but it sure felt like it was.[28]

The evolutionary strategy of coordination and cooperation that makes our group cohesion so successful is different from that of almost any other species in the animal kingdom. Other species who cooperate may work together so that individuals can care for their own offspring. Humans not only care for their own offspring but also for the offspring of distant relatives. Sometimes individuals do not reproduce at all while still supporting the offspring of family members. *The theory of kin selection* is an evolutionary strategy where individuals support relatives because those relatives are more likely to carry similar genes to them. Our ancient ancestors living in tribal bands could reasonably assume that those living with them shared common genes. Over time evolutionary fitness selected for individuals predisposed to recognize kin—even distant kin—and sacrifice to ensure their survival. This, in the long run, continuously reinforced cooperation.[29]

But, in order for human cooperation to work, it cannot hinge on some sort of even return. If our cooperative genes are to survive to the next generation, it must go beyond a one-to-one tradeoff; the risks and obstacles for broad cooperation are too vast to ensure equal exchange. If we assume equal exchange, cooperation would fail; distrust would undermine the exchange. Why should I help you if I cannot trust you to hold up your end of the bargain? The exchange within the group must be given freely. General cooperation is not enough, and pure selfishness is not going to work in the long run. What is required is the idea of *reciprocal altruism*, where the individual you cooperate with truly wants to cooperate with you. Altruism cannot be a one-way street where only one person is altruistic. If there were too many freeloaders, the cooperative genes would not be selected as altruists work and sacrifice, ultimately selecting their genetics out of the group. The altruism must be reciprocated where group members treat other members of their group as *honorary relatives* as we support them, defend them, and even fight for them.[30]

Those of us in the West, and particularly the United States, emphasize individualism and the choices we make. We too easily discount the power of our cooperative brains. We are the primate version of an ant colony, a type of superorganism built on cooperation and coordination overrunning the planet. Individually, we accomplish little. As von Hippel writes,

> We are the fiercest predator on the planet by virtue of the power of our minds, but even human minds aren't that special on their own. If you drop one of us naked alone into the wilderness, you just fed the creatures of the local forest. But if you drop one hundred of us naked into the wilderness, you've introduced a new top predator to this unfortunate stretch of woods.[31]

But even with our cooperative powers, we clearly do not live within a cooperative utopia. Liars, cheaters, and free riders have shaped our evolutionary history as much as kin selection and cooperation. Yes, humans developed altruism, but we also acted with self-interest.[32] Copying from others is an important aspect of social learning, and, as such, it is also an avenue for one individual to take ideas from another individual and use them to the disadvantage of the person who discovered or invented them. Intellectual theft is part of social learning, and if that theft is not put in check, then social learning does not benefit the larger group. If free riders can further their genes without having to expend their energy, then why wouldn't they? And if innovators could not benefit from their own innovations, they why expend the energy to innovate? Thus, humans have developed a kind of *cognitive immune system* to protect against free riders. The human tendency toward *moralistic aggression* by turning on members of our own group if they threaten the strength of that group protects the group from its own members. So if people deviate from the established social norms, then they are pushed out of the group.

> Reciprocal altruism is the source of friendship, gratitude, sympathy, guilt, innate sensitivity to cheaters, generosity, withholding help to other people who do not reciprocate, a sense of justice or fairness, and even forgiveness. Each of these either encourages us to enter into cooperative relationships or protects us once we do. The fragility of reciprocal altruism and the psychological complexity even its simple acts require might be why it is surprisingly difficult to find in nature, outside of humans.[33]

The human sense of fairness is an important evolutionary step because it becomes a way to mitigate self-interest. Fairness acts like an enforcement mechanism guiding our own interactions with others so that we do not take advantage of them and so that they don't take advantage of us. But it also helps us judge the interactions of others as a third-party observer. Our feeling of fairness helps us recognize that it is wrong to take advantage of others and can push us to punish those who are overly selfish. Our social world is a marketplace built on reputation where we use social cues to judge others. We give trust to those we know, are more willing to trust people who feel that they belong to our group, and we are suspicious of outsiders—rightly or wrongly.[34] Our social awareness is highly attuned to the groups to which we belong, recognizing our place within the whole. We must judge when to be obedient to the group and when to try to push against the group if necessary. We are calculating reward, punishment, self-interest, and the safety of being part of the group.[35] Our desire to remain in the group can be so strong that we actively deceive ourselves, even adhering to group beliefs in the face of counterevidence.[36] Mercier calls our psychological stance toward others one of *open vigilance*, where we must be open to cooperation and the benefits that come from the group while being vigilant against those who would deceive us.[37] In the long run, gullibility is evolutionarily maladaptive.

In our ancient, hunter-gatherer existence, in-group pressures such as deciding to cooperate and avoiding deception were not the only pressures at work. Part of our allegiance to our own group came from the pressures—and often fear—of other groups. We might imagine that sometimes groups might have worked together in terms of trading, but more often, neighboring tribes presented danger.[38] In our ancestral past, tribal groups competed for territory and resources. Strong groups thrived while weaker groups did not. Groups with better organization, better communication, and other factors related to the size and cohesion of the group ensured that their genetic lineage continued. Thus, the cooperative factors within the group were shaped by competition with external groups. Groups with weak cooperative makeups could not compete with efficient groups.[39] Our psychology has built in *parochialism*, resulting from an instinctive hostility toward people who are outside of our group. Our own group represents safety. External groups represent a threat.[40]

> Humans evolved to be highly cooperative, but the underlying evolutionary pressure was a fight for survival. Our cooperative nature evolved to make us fierce competitors. So, it should come as no surprise that our cooperative nature doesn't extend automatically to members of other groups. Indeed, other groups were often a serious threat to our ancestors' survival, so cooperation across group boundaries relies on a very tenuous form of trust. Due to the fact that fairness is relative, distrust between groups is threatened whenever we perceive another group to be benefiting more from an agreement than we do, even if that agreement is clearly more beneficial than no agreement at all. Lastly, because we hypocritically perceive the motives of our own group positively but the same motives of other groups as suspect, we are unwilling to extend the benefit of the doubt to other groups but are dubious when other groups fail to extend the benefit of the doubt to us.[41]

In-group and external pressures have shaped how we interact with others. Feelings of generosity, charity, family, and respect as well as those of jealousy, cowardice, selfishness, and betrayal come from the complexities of our group-based existence. We are at once altruistic and distrustful. We are drawn to groups and desire to belong, but we should also take care to note that our allegiance to a group exists in differing degrees of durability. There is no doubt our direct relatives typically remain our strongest group connection. There are many groups that are fleeting, calling forth little in the way of true devotion. Groups form, reorganize, and go away regularly in our lives. Our evolutionary heritage sets the stage for the complexities of our social interactions.[42]

Our socialized brain has undergone changes resulting from this socialization. Like so many other aspects of the brain, there is not one area that is part of social functions, but it is the combination of brain areas that make this possible. Both higher and lower functions come together in our social brain. For instance, the amygdala, an evolutionarily "older" part of the brain beneath the cortex is thought to be active in recognizing in-group versus out-group membership. We discussed the amygdala when we discussed fear and automatic processing. The amygdala gets very active when it comes to recognizing faces and especially in recognizing emotional faces. It acts outside of consciousness within a split second. In contrast, the prefrontal cortex is a "newer" part of the brain that is activated when we are thinking about different aspects of ourselves. Feelings such as self-esteem are important in terms of how well we feel embedded in the social groups around us.[43]

Pagel shares a theory that consciousness itself resulted from dealing with complex social relationships. Cultural norms that hold together groups shift and change to meet new needs.[44] Additionally, addressing group decision making requires recognition of multilayered interactions with others. One area of speculation is that consciousness itself came about to offer the mental dexterity to deal with these needs.

> Life in a complex social environment such as our own requires us to make decisions about a fluid and constantly shifting situation. The role of a conscious mind might be to weigh up alternative courses of action sent to us from our subconscious minds. This role might be given over to our conscious mind rather than allowing our brains to follow some rule of thumb or algorithm because the social contingencies multiply endlessly—"if I do this, that might occur, and then she might do this or he might do that and that would lead to this. . . . " If not merely a problem of contingencies, the rapid pace of cultural change means that new situation constantly arise and these require conscious deliberation rather than less flexible subconscious rules . . . it might be that

> precisely because of the complexity and novelty of the social relations we regularly engage in, we need something that works in real time and is flexible.[45]

Our society is held together by genetic bonds. It is also held together by the cultural systems that connect to other people who are not genetically related to us. Our underlying psychology has been largely unchanged for thousands of years, even as the cultural rules overwritten on that psychology are changing very quickly. So consciousness may have resulted from social pressures, managing culture-built complexity in the mind, allowing us to dynamically process situations.

For those of us in libraries and classrooms, the social mind offers an important perspective on how we process information. No matter how we feel on the matter, we are deeply connected to others. Culture is a type of operating system that we inherit upon birth. Ideas propagate like genes, holding groups together. Our social brain has shaped how the mind operates. So, to know something is to be shaped by social forces even if we do not see them at work around us. The groups to whom we belong push and pull us, promoting some ideas and resisting others.

Notes

1. Mark D. Pagel, *Wired for Culture: Origins of the Human Social Mind* (New York: Norton, 2013); Alison Gopnik, *The Gardener and the Carpenter: What the New Science of Child Development Tells Us About the Relationship Between Parents and Children* (New York: Farrar, Straus, and Giroux, 2016); William von Hippel, *The Social Leap: The New Evolutionary Science of Who We Are, Where We Come from and What Makes Us Happy* (New York: Harper Wave, 2018).
2. Pagel, *Wired for Culture*, 46.
3. Pagel, *Wired for Culture*; Gopnik, *Gardener and the Carpenter*; von Hippel, *Social Leap*.
4. Given the impact that humans are having on the health of the planet, we may be lucky to be as successful as *homo erectus*. Our 200,000–300,000 years may not seem very impressive when compared to the 2,000,000 years of *homo erectus*.
5. von Hippel, *Social Leap*.
6. von Hippel, *Social Leap*.
7. von Hippel, *Social Leap*.
8. Pagel, *Wired for Culture*.
9. Pagel, *Wired for Culture*.
10. Pagel, *Wired for Culture*.
11. Pagel, *Wired for Culture*.
12. Pagel, *Wired for Culture*, 13.
13. Pagel, *Wired for Culture*, 21.

14. Pagel, *Wired for Culture*.
15. Pagel, *Wired for Culture*.
16. von Hippel, *Social Leap*, 136.
17. Pierre Bourdieu, *Distinction: A Social Critique of the Judgment of Taste* (London: Routledge, 1984).
18. E. O. Wilson, *The Social Conquest of Earth* (New York: Liveright, 2012).
19. Pagel, *Wired for Culture*.
20. Pagel, *Wired for Culture*.
21. Pagel, *Wired for Culture*; Joseph LeDoux, *The Deep History of Ourselves: The Four-Billion-Year Story of How We Got Conscious Brains* (New York: Viking, 2019).
22. Pagel, *Wired for Culture*, 275.
23. Pagel, *Wired for Culture*; James E. Zull, *From Brain to Mind: Using Neuroscience to Guide Change in Education* (Sterling, VA: Stylus Publishing, 2011).
24. Zull, *From Brain to Mind*.
25. James Surowiecki, *The Wisdom of Crowds: Why the Many are Smarter Than the Few* (London: Abacus, 2014).
26. Surowiecki, *Wisdom of Crowds*.
27. Pagel, *Wired for Culture*; von Hippel, *Social Leap*.
28. von Hippel, *Social Leap*.
29. Pagel, *Wired for Culture*; Robert M. Sapolsky, *Behave: The Biology of Humans at Our Best and Worst* (New York: Penguin Books, 2017), 507–8.
30. Pagel, *Wired for Culture*.
31. von Hippel, *Social Leap*, 106.
32. Nate C. Carnes and Ronnie Janoff-Bulman, "Restraining Self-Interest or Enabling Altruism: Morality and Politics," in *Social Psychology of Political Polarization*, ed. Piercarlo Valdesolo and Jesse Graham (New York: Routledge, Taylor & Francis Group, 2016), 123–42.
33. Pagel, *Wired for Culture*, 190.
34. Pagel, *Wired for Culture*.
35. Sapolsky, *Behave*.
36. von Hippel, *Social Leap*.
37. Hugo Mercier, *Not Born Yesterday: The Science of Who We Trust and What We Believe* (Princeton: Princeton University Press, 2020).
38. von Hippel, *Social Leap*.
39. Wilson, *Social Conquest of Earth*.
40. Pagel, *Wired for Culture*.
41. von Hippel, *Social Leap*, 208.
42. Sapolsky, *Behave*.
43. von Hippel, *Social Leap*; Sapolsky, *Behave*; Gina Rippon, *Gender and Our Brains: How Neuroscience Explodes the Myths of the Male and Female Minds* (New York: Pantheon Books, 2019).
44. Pagel, *Wired for Culture*.
45. Pagel, *Wired for Culture*, 329–30.

PART II

THE FEELING OF KNOWING

The memories that we hold and the content of our knowledge are separate from the feeling of knowing. This mental sensation provides an unconscious, metacognitive assessment of what we know. Our unconscious processes emerge from our schemas, which rest on culture and the theory of mind. This section highlights important metacognitive areas of psychology: source monitoring, and conflict monitoring. It also considers strategies for how the mind operates, including heuristics, rationality, and reason. This section also takes a step outside of neuroscience and psychology; it brings philosophy into the discussion. Social epistemology, an area of philosophy, offers an avenue for judging the ways that groups produce knowledge.

CHAPTER ELEVEN

The Happiness of Pursuit

In baseball, the hidden ball trick is a strategy that is tons of fun. When utilized, the defensive team deceives a base runner as to the location of the ball in order to tag them out. The pitcher acts as if the ball is in glove and walks back to the pitching mound; all the while, the first basemen actually has the ball. Thus, *hidden* ball. The pitcher walks up and acts as if he is preparing to pitch. Then, when the base runner steps off the base, the defensive player makes an easy tag. (YouTube is full of hidden ball trick highlights if you want a break from cat videos.) Deception is a common strategy in sports whether it is a bluff in poker, a fake handoff in football, a fake pass in basketball, or faking out a goalie in a penalty kick in soccer, among many examples. When we purposefully use deception, in sports or otherwise, we utilize a skillset that other animals do not seem to exhibit. We have the ability to predict what other people will do within a given situation. We are able to put ourselves in the shoes of others, think about what they might do, and then act in response to them. We can anticipate their moves, understand the meanings behind their actions, and also guess at the feelings behind their actions.[1] Mercier calls these *mind-reading mechanisms*.[2] They make up what psychologists call the *theory of mind*, which is important to our cooperative and social systems including learning and teaching.

Theory of mind is not just about deception. It allows us to consider that a friend might be hungry when they come for a visit because we anticipate their needs. Theory of mind helps us recognize that someone may be unhappy if they just dropped their cake onto the floor. Theory of mind is why we automatically look up in the sky if we walk by other people who are standing around and looking up. We understand that if these people are looking up, there must be a reason. All of these examples happen because we recognize the internal states of other people even if we cannot directly observe them or directly ask them.

> "Theory of mind" is a special kind of cognition in which one has thoughts about other people's mental states. In social interactions we use knowledge about how our mind works to read others' minds—to attribute thoughts, beliefs, and feelings to them, and predict their behavior.[3]

Theory of mind is necessary so that individuals can anticipate the reactions of others. This requires individuals to recognize that others think in similar ways and different ways to themselves. The theory of mind forms a foundational understanding for social interactions.

But theory of mind is not just about how we see other people. It is also that we understand that other people also understand us. Self-conscious emotions such as pride, guilt, and embarrassment come from our feelings as others appraise us. These emotions are important because they help the mind locate us as individuals within the group. They utilize our emotions in order to pass an immediate verdict on our status within the group.[4] As we spend more time in a new group, the better attuned we are to their minds, the more we recognize when to rely on their advice, but also the more that we understand their internal feelings. Humans seem to have an intuition that can judge the skills of others. When we watch others work or have past experience with them, we have an intuition on how successful they will be at future tasks. We are also very good at intuitively judging who has knowledge on what topics by interacting with them. Surely, these skills are far from perfect. But as we interact with new people, we instantly judge, project feelings onto them, and work to gauge their mental states. When we interact with a new group of people, we understand individuals by judging the people around them.[5]

The theory of mind is fundamental to teaching and learning. Chimpanzees, among our closest evolutionary cousins, do not have theory of mind—or they seem to have a significantly underdeveloped one compared to humans—and, therefore, chimpanzees are very bad teachers. Young chimpanzees are very bad learners. For instance, it often takes young chimpanzees ten years to learn how to do a task such as cracking a nut, which many other individuals utilize each day. Chimpanzees around each other are cracking open nuts all the time. It is not a hidden trick but the basic ability to take note of what others are doing, to recognize a reason behind the actions, and then to copy the action to gain the benefit is beyond their ability. Even a basic form of communication such as pointing escapes them. Human children, even when fairly young, can easily follow the gaze of others and easily understand when an adult points at an object to follow. But adult chimpanzees will not follow.[6]

When we teach another person, a basic starting point is for us, as the teacher, to try to understand where the student is in the process. If we are teaching a new skill, we want to understand if they have any past experience. We try to understand what motivates them. Why do you want to learn this? We try to anticipate questions that they may have. All of this is built on the theory of mind. The idea that the teacher can use the student's experience and existing knowledge as a starting point makes human learning very effective. The notion that a student can learn concepts—such as how a process works—through watching a demonstration by a teacher is a foundation of our social learning and all made possible by the theory of mind.[7]

While the mind comes prepared for *social* learning, it also is prepared for learning in general. It's not just that we can learn from copying others; we also can recognize, dissect, and reshape ideas. Even though most of us in educational settings emphasize formal learning, we should not lose sight of the fact that learning is an everyday occurrence. Experience is the source of most of our learning. It is the first foundation for knowing. Every experience changes the brain. The brain in the morning will be different by the evening. Most changes occur on a very microscopic level but there are some that will drastically change behavior. Childhood is the largest period of learning, focusing on exploration and discovery. In childhood, experience is new. We learn by errors. We learn by doing. Through our experiences we build our mental habits, our schemas for how the world operates.[8]

The lengthy human childhood is fairly unique in the animal kingdom. Our large brains take years to fully mature, much longer than most other animals. Humans are quite helpless when born. They are entirely reliant upon the community into which they are born, and it is that community that prepares each member to contribute. In so doing, that community expends significant resources to get a child to maturity, offering their own contribution to the whole. Our species has made this evolutionary tradeoff in order to utilize and prepare our big brains.[9]

Our general arc in life is to move from play-based learning toward goal-based learning. Play is more open and experimental. There is some evidence that play increases flexibility in the brain. Ultimately, it seems that the point of play is to create mechanisms for development that evolution does not need to program out in advance. Instead of building out all the rules beforehand, play allows us to explore and develop and find new solutions.

But in order to encourage play, evolution has played a trick by making it enjoyable. We might be seeking fun, but our mind is learning. The reason for the seeking does not need to be the same as the evolutionary reason. In contrast, goal-based learning focuses on a need. Learning to plant a seed, learning to hunt, or learning to make clothing may be valuable lessons to learn but they are a different type of learning from play.[10]

Our stages of development have different goals and our learning changes to meet these goals. Infants primarily explore a physical world, mastering their own bodies and interacting with what is around them. Preschoolers explore a psychological world with a focus inward. School-aged children work out an externally driven social world. Adolescents take a further step and go out in the world without the protection of caregivers at all. The adolescent brain seems to be more attuned to rewards, driven heavily by the brain's reward systems. Thus, adolescents tend to downplay risks while also seeking social acceptance of peers. At the same time, adolescents' self-control systems are more developed than that of children but still underdeveloped when compared to adult brains.[11] Gopnik suggests that the adolescent mind needs rewards, and developing control systems meant that adolescents need guidance. Over evolutionary history, adolescents were not simply cut loose to learn the life's lessons, but a period of apprenticeship was probably more likely. In order to achieve mastery, teenagers worked with skilled adults to learn important skills.[12] Stanovich reminds us that it is in self-control situations, where we must really engage willpower, that we are most aware that our mind is a democracy. In the adult brain, with fully developed self-control circuitry, the mind is able to override the desires for rewards and short-term gains. The adolescent mind is not so equipped.[13]

As we look at how the human brain learns, we should not lose sight of the fact that a portion of our "learning" follows that of other vertebrates. *Instrumental learning* results from learned behaviors based in reinforced outcomes. For example, we walk by a refrigerator and have an automatic urge to peek in to see what kinds of snacks might be on hand. There are two types of instrumental conditioning. One is based on habit and one is goal directed. Habitual responses tend to come from some *antecedent stimuli.* The stimulus happens first, and the individual responds. The light turns red. We stop the car. The response can become very automatic. Goal-directed responses, on the other hand, are reinforced by punishments and rewards. They require a memory of the outcome and a recognition that taking a specific action in order to reach that outcome. If I answer correctly in class, I will be praised. There is a "habit-versus-action" tension that has evolved based on these types of conditioning. Given different environments it is often better to work habitually (in environments with abundant food for instance) while other times it is better to be flexible and able to adjust (in environments with scarcity for instance). So, as we can see, we are more than social learning. Like all animals, instrumental learning is at work in our minds. The human propensity for learning does not exclude us from similar learning scenarios found in other animals.[14]

But it is the human ability for *deliberative cognition* that makes our learning highly effective. Deliberation uses mental models and runs experiments with them. This allows us to utilize lessons learned through experience, social learning, and instrumental learning, pulling them together into something new. LeDoux argues that it is the cognitive ability of making mental representations along with instrumental learning that helped make deliberation possible.

> Deliberation allows one to envision possible response options and to use practical knowledge stored in memory to evaluate and choose the one that seems most likely to produce a useful outcome. Additionally, through deliberation, disparate pieces of information can be combined across multiple steps of reasoning to rapidly reach a decision. What would take many repetitions of trial-and-error behavior for a new response to be learned via outcome-based reinforcement can be compressed into a moment of internal simulation of the potential outcomes of possible choices.[15]

Stanovich uses the term *mindware* to refer to the raw material based in past learning that can be brought to bear on new situations. Mindware would include strategies, understandings, norms, or experiences. The mind transforms these into *decoupled representations*—schemas—which are mental representations separated from the actual reality before the individual. This is the foundation of deliberative cognition.[16] Our minds are not only reacting to the current moment simply using instrumental learning to react. We can bring forth entire scenarios from our past. We can take our experiences and apply them to new situations. Our mindware is built upon a compilation of memories if nothing else. Utilizing memory involves the memory itself but also a cue to find learned material. Much of our memories draw on *symbols*, often language as a symbol. One representation can bring forth long-forgotten memories.

> Symbols are at the core of memory. . . . All we need is a symbolic cue to trigger reconstruction of a long and complicated memory. For example, the word symbol "camp" may trigger detailed memories of childhood summers. Symbolic cues are our entry to poems, stories, songs, equations, calculations, designs, and

> many other creative activities. Symbols evoke images of our experience. Those images are related not only to concrete experiences, but also the process and nature of the symbolic experience itself.[17]

Symbols are vital to our deliberative cognition. Symbols allow us to name and to share schemas. Symbols allow us to organize and classify memories.

The *naming phenomenon* is part of the integrative function of the prefrontal cortex. This area of the brain is where encoding happens. If we are to recognize another person, we must have in our memory a connection with the auditory process where we heard the name, a sensory process where we recognize the face from the visual input, and somehow the two components must come together and be united within the mind. This is the integrative process at work. A key job of this area is to separate "what" and "where." We recognize differences in things, and we are able to put them into locations and combinations to make meaning. For example, think of the difference between the word *tub* and the word *but*. These are the same combination of letters but are specifically in a different relationship around the letter *u*. Our brain must make sense of that relationship in order to recognize these two words as something different.[18] The what are the letters *t*, *b*, and *u*. The where is the order in which they appear.

As the brain compiles experiences, it becomes easier to expand what it knows. Generally, the brain is more effective when it can connect new experiences to existing understandings. As the brain builds neural networks, it builds connections. The brain learns through connections. Connections to prior knowledge help build pathways to new knowledge. When you are working in an area where you have existing knowledge, it is easier to expand that knowledge. When you are in a new domain of learning, it can be very difficult. Many times there is a need to work through prior knowledge that might be missing. It is difficult to just jump into a new subject.[19]

As new subjects become more familiar, they become easier. When we engage new ideas, our conscious mind actively juggles ideas and strains to make sense. New realizations or skills can be tricky to master at first as neural pathways are first established. But over time, things that were new and awkward can become second nature and can be accessed without effort. The more that they are accessed, the more permanent they will become in your memory. New skills and new knowledge move from intense focus and awareness in consciousness to more be automatic and unconscious. The general direction of learning is from conscious processing to unconscious processing. This only occurs through long-term usage and reinforcement of neuronal pathways.[20]

An essential part of learning involves the role that the brain's reward systems play in shaping behavior. The well-known neurotransmitter *dopamine* drives both motivations and rewards. The release of dopamine is important, driving your mind to want more. But it is not just receiving dopamine that matters. A big part of dopamine is anticipation. When dopamine is held back, we are driven forward. The longer it is held back, the more satisfaction we have when we finally get it.

> Dopamine is not just about reward anticipation; it fuels the *goal-directed behavior* needed to gain that reward; dopamine "binds" the value of a reward to the resulting work. It's about the motivation arising from those dopaminergic projections to the PFC [prefrontal cortex] that is needed to do the hard thing (i.e., to work). In other words, dopamine is not about the happiness of reward. It's about the happiness of pursuit of reward that has a decent chance of occurring.

This is central to understanding the nature of motivation, as well as its failures.[21]

Zull emphasizes the *joy* of learning.[22] It is not just the joy in the moment of comprehension but the joy in the *journey of learning*. Curiosity is the desire to take the journey; the importance of *curiosity* in learning is widely acknowledged.[23] From our earliest moments of exploration as infants to the types of learning we encounter as adults, curiosity matters. The pleasure of learning, the joy, the reward, pushes us to be curious.

In this way, learning can be seen as a kind of multiplier effect where experiences bring about new skills or understandings, and if successful or useful, those skills and understandings can bring about broader skills and understandings. Skills and recognitions become more automatic as processes grow stronger and get transferred from conscious to unconscious processing. Thus, learning grows on itself. As noted above, copying is an important aspect of social learning, but copying alone is not enough. If we only copied, there would never be anything truly new, truly innovative. Each generation would be locked into place with no change. Learning must involve copying what has been done in the past but also experimentation and invention.[24] *Mirror neurons* are fascinating cells in that brain that appear to play a vital role in learning. Mirror neurons fire when we *both* observe a person doing an action and also when we are doing that same action ourselves. These neurons are responsible for "matching" observations of the world with actions that are taken by the body. This seems to be an important step away from simple reflex action. They may be part of our theory of mind and understanding the actions of others.[25]

In order to make these matches, the mind must take notice. The mind's awareness must be active. Before the experience, before the memory is made, before the raw materials of mindware exist, the incoming signals must enter awareness. Most of the time, awareness is the beginnings of learning. Incoming signals may be visual such as words on a page, or auditory such as words spoken by a teacher, but they must gain your attention. As we have noted, the mind runs its simulation for the world given that the brain does not have direct access to the external world. In order for a learning experience to take place, the inputs of that experience must break through the simulation. Your neurons must be stimulated enough to pay attention. When the world around us meets our expectations, we mostly do not notice. We notice patterns and use those patterns to make predictions.[26] We especially notice novelty and variance.

> We are quick to notice things that are out of place or different, and we actually unconsciously look for things that don't belong. This has been a part of human survival since the human race began. Human evolution has counted on the brain being able to detect novelty and determine when things appear different from what we expected. This includes an unexpected movement out of the corner of the eye, abrupt sounds, and other sensory input that is out of the ordinary. This type of sensory detection allow the human species to avoid danger. Novelty detection protected our ancestors from harms; in modern times, it can be expanded to the classroom setting as well.[27]

As you are probably well aware, the mind is not especially wired for sustained attention. Attention jumps around, which makes sense from an evolutionary perspective in avoiding danger, but most of the time it is not especially conducive to deep learning. Deep learning takes focus. The mind needs to practice entering these states of focus where outside inputs are completely ignored. But when entering focused states, the mind uses past experience to filter our inputs and to place attention in one particular direction.[28]

But the attention that often matters most is not the attention to the external world but the attention to the internal. When our brain's simulation notices patterns and novelty *externally*, it is also doing so *internally*. Awareness of our own thinking, evaluating our beliefs about how the world works, and comparing our past experiences to the current moment provides an additional type of *feedback loop*. Awareness is a type of feedback about our mental processes. It is as if the brain self-corrects as it is self-aware. *Metacognition* is a fairly common term within the education literature. It is normally defined as *thinking about thinking*, and by this definition, metacognition is a part of consciousness. Another way to think about metacognition is *awareness of our thinking*. Metacognition is an important part of our feedback loop where we can reflect on the quality of thoughts themselves. It is awareness of our internal world but also a judgment of it.[29]

The mental sensation of *the feeling of knowing* plays an important role in learning; it is the mental sensation that signals to consciousness that we know something. It is the *feeling* that learning has taken place. The feeling of knowing is important to learning because it is a signal that learning has been successful, but at the same time, it is also detrimental to learning because once we feel that we know something, our efforts to learn more may be brought to an end.[30] Crucially for metacognition, the feeling of knowing and our emotional markers can be utilized as reflective tools. It is not enough to just think about our thinking. We need to know how we *feel* about our thinking. We must also recognize our unconscious reactions to our thinking. Do we *feel* that our thinking has been sound? Are we *excited* or *concerned* about our thinking?

> For metacognition *we need to know what we think and how we feel about it; inversely, we must know what we feel and what we think about that*. Metacognition is inherently and integrative process, blending thought and emotion into a unique combination for each of us.[31]

Learning is at its essence a feeling. The feeling of correctness. The feeling of being right. When you learn something, you can feel that you are right, and equally, when you have not quite grasped something, you can feel that too. Learning is by nature reflective. Knowing is by nature reflective. We judge the degree to which we know. And how do we judge? We judge by feeling.[32] Descartes's famous saying "I think, therefore I am" should be modified to "I feel, therefore I know." Often, when faced with a choice, we turn inward and metacognitively evaluate our confidence, and we go with our "best feelings" in the situation at hand.[33]

In the introduction of this book, I started with the idea that we are not purely rational, which is apparent to all of us. But it took us to this point to start to see the various avenues we use to learn. Yes, deliberation (i.e., rationality) is powerful, but it is not the only show in town. We are highly social learners, copying and absorbing ideas from others. We also employ tools used by our evolutionary cousins, such as instrumental learning. Most importantly, our learning has a metacognitive or reflective layer to it. To know something is to have a feeling of knowing.

Notes

1. E. O. Wilson, *The Social Conquest of Earth* (New York: Liveright, 2012); Gina Rippon, *Gender and Our Brains: How Neuroscience Explodes the Myths of the Male and Female Minds* (New York: Pantheon Books, 2019).

2. Hugo Mercier, *Not Born Yesterday: The Science of Who We Trust and What We Believe* (Princeton: Princeton University Press, 2020).

3. Joseph LeDoux, *The Deep History of Ourselves: The Four-Billion-Year Story of How We Got Conscious Brains* (New York: Viking, 2019), 326.

4. William von Hippel, *The Social Leap: The New Evolutionary Science of Who We Are, Where We Come from and What Makes us Happy* (New York: Harper Wave, 2018).

5. Mercier, *Not Born Yesterday*.

6. von Hippel, *Social Leap*; Mercier, *Not Born Yesterday*.

7. von Hippel, *Social Leap*.

8. Abraham H. Maslow, *The Farther Reaches of Human Nature* (New York: Arkana, 1993); Tracey Tokuhama-Espinosa, *The New Science of Teaching and Learning: Using the Best of Mind, Brain, and Education Science in the Classroom* (New York: Teachers College Press, 2010); James E. Zull, *From Brain to Mind: Using Neuroscience to Guide Change in Education* (Sterling, VA: Stylus Publishing, 2011); Alison Gopnik, *The Gardener and the Carpenter: What the New Science of Child Development Tells Us About the Relationship Between Parents and Children* (New York: Farrar, Straus, and Giroux, 2016); Joshua R. Eyler, *How Humans Learn: The Science and Stories Behind Effective College Teaching* (Morgantown: West Virginia University Press, 2018); Terry Doyle and Todd Zakrajsek, *The New Science of Learning: How to Learn in Harmony with Your Brain* (Sterling, VA: Stylus Publishing, 2019).

9. Gopnik, *Gardener and the Carpenter*.

10. Gopnik, *Gardener and the Carpenter*.

11. Laurence Steinberg, "A Social Neuroscience Perspective on Adolescent Risk-Taking," *Developmental Review: DR* 28, no. 1 (2008): 78–106; Gopnik, *Gardener and the Carpenter*.

12. Gopnik, *Gardener and the Carpenter*.

13. Keith E. Stanovich, *Rationality and the Reflective Mind* (Oxford, UK: Oxford University Press, 2011).

14. LeDoux, *Deep History of Ourselves*.

15. LeDoux, *Deep History of Ourselves*, 226.

16. Stanovich, *Rationality and the Reflective Mind*.

17. Zull, *From Brain to Mind*, 164.

18. Zull, *From Brain to Mind*.

19. Tokuhama-Espinosa, *New Science of Teaching and Learning*; Doyle and Zakrajsek, *New Science of Learning*.

20. Tokuhama-Espinosa, *New Science of Teaching and Learning*; Zull, *From Brain to Mind*; Doyle and Zakrajsek, *New Science of Learning*.

21. Robert M. Sapolsky, *Behave: The Biology of Humans at Our Best and Worst* (New York: Penguin Books, 2017), 74.

22. Zull, *From Brain to Mind.*

23. Zull, *From Brain to Mind*; John Dewey, *How We Think* (CreateSpace Independent Publishing, 2014); Eyler, *How Humans Learn.*

24. Gopnik, *Gardener and the Carpenter.*

25. Zull, *From Brain to Mind.*

26. Zull, *From Brain to Mind*; Doyle and Zakrajsek, *New Science of Learning*; Mark Solms, *The Hidden Spring: A Journey to the Source of Consciousness* (New York: Norton, 2021).

27. Tokuhama-Espinosa, *New Science of Teaching and Learning*, 41.

28. Doyle and Zakrajsek, *New Science of Learning.*

29. Tokuhama-Espinosa, *New Science of Teaching and Learning*; Zull, *From Brain to Mind.*

30. Robert A. Burton, *A Skeptic's Guide to the Mind: What Neuroscience Can and Cannot Tell Us about Ourselves* (New York: St. Martin's Griffin, 2014); Virginia Campbell, *Are You Sure?: The Unconscious Origins of Certainty* (Hartford, CT: PYP Academy Press, 2020).

31. Zull, *From Brain to Mind*, 274.

32. Tokuhama-Espinosa, *New Science of Teaching and Learning.*

33. Zull, *From Brain to Mind.*

CHAPTER TWELVE

The Feeling of Knowing

To *know* something requires a feeling. How can this be? What is this feeling and how does it relate to our memories? To answer this, I want to start with the modular nature of the mind. As we've already seen, most of the work carried out by the mind is unconscious. This is true in many situations, but a stark example is that of blindsighted individuals where there is damage to the visual cortex but the eyes are undamaged. In these cases, visual perception does not reach consciousness, so these people cannot see, but the eyes work perfectly well. They still respond to some visual stimuli, such as turning toward a light. The eye still receives visual input and other parts of the mind, outside of consciousness, still react.[1] Blindsighted individuals help us to recognize the modular nature of the brain. Different neural networks work together to perform a function. When one network is damaged or does not work, then that function loses the contribution of the failing portion of the network while the other contributors keep performing their tasks. When we see, we do not experience sight as being modular. We experience a unified whole of seeing.

Our understandings about the world are also modular. Experiences are broken down and encoded into memories stored in different areas of the brain. The hippocampus connects the relationships between stored memory and reassembles them when needed based on context. Memories are not linear narratives stored away in the mind but are constructed components.[2] Our consciousness is seemingly independent from our memories. We are not aware of most of our memories until an external cue brings a memory into awareness. For instance, *what is the name of your favorite teacher*? You probably were not thinking about your teacher until I asked. Your awareness is not tied to this memory but can access this memory. Here's another question: *who was the eighth president of the United States?* Take a second and think about the answer to this one. If you have an answer, *how confident are you in that answer*? Most Americans will recognize that that Martin Van Buren was *a president* of the United States, but only a few astute students of history will know that he was the eighth president. However, with that being said, I would guess that your confidence level on naming the eighth president was probably fairly accurate. Those of you who *knew*, knew that you knew. So I would like to note three different processes at work around Martin Van Buren being the eighth president. There is your conscious awareness, which was happily reading this book without thinking about US presidents. Then, there is the memory of Martin Van Buren. Finally, there is the confidence you hold about your own knowing. That confidence is a *feeling*. When I asked you about your confidence, you looked internally and made a judgment about your knowledge. You expressed a feeling about knowing. You produced that feeling consciously. We can see that consciousness, the memory of the idea, and the *feeling of knowing* are three separate functions of the mind. Just like the example of blindsighted people above, the processing of ideas is also modular, and, critically, the feeling of knowing exists apart from the memory itself. The content is separate from our judgments about that content.[3]

The feeling of knowing is a type of mental sensation that is a part of our conscious experience as described by Burton.[4] *Mental sensations* are the feelings that accompany thinking. They are generated automatically and are differentiated from emotions and affective moods. They include the feelings of knowing, causation, agency, and intention to name a few. They are largely involuntary. The tricky part of mental sensations is that they arise from unconscious processing but, at the same time, they also make up the experience of being conscious. Mental sensations are the equivalent of sensory phenomena *within* the mind. As if they monitor the state of our thinking, they enable an embodied state of thinking (i.e., consciousness). Mental sensations are the feelings that determine *how we experience a thought*. Our subjective experience is wrapped up in these feelings.[5]

> We know the nature and quality of our thoughts via feelings, not reason. Feelings such as certainty, conviction, rightness and wrongness, clarity, and faith arise out of involuntary mental sensory systems that are integral and separable components of the thoughts that they qualify.[6]

Mental sensations help us bridge the gap between conscious and unconscious processing. The feelings around thinking imbue consciousness with a summary of our unconscious thinking.

In survival terms, this is essential. When we need to make a split-second decision or to make a tough choice we often *go with our gut*. For our ancestors hesitation meant death. Mental sensations fuse together intuitions, experiences, and schemas into conscious awareness helping to move us forward. Our minds are geared toward decision over indecision. We can pretend that our decisions are always logical, but if all choices originated from a purely logical standpoint weighing costs and benefits, making entirely arbitrary choices could freeze us in place, but our mind easily makes arbitrary choices—*do I wear the red hat or the blue hat today*? When we arrive in unfamiliar scenarios, we make estimates based on confidence. We may recognize patterns, and we may even look for facts, but when it comes down to it, we often act on what feels best. *We go with our gut*. This is the importance of mental sensations as a part of consciousness.[7]

When it comes to interacting with our world, the feeling of knowing enables us to make decisions and move forward within situations that are often filled with uncertainty. The feeling of knowing itself is a mental sensation that accompanies thoughts, but it is not the same as the thought itself. The feeling of knowing is part of our modular processing. We can think about the feeling of knowing as certainty, rightness, conviction, or correctness. This sense is an important piece of our metacognition, an internal judgment we make about a thought. What does it mean to *know* something? To know something, we have a feeling. Have you ever had an answer right on the tip of your tongue? It is right there. You know that the answer is somewhere in your head, but you cannot quite extract it. That sensation is the feeling of knowing. You are aware of knowing something even if you cannot identify it. Another example is in a moment of confusion, we achieve clarity. We have that *aha* moment. It feels like solving a puzzle. The answers click into place and we understand it and that the answer is correct. That is the feeling of knowing. We can also recognize the feeling of knowing by its absence. Maybe we discover an answer or a possible answer, but we are just not quite sure that this particular option fits what we need. In these cases, we are seeking the feeling of knowing but we cannot reach it. So we can see that the feeling of knowing is different from the content that is known. Sometimes we have the feeling but no content. Sometimes we have the content but our feeling makes us question that content. Sometimes the content hits us along with the feeling all at once.[8]

Burton provides a useful example of the feeling of knowing with the paragraph below. After you read it, I will provide his explanation:

> A newspaper is better than a magazine. A seashore is a better place than the street. At first it is better to run than to walk. You may have to try several times. It takes some skill, but it is easy to learn. Even young children can enjoy it. Once successful, complications are minimal. Birds seldom get too close. Rain, however, soaks in very fast. Too many people doing the same thing can also cause problems. One needs lots of room. If there are no complications, it can be very peaceful. A rock will serve as an anchor. If things break loose from it, however, you will not get a second chance.[9]

Before you read further, feel free to read it again, because once you have the explanation, you will not be able to go back.

When reading this paragraph alone, it is very confusing and the mind struggles to make sense of it. But, with a single word, it all clicks, and that word is *kite*. This paragraph is about a kite. Once you read it again, all of the confusion is gone and there is a feeling of knowing around it. Once we know the secret word, we know that this feels correct and every sentence makes sense.

There are some important aspects of the feeling of knowing that we can highlight. First off, given that the feeling of knowing is separated from the thought itself, the feeling may be attached to the thought after the fact. Sometimes this may come after recognizing new information at a later time. Other times the feeling may be part of the reconstruction of the event itself, as in the example of a Major League batter stating that they were seeing the ball with clarity on that particular occasion even though the ball moves too fast for the human eye to see with any clarity. (See the section on consciousness in chapter 8 for the discussion about seeing the baseball.) Second, the feeling of knowing is tied to the mind's reward systems. There is a benefit to knowing, and as the curious mind seeks answers, it is on the hunt for the feeling of knowing. Achieving this feeling can release rewards within the mind. Third, it then follows that the feeling of knowing is important in learning. If we are learning ideas, then we are imbuing them with a feeling of being correct. Powerful experiences that are repeated create stronger and stronger connections between the decisions that are made and the feeling that the decision is correct. Finally, the feeling of knowing is not a binary state. It is a spectrum of feeling. In order for us to survive, or just in order for us to try new ideas, the feeling of knowing must extend to ideas that have not been tested. Thus, the feeling of knowing may include things like hunches, gut feelings, faith, belief, etc. We could think of this as a spectrum of *vague familiarity* to *concrete certainty*. Indecision could be life threatening, so we must be able to make decisions and test out new ideas. By our very nature, we default toward moving forward.[10]

Within these aspects, we can think of some general ways that the feeling of knowing may arise. We can start with one way that I mentioned previously which is the *aha* moment. This occurs at that special breakthrough moment where the feeling of being correct enters consciousness unified with the thought or idea connected to it. The brain is making some kind of association that is recognized as being correct at the moment it is made.[11]

A second option is when an idea is recognized for the first time, it is evaluated and judged, and in the end determined to be correct. This may follow a process such as weighing evidence or following the steps of an equation. As we follow through the process, the determination feels correct. The feeling of knowledge is connected through the process. We often think that this option is the primary way we make decisions. Our brain can even trick us into seeing this option in places where it may not exist. Our consciousness can build a logical narrative when it may not exist.[12]

A third possibility is the classic *gut feeling*. In this case, we may have a strong feeling of knowledge, but we are unable to clearly connect this to an explanation as to why. In these cases, our unconscious processes are at work, and the feeling of knowing is a signal from the unconscious mind into consciousness. For example, an ER doctor may examine a patient and all tests appear to be normal, but the doc has a gut feeling. She knows something is missing. Her feeling of knowing pushes her based on unconscious cues. So she runs additional tests and discovers an issue that might have been missed.[13]

Finally, the feeling of knowing can present so strongly in some situations that it can feel revelatory. The feeling takes place and explanations for that feeling come later. This is common in mystical experiences where individuals make a great recognition about the nature or truth of their lives or about the universe. This could be a deep meditative moment, a rite of passage, or a psychedelic trip, all of which leave behind a powerful feeling of knowing.[14] William James's discussion of mystical experiences in his book *The Varieties of Religious Experience* captures the idea better than almost anything else:

> Its quality must be directly experienced; it cannot be imparted or transferred to others. In this peculiarity mystical states are more like states of feeling than like states of intellect. No one can make clear to another who has never had a certain feeling, in what the quality or worth of it consists. . . . *Although so similar to states of feeling, mystical states seem to those who experience them to be also*

> *states of knowledge*. They are states of insight into depths of truth unplumbed by the discursive intellect. They are illuminations, revelations, full of significance and importance, all inarticulate though they remain; and as a rule they carry with them a curious sense of authority for after-time.[15] (italics added)

When an individual experiences a mystical state that invokes such a strong feeling of knowing, it is treated as evidence itself. The mind builds a narrative around the feeling, offering explanations, offering justification, or offering reasons for the feeling.

Many times we fall into the assumption that to know something results as the end point of a logical process. We may even admit that the mind is often irrational but still fall back on the idea that knowing is rooted in logical justification—*justified true belief*. But we gain a broader sense of knowing if we accept the following. First, if we accept that the brain is a democracy and that it is modular in nature, then we can see that mental sensations exist separately from ideas. Second, this, then, leads to the recognition that knowing is a feeling separated from other processes. Third, a different process can push us forward and result in a feeling of knowing. Logic is just one of these processes, but not the only one. Fourth, the feeling of knowing can override logic. Many times, it *must* override logic. Certainty must win out over uncertainty, or our very survival is at risk. When we talk about irrationality, we often act as if our brain is broken. Our minds fail us because they do not grasp the rational choice within a situation. But when it appears that irrationality has taken over, it is because our minds are following a different set of rules. The feeling of knowing is being driven by biological processes such as group allegiances or incomplete memories. All of these different processes push the feeling of knowing into consciousness.

There is a sensory quality to the feeling of knowing. Just as our body helps us feel externally, our mental sensations help us feel internally. Crossing the bridge from conscious processing to unconscious processing is a bodily activity. *It is felt*. Examining *felt knowledge* is an attempt to consider how ideas connect with our lived experience. Often when we talk about experiences, we divide them up into various components such as how we think, how we feel, what we remember, the images we see, the desires in the moment, but we do not often consider how to experience these things as a whole. Our mind naturally takes the experience and turns it into *symbolized knowledge*. Our language—and by extension our thought—does not have a way to express the entirety of a moment. But if we think about how meaning is constructed in the mind—including the unconscious mind—meaning goes further than just concepts. Experiences are not discrete units.[16] There is a trend in Western thinking for *disembodied intelligences*. The body is treated as a thing not to be trusted. The body is disconnected from rationality, which has produced a gap in our assumptions about how we know the world.[17]

> Besides the logical dimension and the operational dimensions of knowledge, there is also a directly felt, experiential dimension. *Meaning* is not *about things* and it is not only a certain *logical* structure, but it also involves *felt* experiencing. Any concept, thing, or behavior is meaningful only as some noise, thing or event interacts with felt experiencing. Meanings are formed and had through an interaction between experiencing and symbols or things. . . . Today, however, we can no longer construe "experience" so narrowly. Besides logical schemes and sense perception we have come to recognize that there is also a powerful *felt* dimension to experience that is prelogical, and that functions importantly in what we think, what we perceive, and how we behave.[18]

In trauma therapy, examining bodily understandings has become standard in some circles. The center of recovery is building self-awareness around powerful sensations. In order to gain control of them, the therapist turns the individual inward with the simple but powerful phrase, *notice that*. The goal is to turn inward and to notice how the body reacts to situations and triggers. Before we can be self-aware, before we can intervene in bodily reactions, we must take notice. Noticing the reaction involves noticing the physical sensations and how they impact us. After we notice the physical reactions, we can notice our thoughts, and how our thoughts connect to physical sensations. There is a way that these register in our body. Noticing how the body stores memories and emotions and reactions to them is the first step to changing them and living with them.[19] The examples from trauma therapy offer an important insight into how all our knowledge operates. Knowledge does not live within a domain of symbols and ideas but inside a broader *felt sense*.

When trying to grasp a felt sense, it can be easier to imagine this as a type of physical reaction to knowledge. It is a *feeling*.

> A felt sense is not a mental experience but a physical one. *Physical*. A bodily awareness of a situation or person or event. And internal aura that encompasses everything you feel and know about the given subject at a given time—encompasses it and communicates it to you all at once rather than detail by detail. Think of it as a taste, if you like, or a great musical chord that makes you feel a powerful impact, a big round unclear feeling.
>
> A felt sense doesn't come to you in the form of thoughts or words or other separate units, but as a single (though often puzzling and very complex) bodily feeling.[20]

It is important to note that a felt sense carries meaning but that meaning may not be clear at first. It can easily be ignored or even overrun within the moment. The felt sense is often difficult to communicate in words because it does not come in words. It is like a bodily mechanism that synthesizes large amounts of information on a particular issue or subject. Connecting to the felt sense is a way to connect to the unconscious, just as remembering can walk between conscious and unconscious. We can feel that we've met someone or that we know someone but not articulate it. The felt sense is unarticulated knowledge. We know something but cannot understand how we know it. Connecting to the felt sense is a way to connect to unconscious processing.[21] Genlin outlines his *focusing* process, which is a therapeutic approach that attempts to connect to the felt sense to better understand the self. He outlines six steps:

1. *Clearing a space*: Calm yourself and observe your bodily response to topic. Do not go and explore it but just observe it.
2. *Felt sense*: Pick one problem that may have come to you. Notice it and do not think deeply into it but feel around it. The goal is to feel all of it beyond what you can just think about—not just one facet but the whole of it.
3. *Handle*: Allow a word to come to you that describes this. Stay with this quality of the felt sense until there is a good fit. More than one word may come but one will stay.
4. *Resonating*: Move between the word and the felt sense. See how it feels.
5. *Asking*: Ask yourself what is important about the big picture of this problem. Note the sense again. Try to find an answer and wait for a body shift to happen.
6. *Receiving*: Receive the shift in a friendly way. Stay with it and observe it.[22]

Through focusing, the mind experiences a *bodily shift*. It is more than just understanding a problem through ideas. It is an attempt to push the unconscious mind to open up or even to change. This is especially useful on topics that seem unclear or troubling, but where the words to explain the problem are not apparent. Tempting as it may be, we need to remember that felt meaning is not some sort of magical communion with a higher level of knowledge. Our felt sense is an alternate and often unrecognized way to know things, but it is not necessarily a more accurate way to know.

We commonly recognize the impact of feelings upon intellect. Additionally, things like culture, biology, psychological needs, economic and class factors, and much more impact our intellectual outcomes. But we often do not have an active method for trying to engage these factors working in the unconscious mind. How can we identify our unconscious worldviews? How can we pull out our own biases? If we are to understand a topic and find a meaning, we need to recognize the *felt meaning*. We may recognize that we cannot be objective and that tacit understanding permeates our thinking, but do not utilize tools to confront these understandings. Exploring the felt sense could be one avenue for doing so.[23]

I should note that the felt sense is slightly different from the feeling of knowing, even though trying to pull them apart is hair splitting. The felt sense helps us explore and understand our beliefs. It helps us understand what we know. It is an interface with the unconscious. So we can use focusing—or other techniques—to ask ourselves about an idea or topic and reflect upon our beliefs by trying to interface with our felt sense. The feeling of knowing is related to this, but the feeling of knowing is a better-defined mental sensation. It is the feeling that comes to us when we recognize some sort of truth, when we identify an idea as being correct. We can use our felt sense to explore a particular feeling of knowing, and the feeling of knowing may arise when we are examining our felt sense. They are interrelated but not quite the same thing. Importantly, exploring the felt sense as a way to access unconscious processing may be an avenue to help us better understand the feeling of knowing when it occurs.

I need to emphasize that just because we have a feeling of knowing, that does not mean that this feeling is always correct. It does not mean that our feeling of knowing matches the external world, that it is error free, or that it aligns with the thoughts of others. We must be cautious because the mind may generate a feeling of knowing for a number of reasons. If we follow a familiar line of thinking or if our reasoning matches up with something we've thought in the past, our sense of familiarity may lead us to a feeling of knowing. On the other hand, reasoning that is unfamiliar to us or ideas that we had not considered previously may *not* generate a feeling of knowing and, therefore, help to keep preexisting beliefs in place. In moments of cognitive dissonance, a strong feeling of knowing can keep us committed to beliefs even when there is contradictory evidence. And instead of rejecting incorrect beliefs, we often adjust our attitudes and find a way to incorporate old beliefs around new evidence. Recognizing the feeling of knowing may help to better explain confirmation bias and mechanisms that reinforce existing beliefs. When we encounter new information that makes our existing beliefs more coherent, we rarely take the time to fact check. When this new information makes the feeling of knowing stronger, we don't look back.

We accept it with open arms. The biases, prejudices, and stereotypes hidden within our worldview are all wrapped up in the feeling of knowing. For these reasons, the feeling of knowing cannot be enough. The feeling of knowing may make us feel good because it confirms preexisting beliefs. As we have seen, from an evolutionary perspective, making a decision is preferable to indecision. Certainty is preferable to hesitancy. The very mental sensations that underlie our conscious minds can be the sensations that lead us astray. These sensations are pushed into consciousness from unconscious processes such as intuitions.[24]

When we talked about schemas and the mind's simulation, I mentioned the *process of inference*. When we build inferences, we use past understandings—schemas—and project or create new understandings of how the world might work. Our mind takes what we know and extends it forward. The inferential processes are largely unconscious. They are not choices decided upon by the conscious mind. As these inferences are formed, we are not aware of why or how they are formed. Inferences steeped in the feeling of knowing form some of our most powerful beliefs. We take what we know and apply it unconsciously, resulting in feelings that seem obvious and undeniable.

> People may be aware of having reached a certain conclusion—be aware, that is, of the output of an influential process—but we claim that they are never aware of the process itself. All inferences carried out by inferential mechanisms are in this sense *intuitive*. They generate *intuitive beliefs*; that is, beliefs held without awareness of reasons to hold them.[25]

All of our thoughts, our arguments, our reasons are laced with intuitive beliefs. We may strive for objectivity, but objectivity will always elude us because of our conscious mind's inability to access our unconscious processing, and, further, because of that unconscious processing generating intuitive beliefs that are put in place by the feeling of knowing.

Our social connections also rely upon the feeling of knowing. Trust within groups is a matter of information sharing. How do we decide whom to trust as we employ mechanisms of open vigilance? How do we trust without being deceived? The feeling of knowing comes into play. Mercier calls our ability to evaluate messages *plausibility checking*.

> Plausibility checking is an ever-present filter, weighing on whether messages are accepted or rejected. On the whole, this filtering role is mostly negative. If plausibility checking lets in only messages that fit with our prior beliefs, not much change of mind is going to occur—since we already essentially agree with the message. This is why you often need to recognize the qualities of

> a source of information—that is reliability and of goodwill—to change your mind. There is, however, an exception, a case in which possibility checking on its own, with no information whatsoever about the source, gives us a reason to accept a novel piece of information: when the new information increases the coherence of our beliefs.[26]

In order for plausibility checking to be effective, messages from others must go up against our own feeling of knowing. Some messages will be influential enough to overcome that feeling and to ultimately change our thinking. And, of course, others will not. But how can we do better at seeing a need to change?

The challenge that we face is a difficult one. We know that we are prone to errors and that we carry around our own biases and false beliefs, but in order to guard against ourselves, we need to recognize that it is our feelings that guide us. These feelings do not magically appear but come from unconscious processes. Our conscious mind provides a narrative. For example, we are in a crowd of people and we see a familiar face. If we see a face the brain jumps into making recognitions to determine if this is a face that we know. If there is a match and we feel that this person is an old friend, the moment feels as if this were a conscious process, but in reality, this process is essentially a lower-level pattern recognition network that the brain automatically runs. But this is not what we tell ourselves. This is not how it *feels*. Our consciousness lays a narrative over this lower-level brain process. If we are to be honest in assessing our own knowledge, we must acknowledge that neuroscience is telling us that the *self* is a constructed narrative.[27]

> If as modern neuroscience strongly indicates, the self is an ongoing personal narrative constructed by the very mind that is examining itself, introspection is analogous to interpreting a complex work of fiction. To get a view of oneself that is relatively "in sync" with one's unconscious motives requires a combination of close, detailed analysis, looking at the work from a wide variety of angles (including the views of others), and a broad background knowledge from one's personal and cultural history to the latest genetics of behavior. However, the overriding requirement is that any self-assessment be seen within the light of its biological constraints.[28]

So the question is, how reflective can we be? Can we recognize our limitations in knowing? Can we use our felt sense to examine the feeling of knowing? When we think of *metacognition*, we must recognize that part of this process is a type of self-monitoring. Metacognition is not simply thinking about thinking. It is not only holding beliefs about thinking. There is an unconscious aspect of metacognition built upon inferential judgments with the feeling of knowing at the center. We must monitor to see when the feeling of knowing arises and see if we can use the felt sense to suss out the origins or the meanings that are outside of consciousness.[29]

As Zull states,

> For metacognition *we need to know what we think and how we feel about it; inversely, we must know what we feel and what we think about that.* Metacognition is inherently an integrative process.[30]

Metacognitive decisions such as when to stop looking for information, when to be satisfied with an answer, or even when to recognize that a problem exists that may require further exploration are all based on the feeling of knowing.

By our teenage years, we easily accept the physical limitations of our bodies. We do not think we can jump thirty feet in the air or that we can hold our breath for thirty minutes. But we do not as easily accept our mental limitations. In fact, our mental limitations help us to misunderstand our own mental limitations. Things like depression and anxiety are difficult to break out of, but even at the more mundane level it is difficult to really have a perspective on how we know. We tell ourselves that knowing revolves around rationality and hard facts. But, as we have seen, knowing is a feeling. It emanates from the many unconscious processes that are firing away in our minds and bursting forward into consciousness. Our conscious minds build narratives around knowing without acknowledging that how we know is often out of reach. We see our physical selves as being limited by biology, but we do not recognize the biological limitations of the mind. When we look at a problem and an answer feels so obvious, we need to consider our limitations. We must recognize the hidden biases within our worldview. And when we assume that the mind is rational and logical, we must check that assumption.[31]

For librarians and educators, the question becomes how can we help our students recognize the feeling of knowing? Can we help them build metacognitive tools that help them recognize the unconscious processes at work?

Notes

1. Robert A. Burton, *On Being Certain: Believing You Were Right Even When You're Not* (New York: St. Martin's Griffin, 2008); Virginia Campbell, *Are You Sure?: The Unconscious Origins of Certainty* (Hartford, CT: PYP Academy Press, 2020).

2. Charles Fernyhough, *Pieces of Light: The New Science of Memory* (London: Profile Books, 2013).

3. Burton, *On Being Certain*; Campbell, *Are You Sure?*

4. Burton, *On Being Certain*; Robert A. Burton, *A Skeptic's Guide to the Mind: What Neuroscience Can and Cannot Tell Us about Ourselves* (New York: St. Martin's Griffin, 2014); Robert M. Sapolsky, *Behave: The Biology of Humans at Our Best and Worst* (New York: Penguin Books, 2017).

5. Burton, *On Being Certain*; Burton, *Skeptic's Guide to the Mind*; Campbell, *Are You Sure?*; Mark Solms, *The Hidden Spring: A Journey to the Source of Consciousness* (New York: Norton, 2021).

6. Burton, *On Being Certain*, 139.

7. Burton, *On Being Certain*; James E. Zull, *From Brain to Mind: Using Neuroscience to Guide Change in Education* (Sterling, VA: Stylus Publishing, 2011); Christophe André, *Feelings and Moods* (Cambridge, UK: Polity Press, 2012); Burton, *Skeptic's Guide to the Mind*; Campbell, *Are You Sure?*; Solms, *Hidden Spring*.

8. Burton, *On Being Certain*; Campbell, *Are You Sure?*

9. Burton, *On Being Certain*, 5.

10. Burton, *On Being Certain*; Burton, *Skeptic's Guide to the Mind*; Campbell, *Are You Sure?*

11. Burton, *On Being Certain*.

12. Burton, *On Being Certain*.

13. Burton, *On Being Certain*.

14. Burton, *On Being Certain*.

15. William James, *The Varieties of Religious Experience: A Study in Human Nature Being the Gifford Lectures on Natural Religion Delivered at Edinburgh in 1901–1902* (New York: Longmans, Green, and Co., 1917), 370.

16. Eugene T. Gendlin, *Focusing-Oriented Psychotherapy: A Manual of Experimental Method* (New York: Guilford Press, 1996); Eugene T. Gendlin, *Experiencing and the Creation of Meaning: A Philosophical and Psychological Approach to the Subjective* (Evanston, IL: Northwestern University Press, 1997).

17. Steen Halling and Mical Goldfarb, "Grounding Truth in the Body: Therapy and Research Renewed," *Humanistic Psychologist* 19, no. 3 (Autumn 1991): 313–30; Gendlin, *Experiencing and the Creation of Meaning*.

18. Gendlin, *Experiencing and the Creation of Meaning*, 1.

19. Bessel A. Van der Kolk, *The Body Keeps the Score: The Brain, Mind, and Body in the Healing of Trauma* (New York: Viking Press, 2014).

20. Gendlin, *Experiencing and the Creation of Meaning*, 37.

21. Gendlin, *Focusing-Oriented Psychotherapy*; Gendlin, *Experiencing and the Creation of Meaning*; Eugene T. Gendlin, *Focusing* (New York: Bantam Books, 2007).

22. Gendlin, *Focusing*.

23. Halling and Goldfarb, "Grounding Truth in the Body"; Gendlin, *Focusing*.

24. Burton, *On Being Certain*; Burton, *Skeptic's Guide to the Mind*; Hugo Mercier, *Not Born Yesterday: The Science of Who We Trust and What We Believe* (Princeton: Princeton University Press, 2020); Campbell, *Are You Sure?*

25. Hugo Mercier and Dan Sperber, "Why Do Humans Reason? Arguments for an Argumentative Theory," *Behavioral and Brain Sciences* 34, no. 2 (2011): 58.

26. Mercier, *Not Born Yesterday*, 50.

27. Burton, *On Being Certain*; Burton, *Skeptic's Guide to the Mind.*

28. Burton, *On Being Certain*, 160.

29. Valerie A. Thompson, Nicole H. Therriault, and Ian R. Newman, "Meta-Reasoning: Monitoring and Control of Reasoning, Decision Making, and Problem Solving," in *Cognitive Unconscious and Human Rationality*, ed. Laura Macchi, Maria Bagassi, and Ricardo Viale (Cambridge, MA: MIT Press, 2016), 275–99.

30. Zull, *From Brain to Mind*, 274.

31. Burton, *On Being Certain*; Burton, *Skeptic's Guide to the Mind*; Campbell, *Are You Sure?*

CHAPTER THIRTEEN

Exercising Control over Our Mental Lives

The metacognitive aspects of the feeling of knowing, and the extent to which we can develop them, seem to offer useful possibilities for learning. Two areas of research that can help go deeper on this path are areas of research around source monitoring and conflict monitoring.

Research on the *source monitoring framework* looks at the ways we make a judgment about the origin (i.e., source)[1] of a memory. This refers to a whole gamut of possibilities from basic recognitions that a memory originated in a lived experience versus a memory that was imagined or dreamed. This also includes identifying semantic memories such as recognizing that your memory about a place came from a specific book. This can include recognizing that you were not part of stories shared by others as opposed to stories you lived yourself. Part of source monitoring is recognizing the difference between different external sources versus internally generated sources. For example, we must have the ability to recognize the difference between what you thought at the time and what you said at the time.[2]

Additionally, the source monitoring framework can also include features or characteristics of memories such as perceptual information, contextual information, semantic detail, emotional reactions, and cognitive operations (identifying, elaborating, retrieving knowledge). Another way to think about this is that the source monitoring framework is the study of memories about memories. It then follows that remembering the source of a memory relies upon the quality of the initial memory itself. Strains on attention, stress, and other factors may impact how a memory is encoded in the first place.

Additionally, beyond the quality of the information encoded, there is also a need for quality in terms of accessing the memory. So time pressure, stress, distractions at the moment may impact your ability at recall.[3]

Sometimes the sources of memories seem quite clear and unforgettable. The first time I learned about the demand curve was in Economics 101 during my freshman year of college, taught by Dr. Chris Marmé. He was such a great teacher and it was such a compelling lesson, I will never forget! Other times it can be quite blurry, and we may even make guesses about the sources of memories. The first time I learned to conjugate verbs in Spanish must have been in my first Spanish class in my sophomore year of high school, but I have no memory of this.[4]

An important assertion of source monitoring is that memories do not carry around absolute labels that are automatically accessed on recall. Instead, an attribution process takes place that depends on the need for the memory. It is common to misattribute sources or incompletely recall sources. Many times decisions on sources are made quickly and are non-deliberative, but there are times when memories activate a deliberative process where we must consider the source. This takes more time. We can have an internal discussion such as "does this seem plausible?"[5] Source monitoring is extremely important in our ability to exercise control over our mental lives. Keeping experience separate from imagination, connecting memory to experiences, and judging the quality or value of memory gives us a mental order. The neatness provided by source monitoring plays a part in the narrative order of consciousness. Thus, source monitoring takes place within consciousness. Our conscious mind extracts the sources of memories. As such, source monitoring is important in our metacognitive processing. Our internal judgments about how we make decisions, the sources of our beliefs, and the strength of our knowledge rests upon source monitoring. These are reflective aspects of metacognition. We cannot reflect on how our memories are made without connecting memories to their sources. With this being said, it stands to reason that source monitoring connects with the feeling of knowing. When we have a feeling of knowing around a topic, source monitoring is one avenue for examining the strength of that feeling. We may recognize that we know something, but it is through source monitoring that we can try to outline the origins of the feeling as much as possible, at least through conscious processing.

Naturally, the weaknesses around source monitoring are also the weaknesses of our memories. For instance, in situations where we cannot easily identify the source of a memory, we fall back on stereotypes and assumptions. Kuhlmann, Bayen, Meuser, and Kornadt looked at age stereotypes. They note,

> In two experiments, we demonstrated that people rely on age stereotypes during source monitoring: whenever participants cannot remember who made a statement, they were biased to attribute it to the source whose age the statement was stereotypical—even though half of the statements made by each source had in fact contradicted age stereotypes.[6]

They showed that poor source memory increases the likelihood of relying on age stereotypes. This is true in younger and older adults. Older adults tend to have less ability to remember sources so they may rely on stereotypes more often.

Another failure of source monitoring occurs during the reconstruction of memories. If events are similar or sources are similar there may be confusion and that may cause errors in judging the source of a memory.[7] Ever have trouble distinguishing between the book and the movie adaptation of a book? Was Tom Bombadil in the book or movie version of the *Fellowship of the Rings*? Or do you get confused about where you first learned a skill in school? The major challenge of recall is that memory exists outside of consciousness, even though source monitoring resides in consciousness. So, as we try to consciously access memories, we have no grasp on what we are missing.

Additionally, as noted above, memory reconstruction is not an all-or-nothing process. The current context around which a memory is recalled can have great influence over how that memory is reshaped to enter consciousness. Cues in the moment evoke parts of memories but not necessarily the entire memory.[8] An old textbook on the shelf may activate a memory of sitting in a particular class while not activating memories of friends who were in class with you. Or a picture of your family on vacation may activate positive memories of times together while ignoring the arguments between siblings on the drive there.

The failings of memory reconstruction are well recognized in many areas of society. Eyewitness testimony is one of these areas where the weaknesses of source reconstruction can have serious impacts on court cases. This is especially true when a witness makes misattributions that contradict physical evidence. One approach to overcoming these weaknesses is the use of the *cognitive interview*, which is growing in popularity among investigators. This memory tool asks witnesses to reconstruct their memories based on deep details of the situation. They are asked to remember as much of the context—locations, times, details—as possible. The effort involves trying to reconstruct full memories while also making those memories resistant to suggestions, misinformation, or other cues from investigators. This has been found to get more concrete information and increase recall.[9]

Besides source monitoring, there is another metacognitive aspect of knowing. This is *conflict monitoring*, which occurs when individuals notice a conflict or an inconsistent feeling when they give intuitive responses to questions.[10] When faced with some questions, we often rely upon heuristic answers (i.e., shortcuts). Here is a classic example:

A bat and a ball cost $1.10 in total. The bat costs $1.00 more than the ball. How much does the ball cost?[11]

This is a fairly well-known example, so you may have heard of this. When most people come across this question for the first time, their tendency is to fall back on simple subtraction and answer $.10. Most adults are so accustomed to dealing with subtraction that they automatically—intuitively—fall back on subtraction. But, with some examination, we can see that $.10 is not correct:

> If the ball = $.10,
>
> Then to get the cost of the bat, we know that the bat costs $1.00 more than the ball, so the bat = $.10 + $1.00 = $1.10
>
> Together the bat ($1.10) plus the ball ($.10) = $1.20.

Since the original problem notes that "*a bat and a ball cost $1.10 in total*" the ball cannot cost $.10 alone. This intuitive answer arrived at via subtraction cannot be correct. The correct answer is $.05

> If the ball = $.05,
>
> then the bat = $.05 + $1.00 = $1.05
>
> Together the bat plus the ball = $1.05 + $.05 = $1.10.

As I noted, most people get this wrong the first time, and, in fact, even after some explaining, many people still struggle to make sense of this because their intuitive sense to subtract is so strong. But at the same time, even when they are subtracting and giving the wrong answer, many people feel strange about their answer. *They know that something just doesn't feel right.* They are in conflict even if they cannot explain exactly why they feel this way. They have an unconscious sense that their answer is not correct.

Of course, the bat and ball question is purposefully written to push us toward an intuitive response. It is written to activate conflict. As a contrast, here is the same question written without conflict activation:

A bat and ball together cost $1.10. The bat costs $1.05. How much does the ball cost?[12]

This question is straightforward. Simple subtraction provides the answer. Our intuitive reaction aligns with our unconscious processing. There is no conflict from this rewritten version.

Conflict monitoring is another type of *gut feeling*. This is a type of feeling where we feel the internal disagreement of the brain as democracy. But in this case, the democracy cannot reach the outcome. Different factions are at work and are in conflict. We want to fall back on a type of automatic response but something in our unconscious disagrees. Here is another. When you read it, see if you note conflict:

> *In a study 1000 people were tested. Among the participants there were five librarians and 995 bankers. Jo is a randomly chosen participant of the study.*
>
> *Jo is 46 years old and has three cats. On Friday nights, Jo likes to kick back and read a good book. Jo enjoys keeping track of the bestseller lists.*
>
> *What is most likely?*
>
> *a. Jo is a banker*
>
> *b. Jo is a librarian*[13]

When you select an answer, do you note conflict? Of course, you may experience conflict just based upon the fact that I have included it, and you know that I have a reason for inclusion. The correct answer to this example is answer a. This is an example of a *base rate neglect problem*. When given this question, many people fall prey to our assumptions and stereotypes. The description sure seems like a librarian, but this totally ignores the math. If Jo was selected randomly, then there is a much higher probability (995/1000 > 5/1000) that Jo is a banker. There are many examples like this, and there are even more examples from our real lives. These are moments where one answer seems obvious but there is something pushing us, nagging at us, making us *feel* that something is not quite right. We experience conflict.[14]

This feeling of conflict is important because it causes us to pause. In evolutionary terms, this is an advantage. Most of the time, we are able to fall back on unconscious, stereotypical processing. This is more efficient in terms of resources. Conscious processing requires focus. It requires attention away from other things. Why waste resources when automatic processes can do the job? But there are times when our intuitive resources may make mistakes. There are times when the brain as democracy falls short and other intuitive processes grab our attention. We feel this as conflict. When we feel this conflict, our consciousness takes note. Sometimes we may override our decisions and sometimes we may not. But we are aware of the conflict and take notice.[15]

Pennycook, Fugelsang, and Koehler define three stages related to conflict monitoring. First, there is an initial response that is generated due to an external cue. This could be a problem or question that calls for an answer or action. Some sort of decision needs to be made. Within this first stage, an initial response is generated. Second, either conflict is detected or not detected. If it is not detected, then the initial response stands. If it is detected, then a choice must be made. The third and final stage involves reaching a resolution around the conflict. There are two options: a decoupling process or a rationalization process. In *rationalization*, even when conflict is detected, the individual finds a way to justify the initial intuitive response without really considering this response. The response is accepted and then justified. In *cognitive decoupling*, the individual overrides the initial response.[16]

Several facets of conflict monitoring have been observed. One consistent finding is that conflict monitoring results in *response latencies* when compared with non-conflict situations. To put it simply, conflict causes us to pause and think.[17] A related finding with an interesting tie into source monitoring is that as individuals come across information that is in conflict, they pay more attention to sources and are more likely to encode those sources more firmly into memory for later access.[18] Thus, in conflict situations a broader array of neural networks are activated. As the mind detects conflict, various unconscious and conscious processes jump into action. This activation can be seen on fMRI machines where brain activity lights up in a conflict situation.

Research into conflict monitoring does offer one glimpse of hope. Researchers have built a case for *logical intuitions*. Among the many neural networks and intuitive systems that activate around decision making, we can see instances where our automatic processing based on stereotypes and habit can be overridden or at least challenged through unconscious awareness that aligns with logical outcomes. In some cases, our gut response is a logical one.[19]

When we hit moments of conflict, we pause and process. Our mind activates a cacophony of processes at work in any situation. Making a decision is not simply finding the "right" neural process, but it is also inhibiting those that are incorrect. A *belief inhibition process* takes place. Many beliefs are discarded. They are even inhibited from entering consciousness in many situations. In situations where conflict is not detected, there is an inhibition failure. When we fall back on stereotypes or heuristic responses, it is not just that we are taking the path of least resistance or falling into routine. We fail to inhibit these routines. Moments of conflict present the opportunity to put our automatic processes in check. We can kick in conscious processing to weight a decision. The ability to inhibit beliefs seems to be as important in decision making as conscious deliberation.[20]

Conflict monitoring can check the feeling of knowing. We may face a choice and have an intuitive response, but then we feel conflict. When conflict is detected, we pause and consider. Sometimes we may go with our initial reaction and follow that through to a strong feeling of knowing. Sometimes we may go forward and our conflict gives us a weak feeling of knowing. We may select an answer but have a gut feeling that we are incorrect because of conflict. Both conflict monitoring and source monitoring are types of metacognitive processes. They are opportunities to pause and evaluate the degree to which the feeling of knowing is accurate. They are important parts of our experiences. They give us metacognitive control over the world of ideas within our heads.[21]

For librarians and educators, conflict monitoring and source monitoring may represent opportunities for students to explore the processes of their minds. Source monitoring challenges us to track down the beginnings of what we know. How did we get to our beliefs? Conflict monitoring is a chance to pause and struggle with the feeling of knowing.

Notes

1. It is important to note that use of the term *source* means *beginnings*, *initiation*, or *starting point* and not *source* as in a citation or reference.

2. Marcia K. Johnson, Shahin Hashtroudi, and D. Stephen Lindsay, "Source Monitoring," *Psychological Bulletin* 114, no. 1 (1993): 3–28; Beatrice Kuhlmann, Ute J. Bayen, Katharina Meuser, and Anna E. Kornadt, "The Impact of Age Stereotypes on Source Monitoring in Younger and Older Adults," *Psychology and Aging* 31, no. 8 (2016): 875–89.

3. Johnson, Hashtroudi, and Lindsay, "Source Monitoring."

4. Johnson, Hashtroudi, and Lindsay, "Source Monitoring"; Kuhlmann, Bayen, Meuser, and Kornadt, "Impact of Age Stereotypes."

5. Johnson, Hashtroudi, and Lindsay, "Source Monitoring."

6. Kuhlmann, Bayen, Meuser, & Kornadt, "Impact of Age Stereotypes," 884.

7. B. Hunter Ball, Richard L. Marsh, J. Thadeus Meeks, and Jason L. Hicks, "The Reactivation of Associated Information Affects Source Monitoring," *Memory Cognition* 39, no. 5 (2011): 818–26.

8. Ball, Marsh, Meeks, & Hicks, "Reactivation of Associated Information."

9. Chad S. Dodson, Emma Powers, and Mariko Lytell, "Aging, Confidence, and Misinformation: Recalling Information with the Cognitive Interview," *Psychology and Aging* 30, no. 1 (2015): 46–61.

10. Wim De Neys, "Bias and Conflict: A Case for Logical Intuitions," *Perspectives on Psychological Science* 7, no. 1 (2012): 28–38.

11. Daniel Kahneman, *Thinking, Fast and Slow* (London: Penguin, 2012).

12. Janie Brisson, Walter Schaefer, Henry Markovits, and Wim De Neys, "Conflict Detection and Logical Complexity," *Psychologica Belgica* 58, no. 1 (2018): 318–32.

13. Adapted from Wim De Neys and Tamara Glumicic, "Conflict Monitoring in Dual Process Theories of Thinking," Cognition 106, no. 3 (2008): 1248–99.

14. Wim De Neys, Elke Moyens, and Debora Vansteenwegen, "Feeling We're Biased: Autonomic Arousal and Reasoning Conflict," *Cognitive, Affective, & Behavioral Neuroscience* 10, no. 2 (2010): 208–16; De Neys, "Bias and Conflict."

15. Linden Ball and Edward Stupple, "Dual Reasoning Processes and the Resolution of Uncertainty: The Case of Belief Bias," in *Cognitive Unconscious and Human Rationality*, ed. Laura Macchi, Maria Bagassi, and Ricardo Viale (Cambridge, MA: MIT Press, 2016), 143–65.

16. Gordon Pennycook, Jonathan A. Fugelsang, and Derek J. Koehler, "What Makes Us Think? A Three-Stage Dual-Process Model of Analytic Engagement," *Cognitive Psychology* 80 (August 2015): 34–72.

17. De Neys, "Bias and Conflict"; Wim De Neys and Michal Bialek, "Dual Processes and Conflict During Moral and Logical Reasoning: A Case for Utilitarian Intuitions?" in *Moral Inferences*, ed. Jean-Francois Bonnefon and Bastien Trémolière (London: Taylor & Francis, 2017), 123–36.

18. Jason L. G. Braasch, Jean-François Rouet, Nicolas Vibert, and M. Anne Britt, "Readers' Use of Source Information and Text Comprehension," *Memory Cognition* 40, no. 3 (2012): 450–65.

19. De Neys, "Bias and Conflict"; De Neys & Bialek, "Dual Processes and Conflict."

20. Wim De Neys, Oshin Vartanian, and Vinod Goel, "Smarter Than We Think: When Our Brains Detect That We are Biased," *Psychological Science* 19, no 5 (2008): 483–89; Wim De Neys and Samuel Franssens, "Belief Inhibition During Thinking: Not Always Winning but at Least Taking Part," *Cognition* 113, no. 1 (2009): 45–61.

21. Johnson, Hashtroudi, and Lindsay, "Source Monitoring."

CHAPTER FOURTEEN

Our Shortcuts and Bypasses

You will not be surprised to know that the brain takes shortcuts, and this chapter is going to explore some of them. But philosopher John Dewey, who is foundational reading for most of us in education, tried to get us to avoid these shortcuts. He set up a dichotomy between our animalistic "instincts and appetites" and scientific reasoning. He sees reason as our only hope at intervening into uncritical thinking. He notes that our experiences are greatly impacted by the strength or the intensity of the things that happen to us. This intensity biases us in our beliefs. He wants an effort made that experience is more connected to scientific thinking.[1] And it is not so much that Dewey is wrong as that Dewey underplays our ability to intervene. There are forces that prevent us from recognizing conflict and engaging reason. No matter how much we try, our minds are built to make efficient choices. We rely on intuitive thinking first.

As we have seen previously, two pressures underpin intuitive thinking. First, there is an evolutionary pressure to make fast decisions. Individuals who hesitate are more likely to become lunch, so brain mechanisms supporting speedy choices get selected. Therefore, opportunities for conflict to arise and intervene in choices may be reduced. Second, due to these pressures, the mind typically moves most conscious processing into unconscious networks over time (especially for repeated activities). The activity that previously required great concentration and focus eventually becomes second nature and automatic. Despite the illusion of control put forward by consciousness, our brain is actually wired for autopilot.[2] In fact, we often fail to recognize how our intuitive systems work. It has been shown that most individuals are quite consistent in their beliefs when asked on questionnaires or surveys. In the abstract, they remain consistent, but in real-world situations those beliefs fall away.[3] We may consistently answer that we are environmentally conscious and worried about climate change but carpooling with a coworker, biking to work, or taking public transportation all seem quite inconvenient for most people, so we wind up driving alone.

Ultimately, the brain operates by taking shortcuts. Rippon calls the brain a "neural gambling machine" where it generates beliefs and assumptions over a lifetime and uses these to make choices. The brain essentially operates on stereotypes and experience-based assumptions.

> The core of the system is to minimize "prediction error" by speedily and continuously generating and updating priors based on the normal course of events. These will draw on pretty minimal amounts of information to estimate the next step and ensure no surprises, efficiently reducing the need for cognitively wasteful rechecking or "overthinking." In the light of feedback about a mismatch, a quick reconstruction of a new prior will follow. So, our brains navigate us through the world via a combination of predictive-texting-like skills and high-end satnav guidance.[4]

This offers a perspective on Mercier and Sperber's *intuitions*.[5] They define intuition as being a decision or judgment that we make that to us appears to be justified and make sense even though we do not deeply evaluate the reasoning underlying decision. These intuitive judgments are made and accepted. Much of our everyday activities run on a string of intuitive judgments. They describe intuition as "knowing without knowing how one knows."[6] Many intuitive decision-making modules have evolved in us over thousands of years. A good example is selecting food. We can often tell by taste if food is acceptable or rotten. It is not perfect, but if something is very rotten like spoiled milk, you will gag and not be able to drink it. By contrast, shopping for a new car and selecting a car have not evolved intuitively. In this case, we may use reasoning but we may also use other types of intuitions such as social pressures like status of the car brand.

The use of shortcuts by the brain has garnered a great deal of attention in recent decades thanks to the discussion of cognitive heuristics initiated in the 1970s by Kahneman and Tversky in their work on *prospect theory*.[7] In prospect theory, they undercut the long-held view that economic actors sought to maximize their utility as would rational actors. Kahneman and Tversky demonstrated that individuals view risk related to gains and losses quite differently, putting more value on gains. They also looked at anchoring bias—among several heuristics—where individuals make estimates based on initial values that are put before them.[8] The details of this work are less important here than the larger impact they had on undermining the rationalist view of decision making and opening up a line of research connected with heuristic thinking. Kahneman's 2012 book, *Thinking, Fast and Slow*, made these ideas accessible for general audiences. Kahneman defines a heuristic as "a simple procedure that helps find adequate, though often imperfect, answers to difficult questions."[9] More specifically, a heuristic is a mental shortcut that reduces or ignores a great deal of information around a decision and follows a preset algorithm or rule of thumb in order to efficiently arrive at an answer. Over the past decade there has been a heuristics arms race among psychologists and others looking at the use of shortcuts in numerous situations. Metzger and Flanagin offer heuristics that are often used in evaluating information:

- Reputation heuristic: People rely on name recognition of a website or online source in a judgment of the information. Even recognizing a name without really understanding the source is a shortcut people use.
- The endorsement heuristic: People will believe information or a source if other people do also. Known individuals who suggest a source are powerful influencers of others.
- The consistency of heuristic: This is a judgment made by checking consistency of information across different sources. This can require more effort than other heuristics.
- The self-confirmation heuristic: This is basically confirmation bias. People judge information credible if it agrees with preexisting beliefs.
- The expectancy violation heuristic: If a website does not live up to expectations, then the information may be judged as less credible. This could be errors in the website. It could be unexpected navigation or design. It could be giving a user more of an abundance of information than might be expected.
- Persuasive intent heuristic: When bias is overly present, then individuals judge the information as less credible. One example is commercial information that is clearly trying to make a sale. Even if the information is accurate, individuals guard against this and do not want to fall into a trap.[10]

At this point in the discussion, I offer these specific heuristics as examples not so much because of their accuracy or veracity but as illustrations of information-seeking heuristics. There are literally hundreds (thousands?)

of heuristics that have been defined within other domains. One category of heuristics that connects with conflict monitoring is known as *belief-based heuristics*, where believability of a conclusion influences how we judge validity of an argument. Basically, people accept a believable conclusion without actually examining the argument. If a conclusion is believable, and it tends to be in line with mental models, then people do not examine the argument closely at all. If the conclusion is unbelievable, then the people will go back and scrutinize more.[11] Although this is not quite the same as conflict monitoring, there are obvious connections in that expected outcomes are less likely to result in conflict. We gloss over outcomes that fall in line with how we see the world.

We can see how our mental shortcuts and heuristics build a degree of *bias* into our thinking. There is no way around it. We build our mental shortcuts from our experiences, and, thus, we are biased toward the ways that we believe the world to work. I should note that psychologists see *bias* as a systematic error or systematically favoring one perspective. They do not necessarily see bias as some sort of moral compromise.[12] The last few decades of research on heuristics may leave us with the idea that our brains are broken. Much of the value of Kahneman and Tversky's original work—for which Kahneman received the Nobel Prize in economics—was that it demonstrated that the purely rational mind was a myth. People are not purely rational. Kahneman and Tversky demonstrated experimentally that individuals consistently relied on heuristic thinking given specific situations. Their work led to an explosion of research spanning several decades. Entire subdisciplines such as behavioral economics came from them. Entire bodies of work pushed back against the purely rational mind. But the response against rationality would leave a reader to believe that heuristic thinking has doomed our decision making. Mercier's concept of *open vigilance* emphasizes that people are mostly difficult to fool.[13] We are not as gullible as heuristic research would have us believe. Moreover, rationality still plays an important role in our decision making.

I would like to draw some distinctions in terminology that are important in how we understand these facets of research. It is easy to use the terms *intuitions* and *heuristics* interchangeably, but they are not the same thing. Both connect to decisions or judgments that we might make based on a situation or a context. Both take place without conscious examination with the intent on making decisions efficiently. But intuitions are entirely outside of consciousness and are closely connected to unconscious networks in the mind. They are built on past experience and schemas for how the world works. Heuristics, on the other hand, may be built on intuitions but they can have a component of consciousness as well. Our conscious mind can fall back on heuristic thinking when it does not want to devote resources to examining a problem or as it makes assumptions about a situation. Intuitions and heuristics are both shortcuts in decision making.

The shortcuts that we use have a complicated relationship with the feeling of knowing. Thanks to our shortcuts, some decisions may bypass the feeling of knowing altogether. We cannot generate a feeling as part of consciousness if we do not even notice or reflect upon our decisions. We may make a fast choice that does not come into consciousness at all. There is no feeling if we do not notice. There are other times when we may be aware of the choice but are distracted, preoccupied, lazy, or too willing to fall into habits, so we use shortcuts. Our shortcuts may support our feeling of knowing. Our intuitions and our feeling of knowing may form a kind of mental conspiracy leading us in bad directions. Reflecting on and being aware of our shortcuts are the starting point for us to intervene and cut them off as much as possible. For those of us in instructional situations, recognizing shortcuts and pointing them out to our students may be an important component in teaching students to better understand decision making and information utilization.

Notes

1. John Dewey, *How We Think* (CreateSpace Independent Publishing, 2014).

2. James E. Zull, *From Brain to Mind: Using Neuroscience to Guide Change in Education* (Sterling, VA: Stylus Publishing, 2011); Mark D. Pagel, *Wired for Culture: Origins of the Human Social Mind* (New York: Norton, 2013); Virginia Campbell, *Are You Sure?: The Unconscious Origins of Certainty* (Hartford, CT: PYP Academy Press, 2020).

3. Jaime L. Napier and Jamie B. Luguri, "From Silos to Synergies: The Effects of Construal Level," in *Social Psychology of Political Polarization*, ed. Piercarlo Valdesolo and Jesse Graham (New York: Routledge, Taylor & Francis Group, 2016), 143–62.

4. Gina Rippon, *Gender and Our Brains: How Neuroscience Explodes the Myths of the Male and Female Minds* (New York: Pantheon Books, 2019), 114.

5. Hugo Mercier and Dan Sperber, *The Enigma of Reason: A New Theory of Human Understanding* (London: Penguin, 2018).

6. Mercier and Sperber, *Enigma of Reason*, 64.

7. Daniel Kahneman and Amos Tversky, "Prospect Theory: An Analysis of Decision under Risk," *Econometrica* 47, no. 2 (1979): 263–91; Amos Tversky and Daniel Kahneman, "Rational Choice and the Framing of Decisions," *Journal of Business* 59, no. 4 (1986): 251–78.

8. Daniel Fonseca Costa, Francisval de Melo Carvalho, Bruno César de Melo Moreira, and José Willer do Prado, "Bibliometric Analysis Includes the Association

Between Behavioral Finance and Decision Making with Cognitive Biases such as Overconfidence, Anchoring Effect and Confirmation Bias," *Scientometrics* 111, no. 3 (2017): 1775–99.

9. Daniel Kahneman, *Thinking, Fast and Slow* (London: Penguin, 2012), 98.

10. Meriam Metzger and Andrew J. Flanagin, "Credibility and Trust of Information in Online Environments: The Use of Cognitive Heuristics," *Journal of Pragmatics* 59 (2013): 210–20.

11. Dries Trippas, Simon J. Handley, and Michael F. Verde, "The SDT Model of Belief Bias: Complexity, Time, and Cognitive Ability Mediate the Effects of Believability," *Journal of Experimental Psychology* 39, no. 5 (2013): 1393–1402.

12. Mercier and Sperber, *Enigma of Reason*.

13. Hugo Mercier, *Not Born Yesterday: The Science of Who We Trust and What We Believe* (Princeton: Princeton University Press, 2020).

CHAPTER FIFTEEN

Consistent Choosers

Even with the discussions of the feeling of knowing, heuristics, and intuitions, we should not come away thinking that rationality does not exist or that rationality is not important. In fact, rationality and reason are the foundations of human thought. Without rationality and reason, it seems unlikely that humans would move beyond our home ecosystem and spread across the globe.

First, we must understand what rationality is. Defining rationality is very difficult. We often use this term interchangeably with reason or even knowledge. Generally speaking, there are a few things we can say about rationality that seem to be consistent. First, rationality is a type of thinking that we employ in specific types of situations with some sort of goal in mind. That goal might be to identify the *truth* of a situation or to make a choice around a desired outcome. Second, in striving for this goal, we must ground our beliefs in some sort of justification. This could be empirical justifications, the building of arguments based upon logic, or just that our beliefs are consistent from one side of the argument to the other.[1] Even though there is evidence for logical intuitions,[2] we can definitely say that rationality operates within conscious processing. We consider a choice and are actively aware of that choice.

Stanovich defines two types of rationality. The first type is *epistemic rationality*, which focuses on how well our beliefs reflect the actual operations of the world. Do we use evidence of the world around us and reflect that evidence in how we believe the world works? The second type is *instrumental rationality*, which focuses more on reaching goals that we may have.

"Somewhat more technically, we could characterize instrumental rationality as the optimization of the individual's goal fulfillment."[3] Do we make choices based on the evidence around us that will allow us to reach the outcomes that we desire?

Within the domains of economics, mathematics, and philosophy, theoreticians build ideas of rationality on *normative models*. Theoreticians seek to answer the question of how an intelligent agent *should* reason. In other words, given a context and specific set of facts, what is the "correct" answer to a problem? As we have seen throughout this book, our brain does not operate on normative models. But normative models are a kind of benchmark that are often used to determine how well humans perform in tasks involving reason. When we deviate from these models, we must try to understand if this is truly irrationality or some sort of facet in the way our brains work.[4] In the bat and ball problem, the normative answer is $.05. In other contexts, normative answers encourage us to get vaccinated, exercise forty-five minutes a day, or start retirement investments early in our careers. As we know, many people do not follow normative outcomes.

The purest form of rational modeling comes from *rational choice theory*, which is a theorem of mathematics and is at the heart of classical economics. As Pinker states,

> Rational choice is not a psychological theory of how human beings choose, or a normative theory of what they are to choose, but a theory of what makes choices *consistent* with the chooser's values and each other. That ties it intimately to the concept of rationality, which is about making choices that are consistent with our goals."[5]

Rational choice theory is built upon some basic axioms:

- **Commensurability**: "A rational agent must care about things and prefer some to others."[6] This is in contrast to non-rational things such as rocks or vegetables.
- **Transitivity**: If you prefer item A to item B, and you prefer item B to item C, then you must prefer item A to item C.
- **Consolidation**: A risky choice that involves chance may not lead to a solid outcome but may lead to a further choice. An individual making a decision should calculate the overall risk for all of the choices.
- **Independence**: This axiom is related to how choices are framed. If you prefer A to B, then a lottery with A versus C is preferable to a lottery with B versus C. The impact of C should not change the selection. If

you choose an apple over an orange, adding a third choice of a banana should not lead you to choose the orange.
- **Consistency**: If you prefer A to B, it is a better gamble to have some chance of getting A with some sort of chance of ending up with B, as opposed to a certainty of settling for B. A partial chance is better than nothing.[7]

Our purpose for discussing rational choice theory here is not to list out all the axioms or to explore any of them in depth. Instead, rational choice theory presents a type of classical model for decision making. It offers a contrast for how the mind actively makes decisions. Rational choice theory seems like extending rationality to the thousandth degree.

I need to note that *logic* should not be equated with rationality. Logic is a type of thinking or even a tool that can be utilized in rational thought, but logic does not stand alone for rationality even though those words are used interchangeably in some circumstances.[8] The term logic is used in many different ways, but overall, formal logic is thought to be a method of reasoning that comes to valid conclusions utilizing argumentation built on premises. Similar to studying rational choice theory, studying logic presents a formal approach to the structure and form of decision making. However, it is clear that formal logic does not exist in the wild. When we face decisions, we are not constructing inductive or deductive statements. In our lives, content matters more than structure, and it is not surprising that our minds do not operate on this purely formal form of thought.[9]

Both logic and rational choice theory revolve around the difficult issue of *truth*. What counts as truth? Pinker argues that even those people arguing that truth is relative are making a claim toward a type of truth. The real debate may be how much truth is knowable. He notes that we may accept the idea that there is objective truth while also accepting the idea that we may not know what it is and, even more so, may not be able to ever achieve it.

> But the conviction that [truths] are out there and licenses us to develop rules that we can all abide by that allow us to approach the truth collectively in ways that are impossible for any of us individually.[10]

In some instances, the truth is apparent and can be agreed upon. For example, if we presented the bat and ball problem to a class of thirty undergraduates, it would only take one of them to recognize the answer and explain it to the others and slowly everyone would recognize the correct answer. But in many situations, there is not one correct answer. *Should the federal minimum wage be increased, decreased, or remain the same?* There is no single answer to this question. In order to answer this, we can use a type of rationality that pulls together information, experience, observation, and, importantly, beliefs about how the world *should* operate. We can each find our own answer, but there is not one answer agreed upon by all.

Pinker calls this real-world rationality *ecological rationality*.[11] It is different from formal rationality in that these are the decisions that people make out in the world as they commingle different types of knowledge and logic to make decisions. He calls this a "hybrid system" that can draw from formal systems of rationality, but it also draws on experience and other decision-making functions of the brain. Stanovich calls this real-world rationality an *organismic-level concept*. He sees this as the utilization of what he calls the *reflective mind* (i.e., the conscious mind) and the *algorithmic mind* (unconscious mind).[12]

> To be rational, an organism must have well-calibrated beliefs (reflective level) and must act appropriately on those beliefs to achieve its goals (reflective level). The organism must, of course, have the algorithmic-level machinery that enables it to carry out the actions and to process the environment in a way that enables the correct beliefs to be fixed and the correct actions to be taken.[13]

Taken together, Pinker and Stanovich emphasize that we should consider rationality to be something beyond the formal perspective that we study in philosophy or mathematics. Rationality as it is employed in our lives is quite complicated, drawing on our goals and various ways that we process situations. Many types of studies that psychologists employ rely on formal rationality that may not actually exist out in the world—things like trolley cars speeding at tied-up individuals on the tracks. Much of our study of how we think looks at normative outcomes acting as if individuals have no other knowledge outside of the premises and conclusions defined within the normative problem.

Similar to the feeling of knowing, our minds have a very strong *sense of reason*. We feel that one thought leads to another thought. We can't help but perceive our thoughts in a linear fashion. We have a feeling of order to our mental lives. But this order hides the messiness of the mind. Burton notes that our thoughts arise from an "underlying simmering cognitive stew" within our unconscious mind.[14] Just as we are not always aware of our heart beating, we are not aware of our intuitions. We may be quick to assume that our decisions rest upon a structure of rationality even though other brain processes are at work. One of the goals of consciousness is to provide a unified narrative in order to maintain the feeling of unity and direction. This is probably a useful function, but it also may hide underlying desires, schemas, fears, and needs that drive our thinking.

When we experience mental sensations such as the *feeling of knowing* or the *sense of reason*, we are experiencing a summary of underlying mental processes. This is the brain-as-democracy at work. Various schemas and intuitions built up over a lifetime activate along with the evolutionarily wired processes such as the drive for calories, the need to belong, or the need to protect others. The summary of this activation are these feelings that push us to make a decision. A challenge that we face is to recognize to what degree we can step away from these feelings. How can we interpret the processes at work? Often, especially in educational settings, the phrase *critical thinking* is bandied about. It seems that most educators think that critical thinking is important, and it often seems that everyone from philosophers, to writing teachers, to speech teachers, to historians, and more teach critical thinking. In educational settings, discussions of rationality lead to discussions of critical thinking skills. There is no way around it. Generally, critical thinking seems to center on some sort of metacognitive ability to self-regulate and overcome desires. As Stanovich states, "Critical thinking is often thought to entail the ability to decouple prior beliefs and opinions from the evaluation of evidence and arguments."[15] The line of thinking goes: we can deploy critical thinking skills if we can step away from our beliefs and try to get some sort of objective perspective. Stanovich defines the following thinking propensities that enable the self-regulation:

- collecting information prior to making a decision,
- gaining multiple points of view on any issue,
- recognizing the strengths and weaknesses of one's own arguments,
- seeking positive and negative outcomes prior to making a decision, and
- grasping nuance while avoiding absolute stances.

To me, these propensities fall in line with what most people think of as critical thinking. And for the most part, trying to understand how critical thinking works is probably a great idea.

> Critical thinking is a skill acquired in the same way as learning how to play the piano. Just as we establish circuitry for piano playing, we establish representational maps for how to think. If a present line of reasoning matches how we have thought in the past, it is more likely to generate a sense of familiarity and correctness. Conversely, trying a new line of reasoning is likely to feel strange,

> unfamiliar, and incorrect. The greater our reliance on such involuntary mental sensations as familiarity and sense of correctness, the more likely we are to persist with a belief that our logic is impeccable even when presented with potentially contradictory evidence.[16]

Thus, we cannot think critically without understanding and accounting for the impact of our mental feelings, such as the feeling of knowing. Pinker's ecological rationality[17] and Stanovich's organismic-wide rationality[18] both try to do this. They do not simplify rationality down to pure information processing, but instead, try to account for the different processes utilized by the mind. We have to recognize that our minds cannot easily rise above the systems that produce the feeling of knowing, while at the same time we need to attempt to be introspective around this feeling.[19] We must move toward some sort of reflective thinking.

Ironically, one of the obstacles to our reflective thinking is that we are so good at rationalizing our choices that we do not pause to reflect. Mercier and Sperber note that we are *rationalization machines*.[20] Connecting our beliefs to reason and evidence comes quite easy. But just because we are good at making arguments, that does not mean we are good at making *successful* arguments. In fact, if our brains were intuitively wired to operate on a purely rational basis, our natural tendency would not draw us to find supporting evidence. If our reasoning faculties were truly meant to be purely rational, our reasoning should be drawn to counterfactual sources and ideas that contradict our current thinking. We would instinctively try to disprove our beliefs. But most people do not think in this way. When we use reason, we often use it to prop up our existing beliefs.[21] It seems obvious that we use reasoning, but it also seems just as obvious that our reasoning fails us. If this is so, then why should we have this reasoning capacity at all? How has this helped us?

Mercier and Sperber present a convincing explanation rooted in our social evolution. They note,

> The main role of logic in reasoning, we suggest, may well be a rhetorical one: logic helps simplify and schematize intuitive arguments, highlighting and often exaggerating their force.[22]

They argue that reason has two main functions. First, reason is useful for producing arguments to support our intuitive beliefs that come from unconscious processing in our minds. Second, our reasoning abilities are utilized to evaluate the arguments presented by others.

Traditionally, in Western thought, both philosophy and psychology treat the mental faculty of reason as a capability to help the individual process information better. But most of the time that reason is put into practice, it is to produce reasons that are used to argue with others, agree with others, or build knowledge with others. We do not use reason individually. Most of the time we do not use our reason to evaluate our own reasons for believing or not believing things. If we learn nothing else from decades of research on confirmation bias, we should learn that we are spectacularly bad at evaluating our own reasons. But our reasoning capabilities are at their best when we evaluate the reasoning of others. As noted earlier, we do not want to be fooled by freeloaders. Therefore, we have become good at picking apart the arguments made by others.[23]

Even though we often tie the mental faculty of reason to logic or formal rules for decision making, this assumption doesn't hold up. In practice, reason is much more haphazard, opportunistic, and eclectic. The role of logic is often more rhetorical. Logic is a schema that helps to explain and lay out intuitive arguments that arise from the feeling of knowing. Intuitive ideas come first. Logic is added after the fact.

Reason serves an evolutionary function connected with coordinating group actions. Reason evolved among small bands of humans living together. The significant decisions in life were made by the group. Thus, when we produce reasons, we do so within a social context where we recognize the need to connect with, challenge, or navigate our group. Reasons are a way for individuals to socialize on an informational level. They open up an opportunity for us to connect with others or challenge others. When actions may go against the norm, reasons provide an explanation that makes unusual actions acceptable. Reasons are a way to simplify our own internal processes and turn them outward into the social sphere. If we follow this line of thought, we can see how reasons and reasoning did not evolve to seek out capital-T Truth. Reason evolved to present arguments expecting others to challenge, accept them, or offer counterarguments. The group goals are foremost.[24]

This group context changes how we view well-studied constructs like *confirmation bias*. Mercier and Sperber see confirmation bias as a misnomer. Reasoning is not about confirming. Reasoning naturally falls in line to support preexisting beliefs. Reasoning is a systematic effort to find ideas that support our beliefs. It is not just confirming but actively finding support. They use the term *myside bias* to describe this "feature" of reasoning. Myside bias seeks to find all types of reasons, strong and weak. The individual decision maker can evolve poor individual reasoning skills, because reasoning evolved expecting a group outcome. We can put forth an incorrect or lazy answer because in a group context there would be a pushback and a drive to more rigorous reflection and eventually better answers. This may be why some of the psychology research is so surprising. Studying how individuals make decisions is like only studying a part of a larger system. It's like trying to understand chess by only studying how the pawns move.[25]

As noted above—and really the point of this entire chapter—rationality exists. It is real. We have the ability to examine—and make—arguments based on evidence. We can weigh the impact of logic. But when we take myside bias into account, we note that we are especially bad at doing this to our own arguments. In other words, we are not great at overcoming the feeling of knowing. The idea that we can learn to utilize reason as a means to intervene against intuitive processes just doesn't work. But we are actually pretty good at evaluating the arguments of other people. We can pick apart the poor and lazy arguments that others make. You can probably recognize the weakness of social reasoning, most notably the impact of *groupthink*. When like-minded people discuss something that they already agree upon, they end up creating reasons to strengthen that belief. They do not challenge it and take advantage of the features of the group interaction. Living in a modern affluent society is different in significant ways from the kind of societies in which reasoning evolved. Reasoning evolved over hundreds of thousands of years while the internet has only been around a few decades. We have a greater degree of information coming at us as well as a greater diversity of individuals interacting with us in our everyday lives than our ancestors did. Because of this, reason is often used in different ways from its evolutionary roots. Individuals acting alone can reason themselves into all kinds of beliefs that most people would call irrational.[26]

An important aspect of this social nature of reasoning is that not only can we pick apart the bad arguments made by others, but we can also see when they are right. We can even change our own minds. Most of the time when this happens it is because something externally, and more often someone externally, forces us to examine our own beliefs. This is especially likely in situations with high degrees of trust. Humans evolved in small bands of people who literally relied upon each other to survive. The trust of in-group members was generally strong. *Epistemic trust* is vital to good decision making because it allows us to step around myside bias and look inward. *If my tribe members disagree with me, maybe I am wrong?* One hundred thousand years ago, we lived with people whom we trusted intimately, and those people whom we didn't trust were probably outsiders competing for survival. Today, in contrast, most of the people with whom we interact have low levels of personal trust. We often do not know the other people around us at all. This is a mismatch for our reasoning capabilities. If we have a personal goal to be more rational, or at least to reason better, joining trusted groups of people with diverse points of view seems like a step in the right direction.[27]

The challenge with myside bias is that modern humans do not live in small bands of trusted people. In fact, the "tribes" to which we identify are shifting and more tenuous than in previous generations. We do not belong to one primary group that defines us but are part of a patchwork of allegiances. These may include our actual family, places where we live, sports team affiliations, political parties, race and ethnic groups, driving a Ford truck over a Chevy, drinking Coke or Pepsi, listening to hip-hop over rock, and many more. These various parts of our identity can be activated and influence our decisions in different directions. As we make choices or we get into arguments with others, our unconscious process pushes us to support our tribes and our reason kicks in to support our existing beliefs. We act on whichever parts of our identities that are activated. We are more likely to seek out *hypothesis-consistent evidence* as opposed to evidence that can disconfirm our beliefs. Often individuals *want* to be fair and objective. They even try to be in many cases but once they are committed to an idea it is difficult to change. This is especially difficult when considering highly charged topics. This general phenomenon is known as *motivated reasoning* within social psychology and political science. Within the motivated reasoning research, we see individuals seek out desired outcomes without weighing evidence.[28] Motivated reasoning exists due to the combination of the feeling of knowing on a topic, myside bias in reasoning, and our tribal instincts to support those who belong to our group and oppose those who do not.

With all of this being said, we may despair that there's no way around our bias or the other traps of our unconscious minds. But most writers do provide some hope for reflective thinking. The ability to intervene into intuitive responses, evaluate our own metacognitive stances, and consider the nature of our own evidence is possible. Mercier and Sperber do note that we can reach reflective conclusions. But we must do so while navigating intuitive decision making.[29] This is a complex process. Gendlin emphasizes the fact that meaning is constructed through the interaction of our unconscious processes (experiencing) and our conscious mind (symbolic thinking). He writes,

> Meaning is *formed* in the interaction of experiencing and something that functions symbolically. Feeling without symbolization is blind; symbolization with feeling is empty.[30]

He views the exploration of the *felt sense* as the key reflective act. This is the means whereby the conscious mind can attempt to examine unconscious processing. When we examine an idea, notice how the body responds to this idea; that reveals the hidden processing, underlying feelings, and submerged affective states. We can try to understand our feeling of knowing (or lack thereof). As we take rational stances on the issues that challenge us, we must interrogate this rationality from the assumptions we make to the ways that the schemas we hold frame our logic. We need to recognize that thinking on our own is not the best approach or best use of our reasoning. But we also must look inward before we can argue outward.

Librarians and educators can recast rationality and critical thinking skills. It is not enough to employ logic and weigh evidence. We cannot just evaluate our sources and hope to find better information to use in arguments. If we are to be rational, we must first evaluate our own feeling of knowing as best we can. What are the origins of the feelings we hold around a topic? Can we see them?

Notes

1. Steven Pinker, *Rationality: What It Is, Why It Seems Scarce, Why It Matters* (London: Allen Lane, 2021).
2. Wim De Neys, "Bias and Conflict: A Case for Logical Intuitions," *Perspectives on Psychological Science* 7, no. 1 (2012): 28–38; Wim De Neys and Michal Bialek, "Dual Processes and Conflict During Moral and Logical Reasoning: A Case for Utilitarian Intuitions?" in *Moral Inferences*, ed. Jean-Francois Bonnefon and Bastien Trémolière (London: Taylor and Francis, 2017), 123–36.
3. Keith E. Stanovich, *Rationality and the Reflective Mind* (Oxford, UK: Oxford University Press, 2011), 6.
4. Stanovich, *Rationality and the Reflective Mind*; Pinker, *Rationality*.
5. Pinker, *Rationality*, 175.
6. Pinker, *Rationality*, 176.
7. Pinker, *Rationality*.
8. There are many branches of logic and thousands of years of philosophy and mathematics dealing with logic. It is not useful or necessary to explore them all here. This mention of logic is meant as an acknowledgment of this history.
9. Pinker, *Rationality*.
10. Pinker, *Rationality*, 40.
11. Pinker, *Rationality*.
12. Stanovich, *Rationality and the Reflective Mind*.
13. Stanovich, *Rationality and the Reflective Mind*, 37–38.

14. Robert A. Burton, *A Skeptic's Guide to the Mind: What Neuroscience Can and Cannot Tell Us about Ourselves* (New York: St. Martin's Griffin, 2014).

15. Stanovich, *Rationality and the Reflective Mind*, 135.

16. Burton, *Skeptic's Guide to the Mind*, 70–71.

17. Pinker, *Rationality*.

18. Stanovich, *Rationality and the Reflective Mind*.

19. Robert. A. Burton, *On Being Certain: Believing You Were Right Even When You're Not* (New York: St. Martin's Griffin, 2008).

20. Hugo Mercier and Dan Sperber, *The Enigma of Reason: A New Theory of Human Understanding* (London: Penguin, 2018).

21. Mercier and Sperber, *Enigma of Reason*.

22. Mercier and Sperber, *Enigma of Reason*, 7.

23. Mercier and Sperber, *Enigma of Reason*.

24. Mercier and Sperber, *Enigma of Reason*.

25. Mercier and Sperber, *Enigma of Reason*.

26. Hugo Mercier and Dan Sperber, "Why Do Humans Reason? Arguments for an Argumentative Theory," *Behavioral and Brain Sciences* 34, no. 2 (2011): 57–111; Hugo Mercier, Pierre Bonnier, and Emmanuel Trouche, "Why Don't People Produce Better Arguments?" in *Cognitive Unconscious and Human Rationality*, ed. Laura Macchi, Maria Bagassi, and Ricardo Viale (Cambridge, MA: MIT Press, 2016), 205–18; Mercier and Sperber, *Enigma of Reason*.

27. Mercier and Sperber, "Why Do Humans Reason?"; Mercier, Bonnier, and Trouche, "Why Don't People Produce Better Arguments?"; Mercier and Sperber, *Enigma of Reason*.

28. Ziva Kunda, "The Case for Motivated Reasoning," *Psychological Bulletin* 108, no. 3 (1990): 480–98; Milton Lodge and Charles S. Taber, "'Why People "Don't Trust the Evidence': Motivated Reasoning and Scientific Beliefs," *Annals of the American Academy of Political and Social Sciences*, March 2015, 121–33; Charles Taber and Milton Lodge, "Motivated Skepticism in the Evaluation of Political Beliefs," *American Journal of Political Science* 50, no. 3 (2006): 755–69.

29. Mercier and Sperber, *Enigma of Reason*.

30. Eugene T. Gendlin, *Experiencing and the Creation of Meaning: A Philosophical and Psychological Approach to the Subjective* (Evanston, IL: Northwestern University Press, 1997), 5.

CHAPTER SIXTEEN

Nebulous, Slippery, and Poorly Understood

The challenge for us in the classroom and for us in our libraries—and ultimately for us as individuals—is even if we recognize the feeling of knowing, even if we understand how to utilize rationality, even if we understand that our minds are modular, what do we do with it? If we are part of larger groups that direct our knowing, what does this mean? As we engage with knowledge that has been handed down to us, how do we interrogate it?

Let's begin by considering a couple of examples of knowledge creation and the group context around them. First, we can look at a process of knowledge acquisition that is clearly dictated by group norms, namely *scientific knowledge* in areas such as medicine, physics, engineering, or other endeavors. Even those of us with rudimentary understandings of these areas of knowledge recognize the role of the larger scientific community in building knowledge. Laws, theories, methodologies, and even subdivisions within disciplines are all negotiated within a larger group context. The practices of sharing findings, seeking funding to further research, and the applications of findings are obviously built within groups. We also know that these groups are not monolithic. Membership is loosely defined as individuals enter and leave the larger conversation. Some individuals are at the fringes and others are recognized as central actors within the larger enterprise. In talking about scientific knowledge, Longino writes,

> What deserves the honorific "knowledge," on this view, is an outcome of the critical dialogue about observation, reasoning, and material practices among

> individuals in groups holding different points of view. It is constructed not by individuals, but by an interactive dialogic community.[1]

A second example on the other end of the spectrum is *testimony* passed from one individual to another. Most of the information we receive in our daily lives does not come from the things we read, the videos we watch, or the alerts we receive on mobile devices. It is, in fact, the information spread to us directly from other people. When an individual gives testimony—whether formal or informal—this is a statement of their belief about the world. This puts the receiver in touch with the schemas and influence of the individual giving the testimony. And while the interaction may only occur between two individuals, this interaction is built on a foundation created by the larger community. The context could be a place of employment, a school, a religious congregation, or just two neighbors who happen to meet up. Nonetheless, the individuals must navigate within larger group dynamics. Shared language, behaviors within specific spaces, levels of formality, differences based on perceived social standing, and countless other examples are defined—whether specifically or loosely—by the larger group. When individuals come into contact, they are not creating their own language that is just shared between them. They are not forming roles and relationships anew. The most awkward or even embarrassing situations take place when individuals misunderstand social cues and do not operate within the expectations of others. Thus, when one individual provides testimony to another, this is never a transfer of raw fact. This is knowledge that is necessarily constructed within a larger context predefined by the individual involved.[2]

So far in this book, I have largely drawn from neuroscience and psychology, examining how the mind makes knowing possible. We can now start to get a broader view of what it means to know something. First, we have seen that new processes in the mind move from the conscious level requiring focus and effort toward unconscious processing where they are automatic and more efficient. While not always the case, this is generally an advantage in terms of evolutionary selection. Second, as we interact with the world, those automatic processes build a predictive model of how the world works. Past experiences help us to understand the present and anticipate the future. Third, our schemas and mental processes interact on the conscious and unconscious levels, producing the feeling of knowing and providing a metacognitive summary of what we know. Fourth, on top of this, a large amount of our efforts in building schemas is devoted to understanding other people. Culture is part of our mental technology that imprints itself on our minds. It connects us with others and guides us in a range of interactions. Fifth, as individuals, our mental faculties of reasoning have evolved within groups. Reasoning is a social and cultural process. Schemas, culture, the feeling of knowing make us a part of something larger. Not just individuals but the individual becomes components of knowledge.

We must make this important distinction. It is not just enough to say that the brain is social. We must take this one step further and say that knowledge, as an outcome of knowing, is something made possible only by the group. As we saw with the examples of the scientific enterprise and individual testimony, a single mind alone is not enough because no single mind is ever really alone. Kornblith notes,

> Knowledge is a socially mediated phenomenon. That social factors play a role in the production of belief is sometimes transparent, as in cases of deference to expert opinion. But the influence of social factors extends far beyond such cases and provides our entire corpus of beliefs. The influence of social factors begins at birth, for language is not reinvented by each individual in social isolation, nor could it be. Because language acquisition is socially mediated, the concepts we acquire are themselves socially mediated from the beginning. Social factors shape the way in which we view the world in subtle and pervasive ways.[3]

The transmission of culture and the creation of communities require coordination of the actions of individuals. The individual must understand how they fit into the group, but even more importantly, groups of people come together to institutionalize their knowledge. Academic disciplines, religions, publications, and governing bodies, among countless examples, produce meanings that outlive the many individuals who join them. Society is an effort to organize the labor of knowing, capturing learning, growing ideas, and sharing it with the next generation.[4]

But, as we organize knowledge by forming larger and more complex groups, the one thing that the psychology and neuroscience do not do is consider our relationship to *truth*. They have brought us to the feeling of knowing, but one thing that the science does not do is consider *truth*. They do not consider the relationship between group knowing and the truth. As groups build beliefs, how accurately are those beliefs reflected in the world? In what ways do groups as they form institutions interfere with or hinder accurate understandings of the world around them? It's not enough just to say that the feeling of knowing is built around social interactions, to recognize that knowledge is reliant on social structures, or to view knowledge itself as a product of groups. We need strategies for evaluating how groups construct knowledge and how this relates to the feeling of knowing.[5]

Social epistemology is a branch of philosophy that considers the relationship of group knowledge to the successful navigation of the world, and I think it offers a perspective on the feeling of knowing. Social epistemology centers on questions related to the degree to which knowledge is individualistic or social. It can be set in contrast to an area of study like the sociology of knowledge, which is empirically based and sets out to define what counts as knowledge within particular settings and the social conditions impacting knowledge creation. Social epistemology, on the other hand, is especially concerned about the systematic production of knowledge and the degree of success that these systems have in creating useful knowledge. Or, simply, it looks at how well groups perform at creating true knowledge.[6]

We employ a wide range of epistemic systems throughout society. Not only do these produce knowledge, but they also produce a perspective on what counts as truth or at least measurements of accuracy around information. Humans have classified and organized the world into information relationships. We have transformed the natural world into information systems whether it be Linnaeus's hierarchy of living things, the standardization of time zones and calendrics to make time universal, or the use of zip codes to classify geography. We have also built epistemic systems to enable society to function including systems of creating and adjudicating laws, economic measures for understanding the usage of limited resources, and political systems that distribute power. Social epistemology studies these and much more by looking at their properties and levels of success.[7]

It is important to note that social epistemology emphasizes the role of truth in epistemic systems that Goldman calls *veritistic value*. He outlines a two-part approach. First is a *fundamental* state of veritistic value—or disvalue. This considers the degree to which practices are accurate or in error. Second, practices also have an *instrumental* value as they support or obstruct the acquisition of the fundamental value. So we could consider the fundamental value that something like the unemployment rate tells us about the actual world. Does it accurately represent the reality of unemployed people as a whole? We can also think instrumentally in terms of how that rate is produced. Who is included or excluded in the measurement? What kinds of work is counted within the rate? For Goldman, truth is often a goal and not a definitive destination. We may never reach a state of absolute truth in many realms, but we must keep moving toward it. He notes that traditional epistemological approaches look at a proposition and consider three options: accept, reject, or withhold judgment. He moves to complicate belief by allowing for infinite degrees of belief. Truth can be nebulous, slippery, and poorly understood, but we must strive to reach it. Not just that—we must strive to examine and understand *how* we can get to it.[8]

A key debate within social epistemology that has relevance for our considerations here is the tension between the individual as a knower and the group as an agent of knowledge production. If the individual is reliant upon group norms and social constructions, to what degree is the individual an individual? Conversely, if the group is made up of individual knowers, does the group—a supposed agent of knowing—even exist?

In this debate, theorists who believe that groups are only made up of individuals support the view known as *ontological individualism*.[9] At the extreme, these theorists see individuals acting within groups but do not acknowledge that groups exist on their own. Group influence over the individual is incidental. Traditional, Western epistemology was pushed in this individualistic direction through many philosophers but most notably Cartesian epistemology, which placed the individual in a position to recognize knowledge without relying on others at all. This reductionist path strengthened over centuries has been difficult to shake.[10]

Most theorists who fall on the individualistic side do acknowledge the impact of groups, but they also emphasize the development of the individual's mind. From our first interactions with the world at birth, our minds are building our schemas of the world. These schemas are influenced by the people around us who give us our culture and explanations of how the world works. By the time we are old enough to judge the veracity of our own beliefs, our beliefs are already well established and locked in place. But just because our minds are influenced by others, that doesn't mean that they are unable to recognize and react to this influence, as Kornblith writes:

> The fact that we must make use of our processes of belief acquisition in order to investigate them does not rob the inquiry of its point, nor does it preclude the discovery that there are important defects in the process as we are born with. The same may be said of the analogous investigation of social factors in belief formation.[11]

She emphasizes that ultimately the mind makes its own perceptual recognitions that are individually created. Social factors play a significant role in how we perceive the world, but in the end, the individual sets their own direction.

Those in the ontological individualism camp can point out two important judgments that individuals make. First, we judge our own beliefs. When we judge our own beliefs, we employ principles called *doxastic practices* that combine our own experiences, the schemas we construct, and the social beliefs given to us by others. These doxastic practices have an evaluative side. There are procedures and criteria for making judgments about accuracy of beliefs. These could be from sensory inputs or from outside information. No matter the inputs, they are interrelated to each other, evolving over time. We become aware of them as we reflect on the source of beliefs.[12]

Second, as we form our own beliefs about the world and we develop our own theory of mind, we come to understand that other people have beliefs, and we can judge their beliefs. The mere fact that we can make judgments about the beliefs of others demonstrates our ability to work outside of the group dynamic. We have some degree of *epistemic egoism* where we rely on our own beliefs and make judgments about the beliefs of others.

Another argument on the side of ontological individualism is that we typically grant trust to individuals. We do not often deal with groups on the whole but with individuals. People we know well or whom we recognize as especially knowledgeable we grant *fundamental authority*, where we trust them at face value. Others, whom we may not know as well, are granted *derivative authority*, where we may take note of their accuracy on related topics before we trust them. We may give away authority, but we are still making our own judgements.[13]

Fricker largely agrees, noting a difference between individuals who have actual authority based upon the knowledge they hold and those who appear to have credibility based upon various norms defined by society—societal standing, credentialing, age, gender, and other markers that can be used as proxies for actual knowledge.[14] We are often in the difficult position of making judgements as nonexperts about the expertise of others. We do our best to look for the indicators of knowledge while also trying our best to critique actual arguments and beliefs. If possible, we can try to review the views of other experts or even try to measure the success that experts have had in the past.[15] In all of these cases, the individual is acting as an individual making judgements.

For those who see social epistemology as leaning toward the individual, the judgment of group knowledge rests upon the actions and characters of the people within the group. Knowledge does not actually reside in a group but in the group's individuals. The processes and group dynamics that influence—for better or worse—knowledge creation must be judged in terms of reliability and effectiveness. It is not enough to say that groups create knowledge. Groups push and pull, wrestle, coerce, and debate in order to create knowledge.[16]

But not everyone agrees with the individualistic perspective. The other side of the debate follows *ontological holism*, which views the group as something larger than just its members. The interactions within groups are dynamic and produce knowledge that no individual could arrive at alone. A group is not just a reference point that feeds its members input upon which they build knowledge. A group can grasp a wider range of perspectives and take a broader set of actions than an individual. When individuals participate in the group, they are engaging with something larger than themselves, and as such, the group is the predominate point of knowledge creation.[17]

An important factor in group dynamics is the *division of cognitive labor* among group members. This allows groups to approach problems in multifaceted ways as group members coordinate their actions. Members of the group may take actions based on the beliefs of other members even though these beliefs are not apparent to everyone within the group. Sometimes groups are broken into subgroups to take different actions and address different levels of a problem.[18]

Some forms of epistemic justification must be understood at the group level. A professional association issuing guidelines for action is one such example. This is more than just individuals acting within a group. Group-level beliefs generate a basis for action within the group, allowing individuals to recognize how they fall within the larger system. Students within a school or practitioners within a religion are examples of individuals acting within a group belief system. In some cases, group members may take action based on beliefs held by some members of the group that are not apparent or known to the entire group. An employee in a corporation or a member of a military unit may act upon beliefs of those who are in charge of the larger organization even though they do not have a full perspective of those beliefs.[19]

Ironically, some of the most convincing evidence for the power of groups are the instances where individuals refuse to accept seemingly obvious knowledge if it contradicts group belief. When valid information comes in conflict with group coherence and belonging, the desire for coherence often wins out. The idea that individuals can evaluate group beliefs seems tenuous at best.[20] I am sure we can easily bring to mind examples of conservatives and liberals demonstrating their allegiance to the group even in the face of strong contradictory evidence.

We may expect groups to catch errors but there are many times when the group does nothing more than just amplify those errors. So instead of just one individual holding an error, that error is now spread across the group. This happens in many ways, including overconfidence in group members when they are incorrect and a lack of confidence in non–group members when they are correct. Groups are especially susceptible to the *common-knowledge effect*, through which information that is held by everybody is more likely to be utilized because of group agreement. Groups can even, in some cases, lead to more extreme, polarized views as they engage in debates and deliberation. Groups tend to argue one side of the debate more vehemently and are therefore pushed in that direction. Group members with more extreme views tend to demonstrate more confidence in their views regardless of whether they are accurate.[21]

I list these examples of the failures of groups not because groups are more likely to be incorrect than individuals but as an example of the power of groups and the inability of individual members to break away from the group. If put to the question, most theorists acknowledge that there is a push and pull between the individual and the group. Theorists are not absolute individualists or groupists. They understand that decisions come from a complicated process where, at times, the group dominates and rises above the individual, and other times the individual can break away and stand against the group. My goal here is not to declare one view as dominant but to outline the debate as these perspectives shed light on how we know and how we make decisions. Whether from the perspective of an individual within a group or from a group made up of individuals, social epistemology tries to capture the relationship involved with the negotiation of reality—the connection between the internal world of the mind and the external world that we experience. Thus, knowledge is the product of these negotiations. The way we judge this product is through the feeling of knowing.

This is the importance of Goldman's veritistic value.[22] Both Goldman and Kitcher emphasize that the measure of truth is found in the comparison between knowledge claims and the reality we observe.[23] They both argue that *correspondence theory* is an underlying principle of veritistic value. Correspondence theory emphasizes that conceptualizations must correspond to outside reality. Truth must correspond to reality. Goldman describes correspondence theory:

> I would add another ingredient, namely, that items are candidates for truth only if they (purport to) *describe* reality. A desire or a wish, if fulfilled, may have an appropriate correspondence relation to reality in the sense that (a portion of) reality matches or realizes the desired content. But such a desire or wish is not called "true" because it represents what the subject *wants* reality to be like, rather than how the subject *depicts* reality.[24]

Correspondence theory aligns with what neuroscientists teach us about the brain and mind. It is locked away from the external world, comparing its schemas to the inputs it receives. The mind continually monitors and corresponds inputs to expectations. The mind builds its simulation but also updates that simulation to match the external world. But the mind does not do so in isolation. It does so with other minds. Both Goldman and Kitcher acknowledge that absolute reality may not always exist or may not be attainable, but they also warn that the inaccessibility of reality does not force us into relativism. Again, it seems that the negotiation is what matters—the continued examination and exchange as groups try to attain truth. Whether we look at individuals or groups, knowledge requires *truth makers* who make propositions to be judged to fit reality or not.

In educational settings, it seems important for us to not only see individuals before us but to encourage those individuals to recognize their own group memberships. We all are a part of an interconnected world and our groups help us to understand how things work. Therefore, we are part of institutional structures. We form governments, religions, fandoms, corporations, and countless other group actors. It follows, then, that if we examine knowledge created by groups and make judgments of truth, we must consider the structures and relationships that impact that knowledge.[25] If we are to examine our own feeling of knowing, it seems supremely important that we reflect upon how our group memberships are built into this feeling. Our knowing is conditioned upon the ways that groups have built the schemas we carry with us.

Fricker complicates the discussion around social epistemology by reminding us that institutions as well as individuals who are in positions to make knowledge do so within power structures. She notes that there is a moral character underlying knowledge built upon trust in others. We must rely upon others for knowledge. But we also know that groups and individuals will rig the system to their advantage when possible.[26] We saw this with Mercier's open vigilance[27] and Pagel's reciprocal altruism.[28] Cooperation comes with the potential to take advantage of others and the need to protect against being taken advantage of, as we saw in chapter 10. In epistemic terms, knowledge can be a tool for cheating. There is a distinction between the appearance of and actually *having* knowledge. As Fricker writes,

> New forms of competition and self-interest mean that individuals and institutions have something to gain from seeming rationally authoritative when they are not, and from others' seeming not rationally authoritative when they are. But more importantly, there is likely to be pressure on the norm of credibility

itself to imitate structures of social power in such a way that the working-indicator-properties will tend to pick out the powerful and not the powerless. This will amount to an epistemic injustice to the extent that it brings about a mismatch between credibility and rational authority. Where this sort of injustice has developed, the mechanism which enables us to discriminate good informants has deteriorated into a mechanism of (unfair) *epistemic discrimination*."[29]

Any attempt to make judgments of epistemic practices must first recognize the potential negative impacts that power relationships can have. We must recognize that people can be denied epistemic standing based on social identity.

If social epistemology is to be of any use in judging the creation of knowledge adding context to the neuroscience and psychology, these power structures must be taken into consideration. Social epistemology rests upon the assumptions of correspondence theory,[30] which views knowledge as the negotiation between our internal world and external experience. Thus, our internal understandings have some level of correspondence to what we find outside of ourselves. But, as we negotiate the relationship between internal and external, we cannot fall into the traps of objectivism—that have been dominant in Western thought for centuries—where identity is pulled apart from knowledge. We need to be wary of the notion that logic and our senses can objectively make judgments about the nature of the world.[31] As Mahoney writes,

> Noteworthy here is the fact that the two primary and presumably different sources of knowing authorized by classical rationalism and logical empiricism were the mind and the senses. The workings of the mind were to be aided by the laws of logic; the renderings of the senses were to be helped by instrumentation in public inspection. In either case, the object of inquiry was external to the person and the methods of knowing required a disconnection or detachment from that which is known. This has perhaps been the most basic illusion of Western white male epistemology: that reality is a rational order revealed by reason and public sensibility. This is the assumption that lies at the heart of objectivism, a tradition that still dominates contemporary worldviews. In this tradition, truth and reality are singular, stable, and external to the person. Such a view essentially denies plurality, perspective, diversity, change, and the private realm—rendering meaningless any discussion of multiple, personal, or dynamic realities.[32]

As we have seen in the interplay between the conscious and unconscious mind in the feeling of knowing, we must understand that reality is not external to the personal. We need to better understand the forces involved with negotiating the relationship between the internal and external worlds.

As previously noted, *received knowledge*—ideas and information that we did not construct or experience directly—is a major source of how we see the world. Relying on the knowledge of others is vital to our success as a species and is also seemingly built into how our minds interact with the world from infancy. An important part of who we are—how we understand the self—is whom we trust. We are born into systems of trust. Family, religion, government, and any other system of knowledge presents us with relationships centered on trust. Who are the *cognitive authorities* that mold our worldview? What are the epistemic systems that we join in order to navigate the world? In order for us to recognize the knowledge of others, we must understand credibility and authority in others. Credibility and authority are required if we are to participate in communities of knowing. One aspect of the self—who we are—rests upon received knowledge and what level of trust we place on that knowledge.[33]

Answering the question "who am I?" is another way for us to think about self-schemas. The ways that we build our identities also play into our feeling of agency. Our biographical memories, the ways that we see ourselves in the world, the contexts in which we live, tie into the foundational factors of our identity. The societal norms that push and pull on our internal identity are built into our schemas. The power of norms—and the power to be included and not excluded—comes in its invisible nature. Norms are never seen and often not even explicitly stated. But, while norms are not seen, we understand that *we are seen*. Our actions in the world are quite visible and are under judgment against these norms. The true pressure that comes is self-inflicted. We fall in line with the norms in order to seek acceptance and fit into the larger culture. As Foucault writes,

> He who is subjected to a field of visibility, and who knows it, assumes responsibility for the constraints of power; he makes them play spontaneously upon himself; he inscribes in himself the power relation in which he simultaneously plays both roles; he becomes the principle of his own subjection.[34]

Competition between groups pushes individuals to cohere while still competing within the group itself. Group norms set the boundaries for both types of competition. Norms have been put in place around every aspect of society. Norms are a way to push toward homogenization while at the same time pointing out gaps and deficiencies between individuals. As norms push for standardization, they are also used to highlight the differences between individuals. We recognize individualization because we recognize norms.[35]

Therefore, we can reflect back on the old saying *knowledge is power*, which we referenced previously in this book, and cast it in a new light. Yes, knowledge is power and the ability for groups through culture to amass knowledge is a selection advantage in evolutionary terms. But, more than this, *knowledge is also embedded in power*. And if this is true, then knowledge is also built into the inequities within that power. When evolutionary biologists and psychologists talk about culture as a selection advantage, their focus is not on the nature of the embedded power structures within a given culture. The social brain hypothesis[36] and the treatment of groups as "cultural survival vehicles"[37] does not assume equity within groups.

With this taken into account, feminist theoreticians[38] have especially sought ways to move beyond the objectivist or positivist approaches to knowing that assume existing power structures. They take an approach that purposefully seeks out different perspectives. Knowledge is always historically situated. There is always a context around the knower and the thing that is to be known. They emphasize that evidence is *selected* and not simply *found*. Thus, the use of empirical evidence must be accompanied by a situational analysis. The act of knowing is that of constant learning where people and situations are always under examination. This is a move toward relativism, but not a full embrace of relativism. It is more of a recognition that the neutral and supposedly objective foundations of knowledge are neither neutral nor objective.[39] Goldberger calls for *knowing as strategy*. Following this approach, received knowledge is not simply received. When knowledge is constructed, we consider how it is constructed. If we come to a conclusion based on reason, we should consider other avenues to reach this knowledge including bodily awareness—our gut feelings.[40]

These ideas are the foundation of feminist standpoint theory. Standpoint theory is a response to Marx's view that consciousness emerges from interactions between people and the world around them as we live our lives. These interactions shape how we know our world. The interactions also provide limits around what is possible for us to know. The standpoints that we find ourselves in are inherently political because they impact the way that knowledge is produced and therefore distort the way that we see reality. Power structures impact our own standpoint. The societal rewards, the commenting on value, the emphasizing of one thing as important and another thing and not, all reflect our standpoint.[41]

When we take social epistemology and standpoint theory together, we see an emphasis on critical self-examination. There is an emphasis on the reflexive nature of knowing. We must spend time analyzing not just reason but also other avenues, whether conscious or unconscious, that will take us to knowing. This is a call for metacognitive skills. Seeking out different perspectives, examining feelings, recognizing power structures, and interrogating knowing are not just prerequisites that we must get out of the way in order to engage in reasoning. They are, in fact, a layer around reasoning that we must activate.[42] This is a further connection to metacognitive ideas such as conflict monitoring and source monitoring. When we reflect, we can and should look for inherent power structures built into norms.

For librarians and educators, this recognition of power dynamics within knowing—especially knowing as strategy—aligns nicely with Brookfield's classic views on critically reflective teaching. For Brookfield, power is part of teaching that includes our worldview driven by culture so teaching can never be *innocent*. By innocent, he means that we, as teachers, command perfect knowledge of exactly what we're doing in our classroom, that we are perfectly effective. Innocence means that our exact assumptions in meaning are perfectly transmitted to our students. This is a "vicious circle of innocence" related to learning. Reflection helps us break away from this circle. We must recognize the power dynamics in the classroom by also identifying our own assumptions and where those assumptions fall short. Reflection is also a way for us to continue to evolve our thinking and understanding. We are in a mode of "constant investigation." I would argue that Brookfield challenges us, through reflection, to challenge our own feeling of knowing and attempt to recognize how power relationships are built into our own ways that we know the world.[43]

Notes

1. Helen E. Longino, "The Fate of Knowledge in Social Theories of Science," in *Socializing Epistemology: The Social Dimensions of Knowledge*, ed. Frederick F. Schmitt (Lanham, MD: Rowman & Littlefield, 1994), 142–43.

2. C. A. J. Coady, "Speaking of Ghosts," in *Socializing Epistemology: The Social Dimensions of Knowledge*, ed. Frederick F. Schmitt (Lanham, MD: Rowman & Littlefield, 1994), 75–92.

3. Hilary Kornblith, "A Conservative Approach to Social Epistemology," in *Socializing Epistemology: The Social Dimensions of Knowledge*, ed. Frederick F. Schmitt (Lanham, MD: Rowman & Littlefield, 1994): 93–110.

4. William Alston, "Belief-Forming Practices and the Social," in *Socializing Epistemology: The Social Dimensions of Knowledge*, ed. Frederick F. Schmitt (Lanham, MD: Rowman & Littlefield, 1994), 29–52; Kornblith, "Conservative Approach to Social Epistemology"; Frederick F. Schmitt, "Socializing Epistemology: An

Introduction Through Two Sample Issues," in *Socializing Epistemology: The Social Dimensions of Knowledge*, ed. Frederick F. Schmitt (Lanham, MD: Rowman & Littlefield, 1994), 1–28.

5. Kornblith, "Conservative Approach to Social Epistemology"; Alvin I. Goldman, *Knowledge in a Social World* (Oxford, UK: Clarendon Press, 1999).

6. Schmitt, "Socializing Epistemology."

7. Alvin I. Goldman, "A Guide to Social Epistemology," in *Social Epistemology: Essential Readings*, ed. Alvin I. Goldman and Dennis Whitcomb (Oxford, UK: Oxford University Press, 2011), 11–37.

8. Goldman, *Knowledge in a Social World.*

9. Frederick F. Schmitt, "The Justification of Group Beliefs," in *Socializing Epistemology: The Social Dimensions of Knowledge*, ed. Frederick F. Schmitt (Lanham, MD: Rowman & Littlefield, 1994), 257–87.

10. Philip Kitcher, "Contrasting Conceptions of Social Epistemology," in *Socializing Epistemology: The Social Dimensions of Knowledge*, ed. Frederick F. Schmitt (Lanham, MD: Rowman & Littlefield, 1994): 111–34.

11. Kornblith, "Conservative Approach to Social Epistemology," 100–1.

12. Alston, "Belief-Forming Practices and the Social," 29–52.

13. Richard Foley, "Egoism in Epistemology," in *Socializing Epistemology: The Social Dimensions of Knowledge*, ed. Frederick F. Schmitt (Lanham, MD: Rowman & Littlefield, 1994), 53–74.

14. Miranda Fricker, "Rational Authority and Social Power: Towards a Truly Social Epistemology," in *Social Epistemology: Essential Readings*, ed. Alvin I. Goldman and Dennis Whitcomb (Oxford, UK: Oxford University Press, 2011), 54–68.

15. Goldman, "A Guide to Social Epistemology."

16. Kitcher, "Contrasting Conceptions of Social Epistemology."

17. Schmitt, "Justification of Group Beliefs."

18. Schmitt, "Justification of Group Beliefs."

19. Schmitt, "Justification of Group Beliefs."

20. Mikael Klintman, *Knowledge Resistance: How We Avoid Insight from Others* (Manchester, UK: Manchester University Press, 2019).

21. Cass R. Sunstein, "Deliberating Groups versus Prediction Markets (or Hayek's Challenge to Habermas)," in *Social Epistemology: Essential Readings*, ed. Alvin I. Goldman and Dennis Whitcomb (Oxford, UK: Oxford University Press, 2011), 314–37.

22. Goldman, *Knowledge in a Social World*; Goldman, "Guide to Social Epistemology."

23. Goldman, *Knowledge in a Social World*; Kitcher, "Contrasting Conceptions of Social Epistemology."

24. Goldman, *Knowledge in a Social World*, 59.

25. Klintman, *Knowledge Resistance*.

26. Fricker, "Rational Authority and Social Power."

27. Hugo Mercier, *Not Born Yesterday: The Science of Who We Trust and What We Believe* (Princeton: Princeton University Press, 2020).

28. Mark D. Pagel, *Wired for Culture: Origins of the Human Social Mind* (New York: Norton, 2013).

29. Fricker, "Rational Authority and Social Power," 64.

30. Goldman, *Knowledge in a Social World*; Kitcher, "Contrasting Conceptions of Social Epistemology."

31. Michael Mahoney, "Connected Knowing in Constructive Psychotherapy," in *Knowledge, Differences, and Power: Essays Inspired by Women's Ways of Knowing*, ed. Nancy Rule Goldberger, Jill Mattuck Tarule, Blythe Clinchy McVicker, and Mary Field Belenky (New York: Basic Books, 1996), 126–43; Carole R. McCann and Seung-Kyung Kim, "Introduction Section III: Theorizing Feminist Knowledge and Agency," in *Feminist Theory Reader: Local and Global Perspectives*, ed. Carole R. McCann and Seung-Kyung Kim (New York: Routledge, 2017), 351–66.

32. Mahoney, "Connected Knowing in Constructive Psychotherapy," 128–29.

33. Nancy Rule Goldberger, "Cultural Imperatives and Diversity in Ways of Knowing," in *Knowledge, Differences, and Power: Essays Inspired by* Women's Ways of Knowing, ed. Nancy Rule Goldberger, Jill Mattuck Tarule, Blythe Clinchy McVicker, and Mary Field Belenky (New York: Basic Books, 1996), 335–71.

34. Michel Foucault, *Discipline and Punish: The Birth of the Prison* (New York: Vintage Books, 1977), 108.

35. Foucault, *Discipline and Punish*.

36. William von Hippel, *The Social Leap: The New Evolutionary Science of Who We Are, Where We Come from and What Makes Us Happy* (New York: Harper Wave, 2018).

37. Pagel, *Wired for Culture*.

38. There is much potential to explore regarding the feeling of knowing through feminist theory, queer theory, discussions on intersectionality, and related discourses. I mention feminist standpoint theory here as a summary that I hope is digestible. But this chapter hardly touches the surface of the great potential that exists. Discussions of power are complex, but also vital for our understanding of the feeling of knowing. I hope that this chapter is an acknowledgment of this possibility. This is not intended to be a thorough synthesis of these areas of discussion. Discussions of critical theory in general, critical pedagogy in the education literature, and critical information literacy within information science have already blazed a trail forward.

39. Linda Martín Alcoff, "How is Epistemology Political?" in *The Feminist Philosophy Reader*, ed. Alison Bailey and Chris Cuomo (Boston: McGraw Hill, 2008), 705–18; Lorraine Code, "Taking Subjectivity Into Account," in *The Feminist Philosophy Reader*, ed. Alison Bailey and Chris Cuomo (Boston: McGraw Hill, 2008), 718–40.

40. Goldberger, "Cultural Imperatives and Diversity in Ways of Knowing."

41. McCann and Seung-Kyung Kim, "Introduction Section III."

42. Alison M. Jagger, "Love and Knowledge: Emotion in Feminist Epistemology," in *The Feminist Philosophy Reader*, edited by Alison Bailey and Chris Cuomo (Boston: McGraw Hill, 2008), 687–705.

43. Stephen Brookfield, *Becoming a Critically Reflective Teacher* (San Francisco: Jossey-Bass, 1995).

PART III

PATTERNS OF REALITY

This section takes the information science literature and connects it to the feeling of knowing. Here, we consider how the neuroscience and psychology literatures lead us to rethink how we define information and related concepts, such as uncertainty and relevance. How does the current research help us understand information behavior, information seeking, and information literacy in new ways?

CHAPTER SEVENTEEN

Information Science and the Black Box

As a social science, information science has generally focused on what we can see. What observations can we make when individuals seek out and use information? Information is an external item to be held (or at least downloaded on a device). Information science theoreticians who study information behavior and information seeking walk up to the edge of our biology, but they do not cross the threshold. Savolainen notes that information science focuses on the external while he pushes us to turn inward. He observes that the mind is often treated as a kind of "black box" in many theories of information behavior where the mental processes are just a mystery and thrown together in some undefined area of the model. He states that until the internal and external components of information behavior are addressed, our theories "remain somewhat hollow."[1]

Case offers straightforward definitions for information seeking and information behavior that are useful starting points for this discussion:

- "*Information seeking* is a conscious effort to acquire information in response to a need or gap in your knowledge."[2] (italics in the original)
- "*Information behavior* encompasses information seeking as well as the totality of other *unintentional* or *passive* behaviors (such as glimpsing or encountering information), as well as purposive behaviors that do not involve seeking, such as actively avoiding information."[3] (italics in the original)

These definitions address neither how the mind processes information nor the role that the feeling of knowing may play in them. They are silent on the mind's construction of a simulation based upon schemas built out of experience. They do not acknowledge how worldview is a lens through which information is experienced and valued. Ultimately, they do not address the modular nature of the mind and the competing understandings we may have as we encounter information.

Wilson's approach emphasizes *uncertainty*, which may present interesting connections to the feeling of knowing—although Wilson does not make these connections. Wilson proposes a nested model that moves from broadest to narrowest: information behavior, information-seeking behavior, and information search behavior. He notes that information behavior is part of a larger spectrum of communication theory and "human communication behaviour" where, as in many subdomains of the social sciences, researchers grapple with the uncertainty between human thought and human actions (and vice versa). He uses this uncertainty as a lever to move ideas forward. He proposes a problem-solving model for information seeking and the searching process. This has three large stages: *problem identification*, where people are trying to understand the kind of problem that faces them; *problem definition*, where individuals recognize how to answer the problem; and *solution statement*, where a plan to solve the problem is formed. In information search, there is uncertainty at each step, and, therefore, a problem to solve. Again, Wilson does not delve into how the mind processes information and what this might mean, but his emphasis on uncertainty may present interesting possibilities.[4]

One of information science's great voices, Marcia J. Bates, grounds the entire discipline in the social nature of information. She sees information science as facilitating information use and trying to answer three big questions. First, what are the features and laws of information that we can use to make information accessible? Second, how do people understand, create, and use information? Finally, how can information professionals design systems that connect questions one and two? This is a kind of *sociotechnical* stance that connects the mind to technological systems. Her ideas seem to have openings for the social mind and social learning.[5]

In terms of information seeking, Bates goes on to outline "modes of information seeking" that are either directed or undirected as well as being active or passive. Among these modes are *awareness*, which is passive and undirected—that is, "simply being aware" as we move through the world and learn about our world. *Monitoring* is a mode where we are on the lookout for answers to questions or needs but we are not actively seeking answers. This can be through social interactions or through interactions with information sources. Monitoring is directed but still passive. *Browsing*, on the other hand, is a complement to monitoring. It is undirected but active. This could be reviewing updates on a YouTube channel or looking at lists of recent publications where a new item may catch your eye and then you act on it. Bates defines *curiosity*, which is undirected and active. This may involve a general but poorly defined question where our interest is piqued and we poke around for more information. Finally, she defines *directed searching* as directed and active, where we are on the hunt for specific information to satisfy a problem or need.[6] Bates roots her perspectives on information seeking behaviors in our ancient past:

> We have no way to prove this, but it may be that foraging behavior has exapted to browsing or other information seeking behavior. We suspect that, in the act of browsing, human beings have applied a general propensity to sample and select, evolved through millions of years, to sampling and selecting from information objects or sources.[7]

Even though she does not use the terms, Bates's focus comes right up to the mind's conscious and unconscious processing as it interacts with the world. Her emphasis on active and passive approaches draws a difference between consciously interacting with information even as most of our mind's work happens at an unconscious level. Her overarching modes are biologically driven, but she does not delve into that biology. Her emphasis is on information as an external thing to be discovered and not on the way the self, identity, and culture impact how we interact with information.

Johnson offers a direct definition: "*Information seeking* can be defined simply as the purposive acquisition of information from selected information carriers."[8] He offers five general purposes for information seeking: first, to add to an individual's knowledge; second, to make a decision; third, to justify a decision after it has been made; fourth, to gather information to converse with others or to help others; and fifth, to gather information to better communicate with experts especially with medical providers. Given that his research focuses on cancer-related information seeking, this fifth purpose is of particular importance to his work. The importance to decision making in terms of health outcomes is important for patients and medical practitioners. Johnson, like many information science practitioners, has a hidden assumption of rationality underlying these purposes. He treats information as an external object to be tallied up and computed. Information is not absorbed into our schemas and made part of our worldview. Information is not judged based on feelings.

I should note that Johnson does acknowledge the role of personal beliefs and, to some degree, feelings within his process. He goes on to propose his *comprehensive model of information seeking*, where he proposes three broad components of the process: *antecedents*, which are background factors like demographics and personal experiences that impact beliefs about the world; *information carrier factors*, which focus on the characteristics and utility of the information sources themselves; and *information seeking actions*, which are the actual decisions resulting from the information. I present here an overview of a more detailed process, but it is noteworthy that Johnson offers an initial connection between information seeking and personal beliefs. He also recognizes that *locus of control*—the feeling of control over a situation—along with these personal beliefs have a significant impact on information seeking and decision making. But he does not connect these feelings to information processing or posit that our feelings are the foundation for belief. He sees these feelings as a kind of "inertia" around information seeking where individuals struggle to get started or change directions.[9]

In the scholarship around information behavior, there is an initial emphasis on behaviors around documents. Information science's connection to libraries and librarianship is very evident. Retrieving documents, sharing documents, and using documents makes up the historic heart of information behavior, and throughout this work, there is a mysterious link between information and the mechanisms of the mind. Savolainen calls for a shift inward. He casts information behavior as a kind of "discursive formations"—drawing from Foucault—where a phenomenon is delineated through the language around it. The idea of information behavior is set into a type of mental model through which we can explore and build theory. Savolainen pushes us to get to the "unspoken theories" and "fundamental assumptions" within the concept of information behavior.[10] To me, he is pushing us to consider the feeling of knowledge embedded within information that is not easily expressed as words.

Savolainen is not alone in recognizing the need to shift inward. There have been a wide range of information science theorists working to build connections into psychology. Many of them have worked to address emotions and feelings around seeking information and treating them as "residual" effects in information seeking. Savolainen reviewed studies on the motivational aspects of emotions in information seeking. He found three larger trends in this literature. First, he noted the role of emotions in "starting and expanding the information-seeking process." Second, he notes the role of emotions in "limiting and terminating the information-seeking process." Finally, emotions play a major role in "avoiding information seeking," where emotions cause us to not start the process entirely. In all of these roles, negative and positive emotions directly impact motivation, but the major concern seems to be the impact of negative emotions at obstructing success. Few of the theorists address the relationship between feeling and knowing.[11]

Heinström expands on the role of emotions in information acquisition. She emphasizes that in an information environment where overload is the norm, the ability to recognize useful information among the useless information is vital. Most of the information we come across each day is incidental information acquisition, and our ability to make value judgments is not just luck but is influenced by emotional dimensions connected to personality traits. She writes,

> One of the keys behind incidental information acquisition seems to be the ability to enjoy information seeking, whether it is grounded in a genuine interest to learn more about the topic, a relaxed invitational mood, an optimistic personality, or temporary feelings of confidence, certainty, and satisfaction.[12]

Heinström takes this further by drawing on trait theory to outline personality traits that influence information behavior. A personality trait is a pattern or characteristic that differentiates one individual from another. A trait is not dominant or predictive. It is not situational. A trait is a persistent tendency that guides actions. She notes that information behavior theory often treats interactions as purely rational problem solving, often disregarding individual differences and tendencies. Her work in connecting trait theory to information behavior attempts to account for this discrepancy.[13] She outlines the follow traits:

- **Openness to experience**: People who have a "broad invitational attitude toward information" are open to incidental information as well as new information purposefully searched. New information feeds curiosity and the design to explore the world. Individuals who are not open to experience are often closed to new information.[14]
- **Conscientiousness**: Conscientious individuals act with purpose and often persevere in their information seeking. They stick with searches until they reach their goals, valuing high-quality sources that are carefully selected. Less conscientious individuals are often lax and easily distracted within the process.[15]

- **Extroversion and introversion**: Information seeking is often a social interaction, and, as such, there are cases when individuals act as extroverts interacting with others to share and receive information. Additionally, there are also times when introvertive behaviors such as internal analysis and reflection are advantageous. This is a more complex breakdown than the simple extrovert versus introvert dichotomy. There are times when individuals may operate in both capacities even though they may favor one or the other.[16]
- **Agreeableness**: People with levels of agreeableness seek harmony and are more likely to accept the information that they encounter. Individuals who are less agreeable are more critical and less trusting of information they encounter.[17]
- **Negative affectivity**: This trait connects affect and emotions. Low energy states (affective states) and negative emotions such as anxiety direct information activities in different ways. They can drive "frantic" searching as individuals rush to finish, or they may drive information avoidance, where there is too much negativity to engage in the process.[18]
- **Positive emotionality**: Conversely, positive emotionality can drive the process forward as we seek positive feelings, a sense of accomplishment, the excitement from new discoveries, or other positive influences. There are times when strong positive feelings such as joy may obstruct work.[19]

These all represent opportunities to explore the feeling of knowing. They could represent different ways of processing information and perhaps different modules within the mind. Heinström touches on the tendency in mental processing of moving from conscious activity to unconscious processing when emphasizes *flow*:

> At its best, information interaction can become an experience of flow where the seeker becomes focused and fully involved. In flow, exploration becomes an opportunity that inspires, motivates and expands. You forget time and place, and hours go by without you noticing. The experience of flow information seeking often develops through interaction between features of the search system, mood and individual characteristics. Search systems may either allow or, unfortunately, obstruct flow, depending on how user-friendly and functional they are.[20]

Savolainen connects personality to motivation when considering factors that drive information seeking. He considers factors that are driven by internal motivation versus factors that are more pragmatic or purposeful (i.e., accomplishing a goal). In terms of internal motivation, he draws on *self-determination theory* to look at the development and functioning of personality within social contexts. Overall, this theory posits that there is a need to be autonomous and competent while also connecting with others. Individuals seek our optimal situations in order to satisfy intrinsic needs. Conversely, there are also external factors driving motivation. He looks at expectancy-value theories in this regard. From this perspective, achieving goals, finding enjoyment, and connecting with others are among many external factors driving activities. From these theories, Savolainen defines these internal and external pressures that are pushing and pulling on our personality traits as we make decisions with information seeking. These internal and external factors may be another way to see the feeling of knowing as kinds of schemas, aspects of self, or mental processing. The intrinsic needs seem to especially connect with unconscious processing.[21]

Heuristic thinking is another avenue of decision making that has been connected to information science. As discussed in chapter 14, *heuristics* are often thought of as "rules of thumb" or shortcuts in decision making. Heuristics are a way to simplify decision making, especially in situations where there is a great deal of information to absorb. Individuals can ignore the cacophony of information coming at them and focus down on a few pieces to guide them.[22] The discussion of heuristics seems to have a place within information science, especially in terms of unconscious processing of information. The mind relies on shortcuts to save time. Savolainen makes an argument for a fairly positive view of heuristics as he connects them to information science. He emphasizes the "fast and frugal" approach to heuristics that focuses strategies that ignore some facets of information with a goal of making decisions more efficiently. When these approaches are positively correlated to correct outcomes, they are used again in the future.[23] Savolainen identified "conceptual units" that researchers used in information seeking:

- **Familiarity**: Using past knowledge as a substitute in the current situation. This seems to be very prevalent in determining credibility of information sources.
- **Recognition**: Searchers looked for clues that they recognize. What are the cues in the environment that seem familiar that will open up a new direction? The source is ignored or focused upon based on cues connected to recognition.
- **Representativeness**: This is often seen when determining the probability of an event. It's based on the prototypes a person has in his or her

> head. This is used when evaluating information. The genre or discipline of a source may be used to determine if a source is relevant to a search.[24]

Materska largely agrees with this view of heuristics. She sees heuristics in line with the "habits of mind" that are often discussed in educational research. Habits of mind are dispositions in thinking that individuals develop over their lives. She suggests that heuristics as habits of mind are a bridge between information behavior and information literacy. Heuristics are tools that are often intuitively applied to solve information problems. When users search for information, they are using heuristics such as the *consistency heuristic*, where they validate sources against each other, the *self-confirmation heuristic*, when sources confirm existing beliefs, or the *expectancy-violation heuristic*, where the failure to meet expectations make sources appear uncredible.[25]

Arazy, Kopak, and Hadar looked at the use of heuristics in judging information quality. Each person "applied non-systematic search strategies." Additionally, the amount of time an individual focuses on a piece of information depends on the context. There are two important characteristics connecting with context: the degree of motivation that a person has for the subject and the mental resources they are using at the time and what they can afford in terms of regulation for focus. Ultimately, they found that outlining a heuristic, especially for judging information quality, was very difficult, and outlining specific heuristics to the search process was very difficult as each search was highly individualistic.[26] They note,

> We conclude that information quality is an elusive construct that is difficult to measure, and users' quality assessments are subjective and dependent on the manner in which they apply the three heuristic building blocks: search direction, stopping rules, and decision rules, making it difficult for multiple assessors to reach an agreement on a resource's quality.[27]

When it comes to personality traits or to the utilization of heuristics, there seems to be an acknowledgement that reflection and awareness are important in helping individuals—especially students—be successful information users. Given found "macro" and "micro" emotional factors that direct information behavior. These include financial situations, social factors, and everyday concerns such as frustrations with technology. She writes, "The findings presented here point to complex perceptions and experiences that inform students' information behaviors, and that are shaped by the full range of human emotions."[28] Farmer argues that librarians and teachers must work with students to build metacognitive skills to handle the social-emotional reactions that come with information seeking. She found that older students who demonstrated more emotional maturity had more successful information-seeking outcomes. This was especially true for students who had a strong self-perception of themselves as researchers.[29] Savolainen's research on the emotions expressed in online discussion boards would seem to emphasize the importance of teaching social-emotional skills around information. Not surprisingly, he found that computer-mediated (anonymous) discussions around controversial topics were laced with strongly emotional content. The expression of negative emotions was especially easier through anonymous postings.[30]

Another area of information science that intersects information behavior and information seeking are the discussions around cognitive authority. These conversations place knowledge in the position of a relationship between individuals and groups of individuals. These conversations make sense from a social epistemological standpoint, but they often neglect to discuss how the mind values and recognizes truth based on the schemas we hold.

Wilson's book *Second-Hand Knowledge* was a landmark statement defining *cognitive authority* as a concept reframing the way information scientists viewed interactions with information. For Wilson, cognitive authority is a kind of trust that we give away to others. In most information interactions, we are not able to directly test the knowledge of others. We must find indirect measures for assigning trust to outside sources. Wilson considers factors such as author credentials and background, reputation of the publisher, and judgements of plausibility. "The different bases for justifying cognitive authority are all accident-prone, highly fallible guides, but we cannot do without them."[31] McKenzie provides this overview of Wilson's work:

Wilson made several points about *cognitive authority*. First, authority is a relationship between two people. Second, cognitive authority has levels of degrees. Third, cognitive authority is connected to some sort of topical interest. In some cases someone may be an authority, in another cases the same person may not. Fourth, cognitive authority exerts influence over individuals that is different from a kind of administrative authority. This is an influence in thinking. Fifth, Wilson defined the relationship between cognitive authority and credibility, competence, and trustworthiness.[32]

The idea of authority as a relationship between people makes sense within the social mind. Part of our evolutionary advantage is the sharing of information across generations and culture as a vehicle for the sharing. In order for us to accept knowledge from others, we must have systems to judge and understand the quality of that knowledge.

Wilson was writing in a pre-online information ecosystem where information scarcity was the rule and information gatekeepers such as publishers, libraries, and other institutions dominated. The shift to the online environment dramatically altered the conversation. Appelman and Sundar studied how changes in terminology of sources within the online world alter the judgements of message credibility in media sources from readers. *Message credibility* is an effort to look at messages themselves, as opposed to outside factors, and determine what factors build trust with readers. They found that three concepts captured the views of readers: accurate, authentic, and believable. Their findings present an avenue to considering unconscious processing. It's not enough to look at source criteria publication. We must consider these broader criteria.[33]

Rieh took up the mantle from Wilson and made efforts to adapt cognitive authority for the online world. She emphasizes Wilson's central concepts that knowledge is constructed in two different ways: through their own experiences or through second-hand knowledge from others. For their own experiences, individuals are not empty vessels but instead bring their own "stock of ideas" through which they interpret the world. These ideas are heavily influenced by the people whom we find convincing—cognitive authorities.[34] An important aspect of Rieh's work focuses on the judgments we make when using online sources. She differentiates between *evaluative judgments* and *predictive judgments*. Evaluative judgments are based directly on qualitative factors of sources.[35] Rieh explicitly ties these qualitative factors to cognitive authority, noting that they are task dependent but generally included "trustworthiness, reliability, scholarliness, credibility, officialness, and authoritativeness."[36] These were direct judgments based on need. Predictive judgements, by contrast, are indirect judgements made when reviewing search results in a search engine or online database. These rely on domain or system knowledge gained from previous or related experiences. System knowledge seemed particularly useful in searching, especially when individuals purposefully selected *where* (search engine, periodical database, library catalog, specialized website, etc.) to search based on what sources they expected to be most useful. Searchers made predictions based on past experience in order to search in specific locations and review overwhelming amounts of search results. Rieh noted that the inexperienced searchers rely heavily on evaluative judgments while experienced searchers utilized predictive judgments to make their searching more efficient. The important thing for our purposes here is that Rieh demonstrates how previous knowledge and expectations-built experience comes into play with *both* cognitive authority (whom to believe) and the mechanics of searching (where to search and interpreting search results). Additionally, her ideas on predictive judgments offer a perspective on the kinds of systemic knowledge required within academic settings. Searchers must build their own schemas based on past experience to be utilized in future searching.

Rieh, along with Hilligoss, offers a broader perspective on the relationship between credibility and cognitive authority. They note that *credibility* is difficult to define but that the general consensus circles around "believability." Individuals encounter sources of information in their world, and they must make judgments as to how and to what degree they should believe these sources. Hilligoss and Rieh posit that credibility is different from cognitive authority and information quality. Cognitive authorities are people who influence the thoughts of others. Cognitive authorities may be seen as credible, but not all people who are taken as credible on a topic may be cognitive authorities. Information quality is a subjective judgment of usefulness of information. They cite the *elaboration likelihood model* in psychology as a general approach to understanding persuasive communication. This is a model previously used by credibility researchers. That explains changes in the attitude of individuals as they interact with messages. This model includes different aspects such as improving arguments or examining peripheral cues of a source.[37] Ultimately, they define three levels of credibility assessment:

- **Construct**: "Conceptualizations of credibility."[38] This may include things like truthfulness, believability, trustworthiness, etc.
- **Heuristics**: "General rules of thumb that are broadly applicable to a variety of situations."[39] These could be media-related (the type of source), source-related (familiar versus unfamiliar sources), endorsement-based (recommended by a trusted person), or aesthetic-based (visual cues such as layouts and design).
- **Interaction**: "Specific attributes associated with particular information objects and sources for credibility judgments."[40] These could be content cues, source cues, or specific attributes of sources that are used to make judgments such as citations or methodologies of particular sources.

The construct level offers interest and connections to the feeling of knowing. Concepts such as believability are not easily measured and are ultimately a type of unconscious processing determination. Hilligoss and Rieh's approach emphasizes that credibility can be approached from multiple levels. It is dynamic and not singular. It changes based on context and based on media formats. They agree with McKenzie's assessment that credibility and cognitive authority are constructivist in nature where individuals are working through dynamic processes and weighing a multitude of factors in giving trust to the various types of information around them.[41] Again, there are clear connections here to the feeling of knowing. These two authors do not dig deeply into how the brain processes information. They walk right up to the edge, asking us to take the further step.

There seems to be wide acceptance across the information behavior research that much of our information lives are lived internally. Case defines dual problems that there is at once too much information coming at us externally for us to process, *and*, at the same time, our minds are dealing with internal thoughts. This internal activity directly impacts the topics or issues that interest us, the kinds of problems that motivate us, and ultimately, the ways that we make decisions.[42] Todd presents two dimensions of knowledge: internal, private, cognitive knowledge; and external, public, social knowledge. Todd, like many information theorists, directly ties knowledge to the cognitive parts of the mind.[43] Cahoy and Schroeder focus on the "affective domain" of the mind, which they connect with values, attitudes, motivations, emotions, interests, and self-efficacy. They discuss writing learning outcomes for information literacy and emphasize that there needs to be a focus internalizing behavior as opposed to just focusing on surface skills that do not change dispositions.[44] Harada focuses on moving from knowledge as an external thing to knowledge as an internal construction with personal connections.[45] When we review the theories outlined in this chapter, we can see that information science, as a discipline, has been turning its attention toward the mind and has been considering the processes at play from information interacting with the mind and making a change—or not making a change, for that matter.

Notes

1. Reijo Savolainen, "Information Behavior and Information Practice: Reviewing the 'Umbrella Concepts' of Information-Seeking Studies," *Library Quarterly* 77, no. 2 (2007): 109–32.

2. Donald Case, *Looking for Information: A Survey of Research on Information Seeking, Needs, and Behavior*, second edition (Amsterdam: Elsevier, 2007), 5.

3. Case, *Looking for Information*, 5.

4. Tom D. Wilson, "Models in Information Behavior Research," *Journal of Documentation* 55, no. 3 (1999): 249–70.

5. Marcia J. Bates, "The Invisible Substrate of Information Science," *Journal of the American Society for Information Science* 50, no. 12 (1999): 1043–50.

6. Marcia J. Bates, "Toward an Integrated Model of Information Seeking and Searching. Keynote Address, Fourth International Conference on Information

Needs, Seeking and Use in Different Contexts," *New Review of Information Behavior Research* 3 (2002): 1–15. https://pages.gseis.ucla.edu/faculty/bates/articles/info_SeekSearch-i-030329.html (12 Jan 2023).

7. Bates, "Toward an Integrated Model," 6.

8. J. David Johnson, *Cancer-Related Information Seeking* (Cresskill, NJ: Hampton Press, 1997), 4.

9. Johnson, *Cancer-Related Information Seeking.*

10. Savolainen, "Information Behavior and Information Practice."

11. Reijo Savolainen, "Emotions as Motivators for Information Seeking: A Conceptual Analysis, *Library & Information Science Research* 36, no. 1 (2010): 59–65.

12. Jannica Heinström, "Psychological Factors Behind Incidental Information Acquisition," *Library and Information Science Research* 28, no. 4 (2006): 590.

13. Jannica Heinström, *From Fear to Flow: Personality and Information Interaction* (Oxford, UK: Chandos Publishing, 2010).

14. Heinström, *From Fear to Flow.*

15. Heinström, *From Fear to Flow.*

16. Heinström, *From Fear to Flow.*

17. Heinström, *From Fear to Flow.*

18. Heinström, *From Fear to Flow.*

19. Heinström, *From Fear to Flow.*

20. Heinström, *From Fear to Flow*, 120.

21. Reijo Savolainen, "Self-Determination and Expectancy-Value," *Aslib Journal of Information Management* 70, no. 1 (15 January 2018): 123–40.

22. Katarzyna Materska, "Information Heuristics of Information Literate People," *Communications in Computer and Information Science* 492 (2014): 59–69; Ofer Arazy, Rik Kopak, and Irit Hadar, "Heuristic Principles and Differential Judgements in the Assessment of Information Quality," *Journal of the Association for Information Systems* 18, no. 5 (2017): 403–32; Savolainen, "Information Behavior and Information Practice."

23. Reijo Savolainen, "Heuristics Elements of Information-Seeking Strategies and Tactics: A Conceptual Analysis," *Journal of Documentation* 73, no. 6 (2017): 1322–42.

24. Savolainen, "Heuristics Elements."

25. Materska, "Information Heuristics of Information Literate People."

26. Arazy, Kopak, and Hadar, "Heuristic Principles and Differential Judgements."

27. Arazy, Kopak, and Hadar, "Heuristic Principles and Differential Judgements," 419.

28. Lisa M. Given, "Emotional Entanglements on the University Campus: The Role of Affect in Undergraduates' Information Behaviors," in *Information and Emotion: The Emergent Affective Paradigm in Information Behavior Research and Theory*, ed. Diane Nahl and Dania Bilal (Medford, NJ: Information Today, 2007), 166.

29. Leslie Farmer, "The Role of Librarians in Supporting ICT Literacy," *Educause Review*, May 9, 2019, https://er.educause.edu/blogs/2019/5/the-role-of-librarians-in-supporting-ict-literacy (12 Jan 2023).

30. Reijo Savolainen, "Expressing Emotions in Information Sharing: A Study of Online Discussion about Immigration," *Information Research*, 20, no. 1 (2015), http://InformationR.net/ir/20-1/paper662.html (15 Jan 2023).

31. Patrick Wilson, *Second-Hand Knowledge* (Westport, CT: Greenwood Press, 1983), 34.

32. Pamela J. McKenzie, "Justifying Cognitive Authority Decisions: Discursive Strategies of Information Seekers," *Library Quarterly* 73, no. 3 (2003): 264.

33. Alyssa Appelman and S. Shyam Sundar, "Measuring Message Credibility: Construction and Validation of an Exclusive Scale," *Journalism & Mass Communication Quarterly* 93, no. 1 (2016): 59–79.

34. Soo Young Rieh, "Cognitive Authority," in *Theories of Information Behavior*, ed. Karen E. Fisher, Sandra Erdelez, and Lynne (E. F.) McKechnie (Medford, NJ: Information Today, 2005), 83–87.

35. Soo Young Rieh, "Judgment of Information Quality and Cognitive Authority in the Web," *Journal of the American Society for Information Science & Technology* 53, no. 2 (2002):145–61. https://doi.org/10.1002/asi.10017.abs.

36. Rieh, "Judgment of Information Quality," 153.

37. Brian Hilligoss and Soo Young Rieh, "Developing a Unifying Framework of Credibility Assessment: Construct, Heuristics, and Interaction in Context," *Information Processing and Management* 44, no. 4 (2008): 1467–84.

38. Hilligoss and Rieh, "Developing a Unifying Framework," 1473.

39. Hilligoss and Rieh, "Developing a Unifying Framework," 1473.

40. Hilligoss and Rieh, "Developing a Unifying Framework," 1473.

41. McKenzie, "Justifying Cognitive Authority Decisions."

42. Case, *Looking for Information*.

43. Ross J. Todd, "Back to Our Beginnings: Information Utilization, Bertram Brookes, and the Fundamental Equation of Information Science," *Information Processing & Management* 35, no. 6 (1999): 851–70.

44. Ellysa Stern Cahoy and Robert Schroeder, "Embedding Affective Learning Outcomes in Library Instruction," *Communications in Information Literacy* 6, no. 1 (2012): 74–90.

45. Violet H. Harada, "Personalizing the Information Search Process: A Case Study of Journal Writing with Elementary-Age Students," *School Library Media Research* 5 (2002), http://hdl.handle.net/10125/40191 (13 Jan 2023).

CHAPTER EIGHTEEN

~

Patterns of Reality

Of course, within the discussions of information behavior and information seeking, theoreticians have needed to define *information*. It is difficult to theorize about using information when we have not defined the thing itself. Unfortunately, this is definitely trickier than it may seem. "Information" is a term not often used by neuroscientists. Or, at least, information is not a term they use to define a component of the mind or brain. Of course, information is a term used widely in educational settings, in libraires, and in many other places, so I am not suggesting that we jettison its use altogether. However, when we think about information and define the term, we should do so by framing it around the lessons drawn from how we understand the mind to operate.

Early attempts within information science at pinning down a definition for information lean on *information theory* originating from communications and engineering most notably the work of Claude Shannon.[1] Brookes references Shannon's use of signals to transmit messages along channels.[2] Johnson also references Shannon's work in defining channels (newspapers, television, etc.), sources (specific papers, stations, etc.), and messages (articles, broadcasts, etc.).[3] Shannon's work was groundbreaking in ushering in the era of "information technology" by transforming information into a numerical code to be sent across wires—and eventually wirelessly across the air. But, for our purposes, the shortcomings of using this definition to understand how humans interact with information should be fairly obvious. Information theory was at once elegant and practical, but it was not intended to offer a definition of information in a social setting. It was not intended to have behavioral applications.[4] Brookes points out that information scientists—among many others—in applying Shannon's work to people treat the human as an information processing device.[5] He writes,

> The first and severest difficulty is that human cognitive processes are not accessible to "public observation" at the level of detail required. From an information-processing point of view, the human is not the passive receptacle for information outputs of the simple Shannon model, but in active, highly selective combined data base and data bank plus dedicated computer all in his own right: an active "black box" which is the result of a lifetime of information input and output interacting with a unique genetic inheritance and innate developmental program.[6]

Admittedly, humans *are* biologically driven information processing machines, but not in the sense where Shannon's work is applicable. By using Shannon as a foundation for information science, past theoreticians made a common mistake across social sciences at that time. Namely, they tried to apply a positivist perspective driven by an absolutist view of data assuming all human activity can be quantified and decoded. This perspective has been rejected across the social sciences but Shannon's work still surfaces in information science from time to time.

Upon surveying different definitions of information, Case finds five problems that information science has wrestled with in defining information. Definitions become difficult because although they offer a focused definition of information, this focus necessarily excludes specific message types or sources that often are treated as information. Case's five problems are:

1. Utility: Does a source need to be useful to count as information? Does it need to reduce *uncertainty*?
2. Physicality: Must information be captured in a physical medium or does it exist in other places like in nature or in the mind?
3. Structure/Process: Does information require a process behind it? Can it be created accidentally? Does an image count as information? Does a process like a recipe count?
4. Intentionality: Does information require an author or creator to *intend* that a message be sent? Again, can it be sent accidentally and still be called information?
5. Truth: If an idea is proved false, does it count as information? Must information be true?[7]

Case complicates the discussion by acknowledging the long-running discussion about separating *data*, *information*, and *knowledge*. He notes that this has been treated as a hierarchy at times and that different authors have tried to define relationships between these ideas. Case chooses to ignore this debate. In his work, he chooses to use *data*, *information*, and *knowledge* "synonymously" because

> they are usually not clearly delineated in studies of information behavior. Knowledge, however, is strictly a phenomenon of the human mind, whereas data and information are often represented by tangible, physical objects. That information usually has a physical manifestation has often been the key consideration in past studies of information seeking. The way that information seeking is typically approached under the new paradigm, though, is in the sense of knowledge—something in someone's mind—not primarily as a physical object.[8]

For the mind, these terms lose meaning. The focus is on memory, schemas, the simulation, and different types of processing. In understanding information and its relationship to how the mind sees the world, we need to move away from the storage metaphor.

In working toward his own definition of information, Case leans heavily on the work of anthropologist Gregory Bateson,[9] who moves away from the mathematical definition of information and toward something more fundamental, the essence of the term *information*. When we use the term information, we are often referring to both our "external environment" and our "internal world." This is the important aspect to address in connecting with the ways the brain processes information. *Information* brings the world around us into contact with the hidden world of our mind. It is an external stimulus that makes us take note. Accordingly, Bateson saw information as a *perceived difference* in the world, which he called a basic "unit of mind." Drawing on this, Case presents a broad definition, "*Information* can be any difference you perceive, in your environment or within yourself. It is any aspect that you notice in the pattern of reality."[10]

Case's definition of information is especially useful for this book. This line is worth considering again: "*It is any aspect that you notice in the pattern of reality*." Information is not just a book. It is not an article. It is not a YouTube video. It is *any aspect* that helps you see the world differently. But the trick is that you have to see it. You have to *notice* it, which really complicates things, doesn't it? We are constantly bombarded with sensory experiences, discussions, online alters, and so much more that we spend a large portion of our lives learning what to ignore and what not to ignore. The things that we notice build our *pattern of reality*. Just as there is no sound if a tree falls in a forest and no one is there to hear it, there is also no information without a mind noticing those patterns. It takes a mind to recognize the patterns and build reality. As Sturges notes,

> Information is what it is because we are what we are, and we are brains, at the center of a sensory apparatus that feeds us with perceptions, within individuality conditioned by our social existence with other human beings. With the brain as a consistent starting point for our theorizing we are obliged to engage with the questions that formed the disciplinary area of information science in fresh ways.[11]

This view has a clear connection to Dewey's reflective thinking.[12] We overlook the things we expect to see in our world and take note of the things that do not fit into our simulation. This also connects in with Pagel's discussion of algorithmic thinking where unconscious processing deals with most of our interactions with the world until something doesn't fit and conscious processing steps in.[13]

When information scientists define information, the concept of an *information need* typically follows. We can see the discussions of information need in a new light when we consider the feeling of knowing. Wilson draws from the research on human needs as he offers his own breakdown of needs. His formulation undergirds the separation of cognition from affect that is often seen in information science. He defines the following needs:

- "Physiological needs, such as the need for food, water, shelter, etc.
- Affective needs (sometimes called psychological or emotional needs) such as the need for attainment, for domination, etc.
- Cognitive needs, such as the need to plan, to learn a skill, etc."[14]

To be fair, Wilson does acknowledge that "the full range of human, personal needs is at the root of motivation towards information-seeking behavior,"[15] but he makes great effort to pull apart cognition from affective needs. Case views information needs with a kind of instrumentality. Information needs drive us to reach a desired goal or to be "closer to, an end state that I want to achieve."[16] Case goes on to write,

> Many writers on the topic of information needs suggest that it is not a basic human need, comparable to those for food, shelter, security, or companionship. Information needs are said to change constantly with new, relevant sensory inputs. In other words, new questions emerge as old ones are answered or even

partially satisfied. Yet some psychologists with existential leanings see information processing as a basic aspect of being human; they are inclined to see information as a basic human need after all.[17]

Information needs are often discussed in a kind of transactional way where there is a type of deficit—uncertainty—and this deficit is corrected by seeking an outside information source. I am not sure what car to buy so I pick up *Consumer Reports* and talk to friends. But Case pushes us to think deeper about information needs when he notes that *information processing is a basic aspect of being human*. When we think of his definition of information as a pattern *of reality*, this makes sense. As we make sense of the world and build our reality, we are in essence processing information. And, therefore, in this processing, *the feeling of uncertainty* is never far away. Many theoreticians make reducing uncertainty an explicitly stated goal for information seeking and for decision making. The point of finding and using information is to change a *feeling* (i.e., uncertainty). Uncertainty is a state of the mind. It is a lack of clarity about reality. There is an incompleteness connected to the situation or issue at hand. The assumption made by information science is that knowledge (or information) is a solution to addressing this feeling. By finding an information source, we can address uncertainty and feel better about the situation at hand. The idea of uncertainty has connections with the feeling of knowing. We may be able to define uncertainty as a lack or absence of the feeling of knowing. We have a sense of incompleteness and, in the right circumstances, seeking information can resolve this feeling.

We are always working to reduce uncertainty in the world around us. And how do we recognize uncertainty? We recognize it as a feeling. When information scientists discuss uncertainty, they are discussing the feeling of knowing.

The *relevance* of information is another concept that helps us understand the meaning of information. Typically, the information science literature treats relevance as akin to being on topic. Is a given piece of information on our topic? If I am studying the meaning of the First Amendment of the Constitution, then the *Federalist Papers* are relevant to my information need and *The Cat in the Hat* is not. Librarians and information scientists (and many others) are particularly interested in relevance when they work to create document retrieval systems. But again, Case urges us to delve deeper. Relevance may be a statement of topicality but, more centrally, it is a discussion about *meaning*. Discussions of generating meaning are easily connected to the schemas we build in the mind. Our experiences provide the lens through which we see the world and, therefore, we see the relevance of information sources. Relevance is not just topicality but also a reflection of our simulation.[18]

The relevance of information is situational. It depends on the information need and the understanding of the individual, to just name a few factors. This brings us to one of the great challenges facing information scientists in studying information usage, namely, the *context problem*. Information is not applied in the abstract. When studying mathematics we can examine a formula on paper and then apply that formula to the real world and see it in various situations. Information, however, is significantly different. Information does not have much meaning outside of the situation itself. It is the reality or understanding around the situation that makes information relevant. Case notes that *context* is a "particular combination of person and situation that served to frame the investigation"[19] into an information need.

From a neuroscience and psychological perspective, context is particularly important to the recall of memory. Memory is not stored as a unit, but experience is broken into pieces and stored across the mind. As a memory is called into consciousness, it is constructed based on the needs of the moment or the current context. In this way, memory is often incomplete. As we apply information within any situation, we must understand the limits of grasping context and how that impacts our expectations of reality.

It is the context problem that really pushes information science into the realm of social science and away from the realm of mathematics and engineering. Our information ecosystem is not measurable no matter how we might try. There have been attempts to build equations around information usage, following in the footsteps of Shannon and his engineering contemporaries—most notably the work of Bertram Brookes in his so-called fundamental equation of information science.[20] This was not really an equation but a type of mathematical shorthand. Brookes attempted to capture the interaction process of information usage where knowledge held by an individual interacts with new information to make a change. Brookes described this as $K[S]+\Delta I = K[S+\Delta S]$ where K is knowledge, S is structure, delta I is a change in information. This formula indicates that we have existing knowledge structures ($K[S]$) that interact with new information (ΔI), which results in a new knowledge structure. The result, on the right of the formula, is the resulting outcome of this change.[21] Brookes advanced the thinking in the field, and he deserves respect as a scholar, but efforts such as his to describe information use in symbolic functions has largely fallen from favor. I would argue it has fallen from favor because of the context problem.

The context around information is not only challenging to understand but it is difficult to study. Contexts are always changing. They are dependent on the individual. Johnson offers three "senses" around context. First is *context as situation*, where the physical environment, social norms, technology, and other factors come together in a moment that dictates information usage and behavior. After the moment has passed, it can be difficult for researchers to truly understand the factors that came together. Second is *context as contingency*, where the factors around information usage and behavior become the "active ingredients" that impact how we use information. These factors make information conditional around the moment. Information functions in the moment, but again, it is very difficult for researchers to recognize the pieces that come together to influence the contingent momentum of information use. Finally he defines *context as framework*, where the social and information structures merge to define the moment. For example, organizations such as employment or religious groups may define the parameters of information use. This presents its own challenges for researchers in recognizing how information usage will shift depending on different frames.[22]

Again, from these discussions, we can see the fractured nature of information usage. Our patterns of reality are never complete. They are momentary, drawing from experience and worldview within the moment. The feeling of knowing is context dependent. So we can see context as a building block toward knowing but also as a limitation around knowing.

Defining information, information need, uncertainty, and relevance is not enough for our profession. On top of this, our understanding of information must extend to include the social nature of knowing—the social minds and the group nature of knowing itself. Over the past decades, we have seen a wider effort within information science to encompass the social nature of information. Savolainen calls for a "social practice approach" that explores how individuals work collaboratively with others to build knowledge. Furthermore, he notes that information systems impact how this collaboration evolves.[23] He writes,

> Hence the social practice approach sees a mutually shaping relationship between information and collaboration practices and the tools developed for purposes of communication and knowledge sharing.[24]

Savolainen argues for use of the term information *practice* over the use of information *behavior*. His focus on practice helps outline some of the social and contextual issues around information usage. Practice acknowledges application of information like all information behavior models, but practice also calls forth the idea of regular, repeated efforts. It is performative.

Our real-life information interactions are quite haphazard. Sometimes we seek out information and that information causes us to restructure our perspectives, but more often, we incidentally interact with information. Sometimes we miss important opportunities. Other times we interact with information that, unknown to us, will be important in the future. Williamson emphasizes this in reporting findings from his study of everyday information use:

> While respondents purposefully sought information in response to perceived needs, they also monitored their world, at least to some extent, and acquired information which they were not always aware that they needed. The majority of respondents indicated a strong desire to "be informed" about a wide range of information topics for everyday life. How they monitored their world and the extent to which they did so was mediated by their social-cultural backgrounds and values, their physical environments, and their personal characteristics.[25]

Williamson's work emphasizes the importance of viewing information "users" within the information systems—often *social* systems—in which they spend their lives. Johnson helps with this as he studies information use within organizations. Many information-seeking models assume some sort of information gap where users recognize an information need that must be addressed. They have an awareness of an information *deficit* that they take action to address. But Johnson notes that everyday information interactions are more complicated. He outlines situational *ignorance*, where individuals do not recognize an information need because they are unaware. So they may have a gap or a need but fail to act because they just do not see it. He also differentiates ignorance from *ignoring*, where an individual chooses to ignore a potential information need because it does not align with their perspective, preexisting beliefs, or personal benefit.[26] Again, they may have a gap but choose not to address that gap.

We can complicate Johnson's discussion even further when we apply the social nature of knowing to his ideas. Since the mind is embedded in cultural power structures that are reflected in knowledge, individuals do not just ignore information to gain an individual benefit, but they recognize their role within groups and have an incentive to ensure that their group remains dominant. They may purposefully ignore information or purposefully act to keep power structures in place.

A related concept that comes up in the literature is *information avoidance*, where individuals actively avoid information for various reasons. Sometimes individuals avoid information that is uncomfortable or contradictory to their own views. For instance, one avoids specific news channels that may disagree with one's own beliefs. This is a reminder that information is deeply connected with our own identity and the identity of the groups to which we belong. Ourselves and our connections to others play a role in our information avoidance.[27]

If we return to the definition of information as *patterns of reality*, the concepts of information need, information context, and information avoidance are intertwined within how the individual (and groups of people) interact with the world around them. Information is not a physical object crafted by humans—books, texts, messages in bottles—but instead, information ripples throughout the simulation the mind constructs.

Notes

1. Claude Shannon, "A Mathematical Theory of Communication," *Bell System Technical Journal* 27 (July and October 1948): 379–423, 623–56; Claude Shannon and Warren Weaver, *The Mathematical Theory of Communication* (Urbana: University of Illinois Press, 1949).
2. Bertram C. Brookes, "Measurement in Information Science," *Journal of the American Society for Information Science*, 31, no. 4 (1980): 248–55.
3. J. David Johnson, *Cancer-Related Information Seeking* (Cresskill, NJ: Hampton Press, 1997).
4. Tom D. Wilson, "On User Studies and Information Needs," *Journal of Documentation* 62, no. 6 (2006): 658–70.
5. Brookes, "Measurement in Information Science."
6. Brookes, "Measurement in Information Science," 252.
7. Donald Case, *Looking for Information: A Survey of Research on Information Seeking, Needs, and Behavior*, second edition (Amsterdam: Elsevier, 2007).
8. Case, *Looking for Information*, 65.
9. Gregory Bateson and Mary Catherine Bateson, *Steps to an Ecology of Mind* (Chicago: University of Chicago Press, 2008).
10. Case, *Looking for Information*, 5.
11. Paul Sturges, "The Brain at the Centre of the Information Universe: Lessons from Popular Neuroscience," *Libellarium*, 7 no. 1 (2014): 9.
12. John Dewey, *How We Think* (CreateSpace Independent Publishing, 2014).
13. Mark D. Pagel, *Wired for Culture: Origins of the Human Social Mind* (New York: Norton, 2013).
14. Wilson, "On User Studies and Information Needs," 663.
15. Wilson, "On User Studies and Information Needs," 665.
16. Case, *Looking for Information*, 69.
17. Case, *Looking for Information*, 82.
18. Case, *Looking for Information*.

19. Case, *Looking for Information*, 13.

20. Ross J. Todd, "Back to Our Beginnings: Information Utilization, Bertram Brookes, and the Fundamental Equation of Information Science," *Information Processing & Management* 35, no. 6 (1999): 851–70.

21. Brookes, "Measurement in Information Science"; Todd, "Back to Our Beginnings."

22. J. David Johnson, "On Contexts of Information Seeking," *Information Processing and Management* 39, no. 5 (2003): 735–60.

23. Reijo Savolainen, "Information Behavior and Information Practice: Reviewing the 'Umbrella Concepts' of Information-Seeking Studies," *Library Quarterly* 77, no. 2 (2007): 109–32.

24. Savolainen, "Information Behavior and Information Practice," 123.

25. Kristy Williamson, "Discovered by Chance: The Role of Incidental Information Acquisition in an Ecological Model of Information Use," *Library and Information Science Research* 20, no. 1 (1998): 35.

26. J. David Johnson, *Information Seeking: An Organizational Dilemma* (Westport, CT: Quorum Books, 1996).

27. Case, *Looking for Information*.

CHAPTER NINETEEN

Information Literacy and the Skills of Knowing

Since its inception in the late 1970s and 1980s,[1] *information literacy* has dominated the thinking of librarians in teaching settings (i.e., K–12 and higher education) and increasingly in public libraries.[2] I like to think of information literacy as an applied branch of information seeking and information behavior. As such, information literacy offers a perspective on how knowledge is created, accessed, and used.[3] Discussions around information literacy have focused on how one might evaluate and judge information sources. Efforts such as the *Information Literacy Competency Standards for Higher Education*[4] and other standards tried to put form around information literacy. These standards offered the following definition:

An information literate individual is able to:

- determine the extent of information needed;
- access the needed information effectively and efficiently;
- evaluate information and its sources critically;
- incorporate selected information into one's knowledge base;
- use information effectively to accomplish a specific purpose; and
- understand the economic, legal, and social issues surrounding the use of information, and access and use information ethically and legally.[5]

From this definition—and the *Standards* in general—came the recognition that *thinking about and understanding* information was an important aspect of accessing and using information. This may seem like something that should be apparent, but defining *the information need*—thinking about how different types of information may address an information deficit and using that knowledge to set a direction for searching and *evaluating sources*—judging sources that have been discovered—were a move forward in exploring the ways that information interacts with the mind. Individual sources met that need at the end.

The *Standards* made underlying assumptions about knowing. One assumption was that individuals with the same sources would reach the same conclusion. Another assumption that information literacy supported was a traditional, rational model of thought devoid of worldview. The *Standards* follow the traditional Western views that centered knowledge within rationality and posited that feeling interrupts thinking, even though this is not explicitly stated within the *Standards*.

Kuhlthau leveled some of these criticisms against information literacy discussions. Importantly, she connects her Information Search Process (ISP) and its attempt to connect information literacy to emotions:

> Advances in human brain science have verified that emotions are closely associated with thinking and acting. The model of the ISP describes feelings, thoughts, and actions of students in six stages of the research process: initiation, selection, exploration, formulation, collection, and presentation.[6]

I will explore the ISP later, but for now, it is worth noting Kuhlthau's recognition that "brain science"—neuroscience and psychology—had much to offer to how librarians should understand information literacy. Like information science as a whole, information literacy practitioners tended to treat information interactions as a kind of formulaic, logic-driven endeavor where "credible" sources will lead to the "correct" answer.

One important move away from a skills-driven approach to information literacy and toward a more conceptual understanding has been the definition of information literacy threshold concepts. Hofer, Hanick, and Townsend led this move,[7] built upon the work of Meyer and Land.[8] A threshold concept is a kind of knowledge boundary within a discipline that must be crossed in order to understand a topic or discipline. Once a threshold is crossed, a learner cannot go back. Following Meyer and Land's definition, these thresholds are transformative, integrative, irreversible, bounded, and troublesome. Hofer, Hanick, and Townsend present information literacy thresholds:

- **Authority**: "Authority is a form of intellectual trust granted by an individual or community to an information source. It is both constructed, built through expertise and persistent reliability, and contextual, limited to certain knowledge domains or situations and shaped by community norms."[9]

- **Format**: "Each instance of a format shares a common intellectual and physical structure with others like it, and is intentionally produced to support or effect action. Intellectual structure refers to the textual and visual content of a format. Physical structure refers to the organization, design, and medium of a format. These categories are not strict and may overlap."[10]
- **Information Commodities**: "Information is a commodity because it can be described by Marx's model: it is a good or service, has value, and is produced by human labor. Like other commodities that can be bought and sold, information is property that can be either privately owned or publicly available in the commons."[11]
- **Organizing Systems**: "Organizing systems describe, categorize, preserve, and provide access to documents and information about documents. Though often mediated by computers, organizing systems are designed by humans and thus reflect and reproduce human understandings and biases."[12]
- **Research Process**: "The research process is characterized by the formulation of an inquiry based on existing ignorance, the pursuit of information to answer, explore, and/or re-formulate the inquiry, the creation of new understandings in answering the inquiry using an appropriate method, and the communication of those new understandings."[13]

The accuracy of these thresholds or even whether these thresholds exist at all is a fair debate, but for me, the most important aspect of Hofer, Hanick, and Townsend's findings is that this steps toward more meaningful discussions of the mental life around information. Gaining information literacy skills is not a matter of simple mechanics connected to searching and looking at sources but also a matter of how the mind processes the world. They define a type of "liminal space" or "transitional place" that a student enters as they approach an information literacy threshold. This is a part of the learning process that is unique to the learner but ends up with a change in perspective. They note,

> This change occurs in two broad ways. First, learners experience epistemological change. This is a cognitive shift, the extent to which the student understands a new concept. Second, learners undergo ontological change as well. This is the shift in identity they experience as they get an inkling of what it's like to look through a particular disciplinary lens. This means that threshold

> concepts engage learners both cognitively and affectively. Understanding the liminal space helps illuminate the troublesome nature of threshold concepts, because crossing the threshold can be both an intellectual and an emotional experience.[14]

This quote is interesting for two reasons. First, it makes the connection between information literacy and identity. The process of engaging in a topic and reaching for a threshold requires an interface with the self. The individual undergoes a change in thought that cannot be reversed. Second, this quote recognizes the unconscious processing that takes place when working with information.

Hofer, Hanick, and Townsend's work was a refreshing move away from *the Standards* and toward a deeper understanding of information literacy. Their work is a step toward librarians and educators considering how we might address unconscious processing. When we interact with information we must address what is felt as much as what is consciously thought.

Mackey and Jacobson argue that information literacy is important within the ever-changing information landscape because information literacy is a *metaliteracy* that brings together a series of other "literacies" such as digital literacy, media literacy, and more. They expand the traditional definitions of information literacy to include collaboration, participation, production, and sharing of information. Mackey and Jacobson emphasize the role of metacognition in being information literate. In order to participate effectively in the information world, we must be self-aware and be able to self-assess our confidence in our own learning. They emphasize the need for reflection within the learning process and within our connections to information. Mackey and Jacobson emphasize the need for students to be reflective on their information literacy skills in terms of finding and using information.[15] Compton takes metaliteracy and applies it to the idea of *inoculation theory*, where individuals are reflective on their own beliefs in an effort to resist extreme views by working to anticipate counterarguments.[16]

These metacognitive discussions have connections to psychological approaches such as the source monitoring framework and conflict monitoring. When students approach topics, to what degree can we get them to look internally and notice the feelings of conflict that may arise around topics and, further, seek to understand the sources of that conflict?

In our polarized information environment with discussions of misinformation and disinformation, the ability to evaluate and make decisions about information seems all too pertinent. Fisch fears that her work in the classroom has transformed her students from "gullible rubes" who believe anything online into "gullible cynics" who believe nothing at all.[17] A *Project Information Literacy* study echoed these findings. It finds that many students have been "schooled for skepticism." It states,

> An important theme to emerge from our sessions was that no news source could be trusted at face value. This viewpoint did not appear to be a symptom of political partisanship so much as being a pervasive belief among students that they should rely on themselves to decide what to believe. Students attributed this outlook to having come of age as the web has evolved from a collection of dubious websites to a dominant news portal and focal point for their social lives. Many felt they had been schooled to be critical of everything they encountered.[18]

This is not necessarily a bad rule of thumb for students, but it is easy to see how we can tip the balance from healthy skepticism to unhealthy cynicism. This has a clear connection to Mercier's open vigilance, where individuals guard themselves against gullibility and deception.[19]

Head, Fister, Geofrey, and Macmillan suggest efforts to fight skepticism and build awareness in students through building "peer-to-peer learning to nurture personal agency."[20] Gibson and Jacobson offer a similar response for dealing with the "post-truth" information world. They call on libraries to be central academic communities that "model a discourse of trust" with healthy skepticism where students question assumptions in a safe environment, but

> test their [students'] assumptions, reflect on their own deficits in knowledge, address some of their cognitive biases, and develop the emotional "muscle" to deal with ambiguity and the polarization they see swirling around them.[21]

Many others have reached a similar conclusion. For example, Folk agrees that reflective practice is important if we are to bring students into conversations who may otherwise be left out. This is especially true for minority students and others who are part of often marginalized groups.[22] Linvill did a study of identity, political views, and the perceptions of bias in the classroom. He found value in making students aware of their own beliefs and how those beliefs impact their own knowledge claims.[23]

Information literacy librarians and instructors in the classroom could utilize what we know about how the mind processes our world. When it comes to belief, we understand that we use past experience in the schemas as a lens through which we see issues surrounding us. We also understand the group nature of knowing and our innate defensiveness in defending people whom we view as part of our in-group. As we attempt to build new models, we need to understand that combating mistrust is not a matter of finding and delivering the "right" facts. Our desire is often to provide stronger and more credible information sources, but addressing the sources of knowledge is more complicated than this. Cooke stated this desire:

> If consumers of information would take time to make a few simple assessments, disinformation would not be so prevalent or insidious. To become critical consumers of media information, users should question the recency or date of the information (or lack thereof), carefully examine the site's URL, consider the language being used (e.g., language that is dramatic, inflammatory, or absolute), consider the plausibility of the information, and consider the reputation and leanings of the website providing the information. . . . Another question to consider is whether the information is reported elsewhere online (i.e., triangulating information). Although these are seemingly easy tasks, critical information consumption is not automatic, and Internet users need to be taught to evaluate, sort, and effectively use the overabundance of information available online.[24]

Cooke definitely offers a more nuanced discussion than this quote may reveal. But the desire to appeal to better thinking or to evaluation checklists seems like a logical solution to the rise of disinformation. For example, Luhtala and Whiting provide a checklist approach to teaching evaluation. Their list includes authority, purpose, scope, audience, viewpoint, sources, conclusion, features, comparison, reliability, currency, and relevance.[25] These concepts in and of themselves are not without merit in the classroom, but the challenge of the "post-truth" information environment requires more.

Recently, there has been a pushback against the checklist approach in teaching students to evaluate sources. There is a feeling that checklists are too reductionist and get in the way of the larger goals of authority and credibility. Russo, Jankowski, Beene, and Townsend discuss the problems with checklists:

> Checklists can feel good upon completion; there's a sense of accomplishment. Nonetheless, the structure of most source evaluation checklists relies on prior knowledge that readers may not possess. Checklists also tend to treat information sources as worlds unto themselves, rather than recognizable formats with regular patterns connected to recurring situations that can be considered before interacting with the content of a source. Finally, it is difficult to discern how the use of such checklists develops the skills in transferable knowledge necessary for more advanced evaluative tasks.[26]

They draw on genre theory within rhetoric as an avenue to helping students recognize a type of authority within sources. Genre theory emphasizes that standard types of communication approaches exist within domains. These approaches (such as research articles, literature reviews, opinion pieces, etc.) connect to substantive goals and purposes. This allows for judgments about sources beyond the typical checklist. The "container" delivering the information communicates the process used in creating the information, the goals of the information, and, ultimately, value that we as readers may give to that source. Teaching students to understand genres is a way to help them understand the production of knowledge and as such, to judge the ways that groups produce knowledge.

Fielding argues against checklists by focusing on the CRAAP test—currency, reliability, authority, accuracy, and purpose—which is an evaluation checklist used across higher education. This test, like other checklists, is a superficial guessing game based on source cues such as about pages, publisher reputation, author credentials, and use of citations, to just name a few. Fielding notes that none of these criteria actually judges the information itself. These are indirect judgements of the information at best. Fielding used a "lateral reading" strategy with her students to try to directly judge the information source.[27] Lateral reading was put forth by Wineburg and McGrew as a strategy used by professional fact checkers with the hope that this would also be useful for students. Wineburg and McGrew make the distinction between vertical and lateral reading. Vertical reading is a deep exploration of a single source following the checklist approach. In lateral reading, on the other hand, fact checkers move across sources "taking bearings" as to how different authors and sources address the topic. The reader is gaining an actual understanding that can be built up into a quality judgment about the original source. Wineburg and McGrew write,

> Paradoxically, a key feature of lateral reading is *not reading*. Efficient searchers intelligently ignore massive amounts of irrelevant (or less crucial) text when making an informed judgment about the trustworthiness of digital information. But lateral reading doesn't take place in a vacuum. It requires knowledge of *sources*, knowledge of how the Internet and searches are *structured*, and knowledge of *strategies* to make searching and navigating effective.[28]

As an approach, lateral reading still requires judgements about individual sources, but it builds a context and broader understanding around these sources. Caulfield has emphasized the need for students to build skills directly related to fact checking beyond just lateral reading. His online book, *Web*

Literacy for Student Fact-Checkers, outlines his "four moves" required to be effective online information users:

- **Check for previous work**: Look around to see if someone else has already fact-checked the claim or provided a synthesis of research.
- **Go upstream to the source**: Go "upstream" to the source of the claim. Most web content is not original. Get to the original source to understand the trustworthiness of the information.
- **Read laterally**: Once you get to the source of a claim, read what other people say about the source (publication, author, etc.). The truth is in the network.
- **Circle back**: If you get lost, hit dead ends, or find yourself going down an increasingly confusing rabbit hole, back up and start over, knowing what you know now. You're likely to take a more informed path with different search terms and better decisions.[29]

This has been shortened to the acronym SIFT: stop, investigate the source, find better coverage, and trace claims, quotes, and media to their original context. Evanston and Sponsel emphasize this with their study of first-year student news consumption. Students often tried to dig deeply into single articles and fell short in recognizing syndicated articles and understanding the processes behind many news sources.[30] For this discussion, these details are less important than the recognition that the old ideas of evaluating articles is not enough. Students—and the rest of us for that matter—need more than reading strategies and more than better media literacy knowledge.

A number of theoreticians emphasize the need to get to evaluation of "truth." Their conversations avoid considerations about how the mind evaluates ideas around truth. Namely, they avoid considering the feeling of knowing. Saunders and Budd emphasize the need to focus on "truth and fact" and less on surrogates such as author credentials or reputation of publishers. They suggest helping students to look at methods, argumentation, and "truth-claims," emphasizing directly looking at the content of the source.[31] Zakharov, Life, and Fosmire's findings of students' information use emphasize the need for guidance. They found that when students evaluated sources they were most often making direct judgments of source content, but they often did this with a dualistic type of thinking where a source was either correct or incorrect. They did not understand the ongoing conversations around topics and that there are many shades of gray. The students were not well equipped to recognize the contexts of sources and the purposes behind different types of writing.[32]

We must find a way to incorporate metacognitive strategies. Whether it is evaluation checklists, the SIFT model, lateral reading, or other strategies, we need to find a way to incorporate and acknowledge the feeling of knowing. In the end, our individual minds absorb outside views of the world and measure them against our schemas. This is ultimately how we measure truth. We generate a feeling about what we are seeing, witnessing, reading, or hearing. For better or worse, the most compelling sources of data will be measured against our gut feeling, and we must consider whether to follow what our feelings tell us or to find avenues to reconsider that feeling.

There are many discussions that recognize that building information literacy skills goes beyond pure rationality. There are potential suggestions that could push us in useful directions. In discussing the post-truth information world, Cooke discusses "an emotional dimension of information behavior."[33] Cahoy and Schroeder take us deeper. They define the "affective domain" as values, attitudes, motivations, emotions, interests, and self-efficacy. For them, feelings surround the research process, enabling and hampering success. If librarians are to successfully build information literacy skills in students, they must work to embed positive affective skills along the way.

> Anticipating students' emotional responses in the impact of those reactions on acquisition of information literacy skills, both positive and negative, is the first step in articulating affective learning outcomes for students. In addition to noting the anxieties, confusion, or frustration that students may encounter as they develop their research skills, librarians must consider the positive behavioral outcomes that they want their students to develop. Building resilience, persistence, and positive learning dispositions in students requires intentional work on developing focused learning outcomes that build these critical emotional skills in our students.[34]

Stipling emphasized the value of inquiry over information literacy. In her view, *inquiry* more fully incorporates dispositions—attitudes toward learning—also responsibilities, and a view of self-reflection. She writes, "Inquiry is a process of learning that is driven by questioning, thoughtful investigating, making sense of information, and developing new understandings."[35] Gibson and Jacobson advocate for the continued evolution of information literacy as a concept so that students are prepared for the "post-truth information landscape." It is important for students to deal with online uncertainty. They emphasize the importance of working with students to develop "habits of mind" to deal with the "necessary ambiguity of the highly mutable, uncertain, and fragmented information environment of the present."[36] They continue,

> Repeated experiences with these cogent combinations of knowledge practices and dispositions, designed into learning venues, provide students with safe but challenging ways to test their assumptions, reflect on their own deficits in knowledge, address some of their cognitive biases, and develop the emotional "muscle" to deal with ambiguity and the polarization they see swirling around them.[37]

The idea of reflection, again, has resonance. Corrall calls for reflective practice to become a new threshold for information literacy. She connects the need for reflective practice back to theoreticians such as John Dewey and Paulo Freire, both of whom worked to problematize learning while emphasizing the need to use education to take action in the world. Drawing on Schön, she emphasizes the dialog that exists between thinking and doing. Being present in the world to truly make sense of experience is to be reflective.[38] This connects with the discussions of metacognition surrounding information literacy as a metaliteracy.[39] Along the same lines, Corrall also discusses critical information literacy as another avenue for rethinking information literacy utilizing a type of reflective practice.

The idea of reflection and building metacognitive skills as a threshold concept is an important one. As we engage in debates and evaluate arguments, can we recognize our own perspectives and the sources of the schemas we hold? Can tools in psychology such as the felt sense be incorporated into information literacy practice?

Before we can do this, we must consider another avenue of information literacy discussion. These are the efforts around critical information literacy that explore how knowing and information structures connect to group power dynamics. Critical information literacy may be seen as a commentary on how groups form knowledge as suggested by social epistemology. *Critical information literacy* (CIL) developed in parallel to the skills-based approach emphasized by the *Standards*. In fact, CIL can be seen as a reaction to the emphasis on assessment and measurable outcomes within the institutional context. CIL has developed over several decades, creating an increasingly rich literature and pedagogical approaches. CIL applies critical theory—utilizing Marxist thinkers such as Giroux—and critical pedagogy—the likes of Freire—to information literacy. The critical approach to information literacy considers the role of power structures in information usage, access, and production, among many factors. It also considers the overlapping power structures in the modern classroom.[40]

When exploring major power structures addressed in CIL, writers move in several directions. A major area for discussion is around the institutional or organizational factors that define education. Seale notes that institutions seek to preserve themselves and preclude notions that might undermine their authority. She extends this to CIL itself, noting that it too has been absorbed by institutions that undermine the ability to honestly critique the profession.[41] Both Mathiesen and Cope emphasize that institutions—as well as librarianship—work to take a neutral stance. The idea is that educational institutions are places of debate open to all ideas, which underlies a pluralistic society. Of course, they also point out that being neutral supports existing power structures and undermines efforts to strive for equality in terms of class, race, gender, and other struggles.[42] Folk sees information literacy and the related skills as cultural capital within the organizational setting. The collaborative and shared learning environments are accompanied by power relationships within organizations and within society. Information literacy is built within a culture of privilege that may not be easily accessible to students from outside cultures. She notes that librarians can work to make information literacy more explicit and work to undercut some of the biases inherent within institutions.[43] Ferretti offers a similar perspective when she talks about the role of reputation when it comes into conflict with praxis. The reputational pressures within organizations are not only built into the existing power structures, but many times, especially in higher education, reputation is a form of currency. And thus, individuals who build reputational recognition as well as cultural capital are not inclined to advocate for marginalized individuals or to work for equity within the organization.[44]

Obviously, critical information literacy has direct connections to the discussions of power structures in chapter 16. CIL draws from some of the same theoretical sources. The organizational discussions related to critical information literacy emphasize some of the approaches outlined by social epistemology in the ways groups form and create knowledge. We are part of groups because those groups offer advantages through the power that they wield. But the power is distributed unevenly and inequitably. Knowledge is embedded within and created within these group dynamics. Libraries, departments, colleges, and universities are all groups that accomplish work and create power structures.

Another direction taken by librarians thinking and writing about CIL are issues related to various aspects of social justice. Smith offers a critique of academic labor and the need for self-determination. He casts education as an arm of the capitalist infrastructure and that those of us within that infrastructure rely upon the institutions not only for our livelihoods but also for our credibility and value.[45] Seal follows this discussion, noting academic librarianship's acceptance of learning analytics and subsumption into surveillance capitalism.[46] Leung and López-McKnight point out the white supremacy in the background of our institutions that pervades classrooms. They call on librarians considering CIL to value the experiences of students of color and to understand that there are many legitimate paths to knowledge.[47] Cope agrees with this in noting that there are "mainstream" cultural forces pervading information literacy that are assumed to be normalized or to represent the "standard" approach. These mainstream perspectives by their very nature reinforce existing power structures.[48] Mathiesen called for *informational justice* as an important aspect of social justice discussions. For Mathiesen, a key aspect of helping marginalized people and seeking equity is the ability to access, share, and produce information. Establishing informational justice undergirds all efforts at social justice. Without it, the other efforts fail.[49] Douglas challenges educators to rethink the very paradigms around how educators work. She encourages us to build classrooms that are open and personal with a focus on "care." For her practices such as assessment cast the learning environment in terms of measurement and accountability. She recasts this as a caring relationship between teacher and student focused on well-being and support. She asks us to consider how we can reposition all relationships within higher education organizations.[50]

These larger discussions related to social justice push information literacy in particular, and education more generally, as a tool for equity. Taken on the whole, these writers push against the power structures behind knowledge. For our conversation here, CIL offers a useful exploration related to knowledge within the educational setting. Although CIL practitioners and theorists did not always set out to offer commentary on knowledge *per se*, they added to this discussion nonetheless. They frame knowledge as an outcome of different forces, whether it be institutional forces, cultural forces, or economic forces. Learning as an information behavior exists within a dynamic environment that connects the personal situation of the learner to the external power structures within institutions and society. From a social epistemological standpoint, this is a commentary on how groups create knowledge. From the psychological standpoint, this commentary connects with how individuals conceptualize the self in relation to other people.

Pankl and Coleman make a connection directly to meaning. They claim that higher education takes a "neoliberal" approach that focuses on skill acquisition sacrificing critical consciousness and a focus on meaning for students.[51] Cooke's discussion of "critical self-reflection" extends this discussion around meaning. She centers CIL and critical inquiry as a type of "sense-making" that is transformative and inclusive of voices often left at the margins. One cannot recognize the power structures at work in the classroom without understanding oneself from a critical perspective. "Learning has to be a reciprocal and co-created process where human beings, with all their opinions, ignorance, and foibles, relate to one another."[52] Torrell argues for building CIL approaches across the curriculum and not just in composition courses where information literacy skills are commonly emphasized. In so doing, she emphasizes the meaning-making inherent in CIL, "just as writing is, CIL is not just a set of skills but a way of critical thinking and processing information and therefore a particularly valuable piece of the college learning experience."[53] Accardi, Drabinski, and Kumbier note that CIL is a "lens" through which we can see libraries and learnings anew. It is a way to create broader meaning through the individual, making recognitions as to how they interact with the institutions in which we participate.[54] From a larger perspective, CIL takes an epistemological stance where knowledge is not neutral, learning is institutionally bound, and groups of people (organizations, classes, departments, etc.) are culturally bound. All of these forces influence how the brain processes the world around it, and while CIL does not take a directly psychological approach to information literacy and information behavior, it does outline some of the complexities at work. As Saunders and Wong note,

> If we want to be fair-minded, rational people, it is essential that we identify and reflect on our unconscious biases, including recognizing how our society shapes and influences those biases, in order to mitigate the effect they have on our thoughts and actions.[55]

Notes

1. Alison J. Head, Barbara Fister, Steven Geofrey, and Margy MacMillan, "The Project Information Literacy Retrospective: Insights from More Than a Decade of Information Literacy Research, 2008–2022," *Project Information Research Institute* (12 October 2022), https://projectinfolit.org/publications/retrospective (13 Jan 2023).

2. Miriam Louise Matteson and Beate Gersch, "Information Literacy Instruction in Public Libraries," *Journal of Information Literacy* 14, no. 2 (2020): 71–95.

3. Maureen L. Fitzpatrick and Yvonne Nalani Meulemans, "Assessing an Information Literacy Assignment and Workshop Using a Quasi-Experimental Design," *College Teaching* 59, no. 4 (2011): 142–49; Leslie Farmer, "The Role of Librarians in Supporting ICT Literacy," *Educause Review*, May 9, 2019, https://er.educause.edu/blogs/2019/5/the-role-of-librarians-in-supporting-ict-literacy (12 Jan 2023).

4. Association of College and Research Libraries, "Information Literacy Competency Standards for Higher Education," *American Library Association*, 2000, http://www.ala.org/acrl/standards/informationliteracycompetency (12 Jan 2023).

5. Association of College and Research Libraries, "Information Literacy Competency Standards," 2–3.

6. Carol Collier Kuhlthau, "Rethinking the 2000 ACRL Standards: Some Things to Consider," *Communications in Information Literacy* 7, no. 2 (2013): 94.

7. Amy R. Hofer, Silvia Lin Hanick, and Lori Townsend, *Transforming Information Literacy Instruction: Threshold Concepts in Theory and Practice* (Santa Barbara, CA: Libraries Unlimited, 2019).

8. Jan Meyer and Ray Land, "Threshold Concepts and Troublesome Knowledge: Linkages to Ways of Thinking and Practicing within the Disciplines," *Enhancing Teaching-Learning Environments in Undergraduate Courses*, http://www.etl.tla.ed.ac.uk/docs/ETLreport4.pdf (13 Jan 2023); Ray Land and Jan H. F. Meyer, "Threshold Concepts and Troublesome Knowledge: Dynamics of Assessment," in *Overcoming Barriers to Student Understanding: Threshold Concepts and Troublesome Knowledge*, ed. Jan H. F. Meyer and Ray Land (London: Routledge, 2006), 61–79.

9. Hofer, Hanick, and Townsend, *Transforming Information Literacy Instruction*, 58.

10. Hofer, Hanick, and Townsend, *Transforming Information Literacy Instruction*, 82.

11. Hofer, Hanick, and Townsend, *Transforming Information Literacy Instruction*, 105.

12. Hofer, Hanick, and Townsend, *Transforming Information Literacy Instruction*, 132.

13. Hofer, Hanick, and Townsend, *Transforming Information Literacy Instruction*, 154.

14. Hofer, Hanick, and Townsend, *Transforming Information Literacy Instruction*, 5.

15. Thomas Mackey and Trudi E. Jacobson, *Metaliteracy: Reinventing Information Literacy and Empowering Learners* (Chicago: ALA Neal-Schuman, 2014).

16. Josh Compton, "Inoculation Theory and Metaliterate Learning," in *Metaliterate Learning for the Post-Truth World*, ed. Thomas P. Mackey and Trudie E. Jacobson (Chicago: ALA Neal-Schuman, 2019), 63–79.

17. Audrey Fisch, "Trump, J. K. Rowling, and Confirmation Bias: An Experiential Lesson in Fake News," *Radical Teacher* 111 (Summer 2018): 103–8.

18. Head, Fister, Geofrey, and Macmillan, "Project Information Literacy Retrospective," 20.

19. Hugo Mercier, *Not Born Yesterday: The Science of Who We Trust and What We Believe* (Princeton: Princeton University Press, 2020).

20. Head, Fister, Geofrey, and Macmillan, "Project Information Literacy Retrospective," 29.

21. Craig Gibson and Trudi Jacobson, "Habits of Mind in an Uncertain Information World," *Reference & User Services Quarterly* 57, no. 3 (Spring 2018): 190.

22. Amanda Folk, "Drawing on Students' Funds of Knowledge: Using Identity and Lived Experience to Join the Conversation in Research Assignments," *Journal of Information Literacy* 12, no. 2 (2018): 44–59.

23. Darren Linvill, "The Relationship Between Student Identity Development and the Perception of Political Bias in the College Classroom," *College Teaching* 59, no. 2 (2011): 49–55.

24. Nicole A. Cooke, "Posttruth, Truthiness, and Alternative Facts: Information Behavior and Critical Information Consumption for a New Age," *Library Quarterly* 87, no. 3 (2017): 217.

25. Michelle Luhtala and Jacquelyn Whiting, *News Literacy: The Keys to Combating Fake News* (Santa Barbara, CA: Libraries Unlimited, 2018).

26. Alyssa Russo, Amy Jankowski, Stephanie Beene, and Lori Townsend, "Strategic Source Evaluation: Addressing the Container Conundrum," *Reference Services Review* 47, no. 3 (2019): 296.

27. Jennifer A. Fielding, "Rethinking CRAAP: Getting Students Thinking Like Fact-Checkers in Evaluating Web Sources," *College & Research Libraries News*, December 2019, 620–22.

28. Sam Wineburg and Sarah McGrew, "Lateral Reading: Reading Less and Learning More When Evaluating Digital Information," *Stanford History Education Group* (September 2017), 38, https://papers.ssrn.com/sol3/papers.cfm?abstract_id=3048994 (13 Jan 2023).

29. Mike Caulfield, "Web Literacy for Student Fact-Checkers," 2017, https://webliteracy.pressbooks.com/chapter/four-strategies/ (12 Jan 2023).

30. Cara Evanston and James Sponsel, "From Syndication to Misinformation: How Undergraduate Students Engage with and Evaluate Digital News," *Communications in Information Literacy* 13, no. 2 (2019): 228–50.

31. Laura Saunders and John Budd, "Examining Authority and Reclaiming Expertise," *Journal of Academic Librarianship* 46, no. 1 (2020): https://doi.org/10.1016/j.acalib.2019.102077 (12 Jan 2023).

32. Wei Zakharov, Haiyan Life, and Michael Fosmire, "Undergraduates' News Consumption and Perceptions on Fake News in Science," *Portal: Libraries and the Academy* 19, no. 4 (2019): 653–65.

33. Cooke, "Posttruth, Truthiness, and Alternative Facts," 214.

34. Ellysa Stern Cahoy and Robert Schroeder, "Embedding Affective Learning Outcomes in Library Instruction," *Communications in Information Literacy* 6, no. 1 (2012): 76.

35. Barbara Stipling, "Inquiry: Inquiring Minds Want to Know," *School Library Media Activities Monthly* 25, no. 1 (September 2008): 50.

36. Gibson and Jacobson, "Habits of Mind," 190.

37. Gibson and Jacobson, "Habits of Mind," 190.

38. Shelia Corrall, "Crossing the Threshold: Reflective Practices in Information Literacy Development," *Journal of Information Literacy* 11, no. 1 (2017): 23–53.

39. Mackey and Jacobson, *Metaliteracy*.

40. Laura Saunders and Melissa A. Wong, *Instruction in Libraries and Information Centers: An Introduction* (Champaign, IL: Windsor & Downs Press, 2020); Johnathan Cope, "Information Literacy and Social Power," in *Critical Library Instruction:*

Theories & Methods, ed. Maria T. Accardi, Emily Drabinski, and Alana Kumbier (Duluth, MN: Library Juice Press, 2009), 13–27; Elisabeth Pankle and Jason Coleman, "'There's Nothing on My Topic!' Using the Theories of Oscar Wilde and Henry Giruous to Develop Critical Pedagogy for Library Instruction," in *Critical Library Instruction: Theories & Methods*, ed. Maria T. Accardi, Emily Drabinski, and Alana Kumbier (Duluth, MN: Library Juice Press, 2009), 3–12.

41. Maura Seale, "Critical Library Instruction, Causing Trouble, and Institutionalization," *Communications in Information Literacy* 14, no. 1 (2020): 75–85.

42. Kay Mathiesen, "Informational Justice: A Conceptual Framework for Social Justice in Library and Information Services," *Library Trends* 64, no. 2 (Fall 2015): 198–225; Cope, "Information Literacy and Social Power."

43. Folk, "Drawing on Students' Funds of Knowledge."

44. Jennifer A. Ferretti, "Building a Critical Culture: How Critical Librarianship Falls Short in the Workplace," *Communications in Information Literacy* 14, no. 1 (2020): 134–52.

45. Dolsy Smith, "Iterable Ciphers for Insurrection," *Communications in Information Literacy* 14, no. 1 (2020): 28–45.

46. Seal, "Critical Library Instruction."

47. Sofia Y. Leung and Jorge R. López-McKnight, "Dreaming Revolutionary Futures: Critical Race's Centrality to Ending White Supremacy," *Communications in Information Literacy* 14, no. 1 (2020): 12–27, https://pdxscholar.library.pdx.edu/cgi/viewcontent.cgi?article=1407&context=comminfolit (13 Jan 2023).

48. Cope, "Information Literacy and Social Power."

49. Mathiesen, "Informational Justice."

50. Veronica Arellano Douglas, "Moving from Critical Assessment to Assessment as Care," *Communications in Information Literacy* 14, no. 1 (2020): 46–65.

51. Pankl and Coleman, "There's Nothing on My Topic!"

52. Cooke, "Posttruth, Truthiness, and Alternative Facts," 90–91.

53. Margaret Rose Torrell, "That Was Then, This Is Wow: A Case for Critical Information Literacy Across the Curriculum," *Communications in Information Literacy* 14, no. 1 (2020): 128.

54. Marie T. Accardi, Emily Drabinski, and Alana Kumbier, "Beginning and Extending the Conversation," *Communications in Information Literacy* 14, no. 1 (2020): 1–11, https://pdxscholar.library.pdx.edu/cgi/viewcontent.cgi?article=1409&context=comminfolit (12 Jan 2023).

55. Saunder and Wong, *Instruction in Libraries and Information Centers*, 77.

PART IV

KUHLTHAU, DERVIN, NAHL, AND EVERYDAY LIFE INFORMATION SEEKING

Nahl's Affective Load Theory, Kuhlthau's Information Search Process, and Dervin's Sense Making are influential theories that offer an avenue to a broader view of information science that goes beyond cognitive processing. The feeling of knowing casts these foundational theories in a new light, emphasizing that emotion and affect do not just interrupt cognition but are part of how we judge our cognitive processes.

CHAPTER TWENTY

Kuhlthau's Information Search Process

There have been several writers within information science and information literacy who have pointed out the connection between information processing and affect and emotion. Carol Kuhlthau is one of the most important writers who did this and also made a bridge between information literacy and information science. Her work tries to step beyond a purely rational approach to searching. Her *information search process* has been an important model for teaching information literacy skills for several decades. For us, her discussions of how we construct knowledge presents an opportunity to think about the feeling of knowing and schemas within the search process.

Kuhlthau's process is built within the context of the student research process that recognizes the emotional and felt experience during student research. The Information Search Process (ISP) assumes an educational setting where students are working on a project with a discrete beginning and ending that differentiates the ISP from other models of information.[1]

Kuhlthau frames this process as a construction process where the student interacts with information to build their own understanding. For Kuhlthau, construction links both human *thinking* and human *learning*. She writes,

> The constructivist view of learning, which offers insight into what the user experiences, is a particularly valuable way to understand information seeking from the user's perspective. Two basic themes run through the theory of construction. One is that we construct our own unique personal worlds, and the other is that construction involves the total person incorporating thinking, feeling, and acting in a dynamic process of learning.[2]

To me, this construction process as Kuhlthau describes it is where the feeling of knowing can enter the process. As different sources intermingle with our existing knowledge, the searcher builds a new perspective based on what is already known and based on new ideas that are presented.

Importantly, Kuhlthau emphasizes the "total person," where thinking is deeply intertwined with feeling and emotion. The deeper a person goes into the construction process, the stronger the negative feelings they will encounter but also the stronger the positive emotions at the end.[3] Generally, those who employ the ISP as a model for understanding students' research document a range of emotions, both positive and negative. Anxiety is often noted as a primary and powerful emotion during major research projects. Overall, students generally face negative emotions early in the process when the process itself and their own topics are rather nebulous. But as they work and both become clearer, students increasingly have positive emotions. Students felt emotional impact on three dimensions: feelings about the process, perceptions of the task, and affinity to research. They especially found that these different dimensions activated strong feelings of anxiety within students at different stages of their work, whether it was initiating research, managing time, or writing their paper.[4]

The inclusion of emotions and feeling was noteworthy around searching, but we must notice that this description only captures a portion of the role that emotions and feelings might play. Emotions and feelings are treated as factors that interfere with the process or push the process forward. They are not treated as a component of knowledge.

The ISP model has six stages; Kuhlthau defines the stage but also outlines associated thoughts, feelings, and actions within the stage.[5] There is a potential to explore the feeling of knowledge of each of these stages.

- Stage 1: Task Initiation: The individual recognizes a knowledge gap and starts the process to address this gap. Thoughts focus on comprehending the task. Mood opens up the possibilities of the task at hand while negative feelings of uncertainty may appear.
- Stage 2: Topic Selection: The individual defines a topic that gives shape to an initially murky process. Considerations for potential topics are weighted against personal interest, assignment requirements, etc. This step offers some clarity that provides feelings of optimism. But once the selection is made, uncertainty may return.
- Stage 3: Prefocus Exploration: As the process discovers more and more information sources, uncertainty increases and feelings of doubt,

frustration, and confusion can emerge. There are heavy cognitive demands with added affective pressures.
- Stage 4: Focus Formulation: This is often the turning point in the process as insights occur and ideas solidify. This is the key point of construction where ideas become personal and internalized. As confidence increases, cognitive efforts are driven by clearer actions.
- Stage 5: Information Collection: In stage five, the focus is extended as information is discovered and incorporated around the topic. This is an opportunity for deeper idea development. Mood is generally more positive.
- Stage 6: Search Closure: In the final stage, the process comes to an end around feelings of satisfaction and relief. There is a possibility of disappointment if the process does not go as planned.[6]

It is important to note that these changes do not address the *how* question. How does the mind process information? What role do feelings play in recognizing truth or developing our simulation of the world?

Savolainen notes that Kuhlthau does not always make distinctions between short-term affective impacts (feelings) and longer-term states (moods). These are often conflated. There is also an underlying assumption that cognitive factors are the driving force behind the process while affective factors either hamper—in terms of negative impacts—or push forward—in terms of positive impacts.[7]

When applied, librarians and instructors have noted that students do not follow these stages perfectly in order. For instance, students tend to skip stages as they move through the process. Given the ease of access to information enjoyed by most students, it is easy for them to gather sources while entirely skipping or breezing through the prefocus exploration and the focus formulation stages. It is very tempting to gather unrelated sources and piece them together. This is a point where intervention and mediation from a librarian or instructor is important to help students find a focus and continue on to the final stages of the process.[8]

Librarians and teachers have used the ISP with students as a way to address anxiety and negative emotions such as frustration or confusion. Using the process provides stages where discussions can be held where feelings are named. Negative feelings can be attributed to the point in the process as opposed to the students themselves. This provides opportunities for students to seek help and to cope with the feelings that come with the process.[9] Additionally, in college students, there is a relationship between the complexity of sources found utilizing ISP and the epistemological sophistication of the students. As students took a more complex epistemological stance, they found and incorporated sources that match this stance.[10] It is valuable to address the moments of negative emotion that hamper of the search process, but this model does not go further and consider how feelings and emotions construct knowledge.

An underlying premise of Kuhlthau's ISP is that cognition and cognitive activities result in negative emotional reactions that undermine confidence. This is Kuhlthau's *uncertainty principle*. By its very nature, the Information Search Process is one that is ill defined. As noted above, the ISP stages can be helpful in giving students a form to this process, but even with these stages, students must follow the branching, circling, and often confusing paths that information sources may lay out in front of them.[11] As Kuhlthau writes,

> The axiom that information reduces uncertainty is not necessarily the person's experience in information seeking. In certain situations information actually increases uncertainty. This research reveals that prior to formulation people are likely to experience heightened uncertainty in the face of unique, incompatible, inconsistent information that requires construction and interpretation to be personally understood. It seems hopeful for people to *expect* uncertainty to increase during the exploration stage of the process rather than thinking that increased uncertainty is a symptom that something has gone wrong. The expectation that information reduces uncertainty initially may be at odds with the person's experience in actual situations of information seeking.[12]

This discussion of uncertainty has interesting connections to the discussion of uncertainty around cognitive authority that I have already mentioned. But for me this discussion is noteworthy as an avenue to consider the feeling of knowing. The uncertainty principle is a statement about information processing. *Feeling* uncertain is a summatory feeling of unconscious processing interjecting into conscious thought. For Kuhlthau, these feelings—emotions in her terminology—are symptoms that interrupt a healthy process. The symptoms must be dealt with through identification, awareness, and interventions. I do not entirely disagree that we should seek to mitigate anxiety in searching, but I think we can go further. Our avenues into the feeling of knowing present an opportunity at reflection within the process. We cannot know something without feeling that we know it. As uncertainty increases, our mind is processing and moving us away from that feeling.

Equally important for this discussion is the series of corollaries that Kuhlthau defines as a larger part of her ISP model. These are the process corollary, formulation corollary, redundancy corollary, mood corollary, prediction corollary, and interest corollary.[13] Each of these corollaries is a statement on the processes of the mind during the ISP process. They offer a view from an information science perspective as to how brain processes interact with information sources. They each offer hints at the feeling of knowing.

The *process corollary* calls on us to view the whole person within the information seeking experience. Kuhlthau attempts to pull in thinking, emotions, and feelings as important pieces to the construction process. The important part for Kuhlthau is that interacting with information is not a purely cognitive exercise, but instead is an *experience* that involves emotions and feelings. She writes,

> From the user's point of view, information seeking is a holistic experience with thoughts, actions, and feelings interweaving in a complex mosaic rather than as separate, distinct entities. Thoughts unfold through actions and feelings involved throughout. The holistic process of information seeking has not been fully recognized in library and information services. . . . Information searching is traditionally portrayed as a systematic, orderly, and rational procedure rather than the uncertain, confusing process that users commonly experience. After the search is completed, the topic understood, and the problem solved, it is all too easy to look back and deny the chaos and confusion that was actually experienced in the process, but at what cost?[14]

In some sense, Kuhlthau's words presage this text entirely as I try to better understand the holistic experience of interacting with information. This corollary is among a grouping of ideas that pushed my interests forward. But it is also worth noting that Kuhlthau still focuses on the negative aspects of "emotion" and does not consider how feelings are part of how we process experience.

The *formulation corollary* is of primary importance for Kuhlthau. Her step of formulation is really the entire point of the ISP. This is the step where perspective forms when the individual cuts through the haziness of the gathered information and ideas coalesce into a focus. Uncertainty is reduced, and a type of clarity is achieved. The time right before formulation can be quite frustrating, but formulation itself is a recognition. Kuhlthau does recognize that some individuals will not find this focus, and thus will not really experience formulation. But for those who are successful, Kuhlthau emphasizes the importance of formulation and the turn from uncertainty to confidence that takes place. Kuhlthau discusses formulation as a kind of clearing up or wiping away of confusion. For me, Kuhlthau describes the arrival of the feeling of knowing. The moment of formulation is the moment when conscious and unconscious processes come to a consensus. It is important to note that

Kuhlthau's descriptions of confidence and recognition are set in terms of feeling even though she does not directly characterize this as a feeling.

In the *redundancy corollary*, Kuhlthau contrasts expected information that she terms "redundant" with unexpected or surprising information. When individuals come across redundant information, it is expected and immediately recognized as relevant to the search. Unexpected information can be exciting and invigorating. But too much redundant information results in boredom with the process, and too much unexpected information may produce anxiety at having to manage. Kuhlthau's description follows Dewey's reflective thinking[15] and Pagel's algorithmic thinking.[16] The mind builds its simulation based on expectations. When something doesn't fit, we take notice.

Kuhlthau's *mood corollary* reflects her perspective that emotions interrupt cognition. In this case, mood is an attitude that impacts the openness or mental limitations of a search. A mood changes and evolves over the course of the search, impacting how the search unfolds. Negative moods can limit possibilities while positive or excited moods can drive the process forward. Kuhlthau does not differentiate between affect, feeling, emotion, and cognition as I have outlined in this book. But her description of mood is more in line with what I have defined as affect. Setting terminology aside, current neuroscience research would generally support this corollary. Affect has both a valence (positive or negative) and level of arousal (high to low energy). Our affect impacts how we experience the world and what we notice. Kuhlthau's mood corollary aligns well.

The *prediction corollary* is useful in our online searching world. She notes that there are decision points throughout the ISP where individuals must essentially make predictions about where to search, what sources have the most potential, and which ideas would be left behind. She notes that this decision-making endeavor is highly individualistic and is "based on one's existing constructs at the time."[17] As we search, we utilize our constructs—our schemas—as the lens to view the world. At each phase of the information search process, we have no option other than using our views of the world as a filter to make decisions and judgments. We cannot escape the individualistic nature of the individual search process. If information is really defined as patterns or reality, then those patterns necessarily reflect our experience.

Her final corollary is the *interest corollary*. Here Kuhlthau emphasizes that interest drives engagement, which drives the process forward. Her discussion aligns with the understanding of *dopamine*'s impact on learning and seeking knowledge. This corollary also seems to connect with the benefit of new neural pathways building upon existing pathways, or, in other words, new knowledge building on existing knowledge. Both of these play a part in generating the feeling of knowing.

Kuhlthau's ISP was very important in defining the role of feelings within searching for information. Her efforts to emphasize the holistic nature of searching opened up important discussions around information literacy and information behavior. In her words,

> The user's holistic experience and information seeking is not being adequately accommodated. Traditional emphasis on locating sources has detracted from the process of constructing meaning from information within sources. Users center not only on seeking sources of information but also on seeking meaning from sources. Seeking meaning incorporates an individual's cognitive, physical, and affective experiences.[18]

Kuhlthau's work offers avenues for future research. Her ideas reflect the thinking of the time. Research on the mind has advanced quite a bit over these years, presenting us with an opportunity to expand on her insight.

Notes

1. Carol Collier Kuhlthau, *Seeking Meaning: A Process Approach to Library and Information Literacy Services* (Westport, CT: Libraries Unlimited, 2004); Carol Collier Kuhlthau, "Kulthau's Information Search Process," in *Theories of Information Behavior*, ed. Karen E. Fisher, Sandra Erdelez, and Lynne (E. F.) McKechnie (Medford, NJ: Information Today, 2005), 230–34; Reijo Savolainen, "The Interplay of Affective and Cognitive Factors in Information Seeking and Use," *Journal of Documentation* 71, no. 1 (12 January 2015): 175–97.
2. Kuhlthau, *Seeking Meaning*, 14.
3. Kuhlthau, *Seeking Meaning*; Carol Kuhlthau, Janice Heinstron, and Ross J. Todd, "The 'Information Search Process' Revisited: Is the Model Still Useful?" *Information Research* 13, no. 4 (December 2008): 45–59.
4. Kuhlthau, *Seeking Meaning*; Kuhlthau, Heinstron, and Todd, "'Information Search Process' Revisited"; Jacqueline Kracker and Peiling Wang, "Research Anxiety and Students' Perceptions of Research: Part II. Content Analysis of Their Writings on Two Experiences," *Journal of the American Society for Information Science and Technology* 53, no. 4 (2002): 295–307; Wendy Holiday and Qin Li, "Understanding the Millennials: Updating our Knowledge about Students," *Reference Services Review* 32, no. 4 (2004): 356–66.
5. Kuhlthau, *Seeking Meaning*; Kuhlthau, Heinstron, and Todd, "'Information Search Process' Revisited"; Savolainen, "Interplay of Affective and Cognitive Factors."

6. Kuhlthau, *Seeking Meaning*; Kuhlthau, Heinstron, and Todd, "'Information Search Process' Revisited."

7. Savolainen, "Interplay of Affective and Cognitive Factors."

8. Dania Bilal, "Children's Use of Yahooligans! Web Search Engine. III. Cognitive and Physical Behaviors on Fully Self-Generated Search Tasks," *Journal of the American Society for Information Society and Technology* 53, no. 13 (2002): 1170–83; Violet H. Harada, "Personalizing the Information Search Process: A Case Study of Journal Writing with Elementary-Age Students," *School Library Media Research* 5 (2002), http://hdl.handle.net/10125/40191 (13 Jan 2023); Holiday and Li, "Understanding the Millennials"; Kuhlthau, Heinstron, and Todd, "'Information Search Process' Revisited."

9. Kracker and Wang, "Research Anxiety," 295–307.

10. Ethelene Whitmire, "Epistemological Beliefs and the Information-Seeking Behavior of Undergraduates," *Library and Information Science Research* 25, no. 2 (2003): 127–42.

11. Kuhlthau, *Seeking Meaning*.

12. Kuhlthau, "Kuhlthau's Information Search Process," 233.

13. Kuhlthau, *Seeking Meaning*.

14. Kuhlthau, *Seeking Meaning*, 93.

15. John Dewey, *How We Think* (CreateSpace Independent Publishing, 2014).

16. Mark D. Pagel, *Wired for Culture: Origins of the Human Social Mind* (New York: Norton, 2013).

17. Kuhlthau, *Seeking Meaning*, 101.

18. Kuhlthau, *Seeking Meaning*, 189.

CHAPTER TWENTY-ONE

Dervin's Sense-Making

Over the last century, librarians have shifted their focus from collecting and organizing *sources* to thinking about how they can better facilitate the *interactions* between sources and individuals. Of course, librarians still collect and organize, but the information science interest in behavior has become increasingly important. Library science has become an applied social science akin to education. The unit of analysis is the individual, and the focus of research has become addressing the problems and challenges for how individuals use that information. One of the figures who contributed to this shift in focus was Brenda Dervin, with her methodological approach called *sense-making*.[1] Dervin's approach works to address the *how* question that is central to this book. How does the mind process information?

Dervin's approach fits well with discussions of schemas and our mind's simulation. Dervin's thinking originated in communications research. It started with the recognition that individuals select information sources from many options whether inside a library or not, just as an individual may select among many communication channels to communicate to a receiver.[2] *Sense-making*, as the name suggests, refers to the process by which individuals make meaning of their world. At its core is a process, to use Dervin's terminology, of "radical constructivist position" where the individual creates meaning from the moment.[3] The present is in a constant state of construction as the individual builds understanding. From an information science perspective, the focus is not on information systems but on the individual making meaning within those systems. At times, this means that individuals create this meaning in conjunction with others. Other times, individuals create meaning through sources.[4]

Importantly, sense-making is not just a purely conscious endeavor. She doesn't use the term, but she attempts to account for unconscious processing. Sense-making recognizes and even emphasizes the role of experience and feelings in understanding the world. Dervin recognizes a kind of embodied knowledge where the individual draws on deeper sources than just rationality and logic alone. The individual does not come to conclusions with unyielding logic, but instead is a dynamic force that can change and recognize the world differently as they experience. In this way, sense-making is a kind of dialog where understanding evolves and adapts.[5] Foreman-Wernet offers this summary:

> The Sense-Making methodology carefully articulates an alternative philosophical perspective that straddles the polarities of the modern and postmodern worldviews. Sense-Making assumes: 1) that both humans and reality are sometimes orderly and sometimes chaotic; 2) that there is a human need to create meaning, and knowledge is something that always is sought in mediation and contest; and 3) that there are human differences in experience and observation. Dervin sees human difference in observing as a strength of the species rather than a weakness. Because of the human need to create meaning and to establish facts—and despite the uncertainties of our knowledge—we are able to circle phenomena from different perspectives and at different times. This circling process then provides the means for us to arrive at a more comprehensive, more fully informed, potentially more useful set of understandings of the situation.[6]

This discussion would seem to connect with the felt sense as a type of bodily interface with unconscious processing. Dervin encourages us to wrestle with ideas and observe meanings within ourselves. The feeling of knowing would have a home within Dervin's approach.

But sense-making is more than just a description for how humans interpret the world. Dervin also envisioned and employed sense-making as a set of methodologies. Dervin used sense-making as a kind of qualitative approach to understanding information behavior. Through these methods, the researcher enters into a kind of dialog with participants where they work to construct an understanding of a moment. This could be done through a moment-by-moment discussion of a particular timeline or creating understandings from multiple perspectives. Sense-making is a tool that allows participants to create and describe deep knowledge around their interaction with information and the larger world.[7] Again, she offers deep connections to the feeling of knowing and the felt sense.

A central tenet of sense-making is the idea of *discontinuity*,[8] also called the *gap idea*.[9] Dervin casts the idea of discontinuity as important in understanding the human condition where experience is marked by breaks in continuity. Not only can we not directly share our own experiences with others, but, often, our own experience is evolving and changing where—within moments or over years—we do not share the same experience with ourselves. In the realm of communications, the idea of studying the gaps focuses on what is lost when ideas are articulated into messages, when messages are transformed by communication channels, when channels reassemble messages, and when receivers access those messages. Discontinuity is a constant in human experience warped by cultures, language, institutions, history, physical space, and many other factors. Discontinuity is a useful way to think about the modular nature of conscious and unconscious processing. Our minds build meaning around the current moment, using past experiences. They do so within systems of knowledge and power structures outlined by history.

It is important to note that in sense-making, "emotions" are a part of the situated moment that is constantly in flux. Emotions are a part of the "informing" process, but they are viewed as surrounding this process in various ways. They may act as a motivating force to bring about action. Emotions may also result from discoveries along the way in the use of information. They may also help or hinder the process. Dervin does not separate emotion and feeling. For her, emotions are something apart from cognition and information processing. Emotions are part of the situated moment, but they are treated almost as a state of being that impacts information use. Feeling does not represent information processing. As Dervin and Reinhard state,

> Sense-Making positions "emotions" as situated sense-making orientation in a confluence of sense making orientations—in effect, as a potentially transitory orientation toward a moment in time-space that could potentially be motivating or inhibiting, helpful or hindering, facilitating or interfering, but always informing to greater or lesser degrees.[10]

To some degree, sense-making aligns well with much brain science. Her work brings unconscious processing into the discussion. The goal of recognizing the changing and varied nature of decision making feels like a good description of the brain as a democracy. The brain uses different types of processes that shift and change based on the current moment. But sense-making does not recognize the role of feeling as an expression of the different processes at work.

Notes

1. Prudence W. Dalrymple, "A Quarter Century of User-Centered Study: The Impact of Zweizig and Dervin on LIS Research," *Library and Information Science Research* 23, no. 2 (2001): 155–65.

2. Dalrymple, "Quarter Century of User-Centered Study"; Lois Foreman-Wernet, "Rethinking Communication: Introducing the Sense-Making Methodology," in *Sense-Making Methodology Reader: Selected Writings of Brenda Dervin*, ed. Brenda Dervin, Lois Foreman-Wernet, and Eric Lauterbach (Cresskill, NJ: Hampton Press, 2003), 3–16.

3. Brenda Dervin, "From the Mind's Eye of the User: The Sense-Making Qualitative-Quantitative Methodology," in *Qualitative Research in Information Management*, ed. Jack D. Glazier and Ronald R. Powell (Englewood, CO: Libraries Unlimited, 1992), 61–84.

4. Dervin, "From the Mind's Eye of the User"; Dalrymple, "Quarter Century of User-Centered Study"; Brenda Dervin, "Comparative Theory Reconceptualized: From Entities and States to Processes and Dynamics," in *Sense-Making Methodology Reader: Selected Writings of Brenda Dervin*, ed. Brenda Dervin, Lois Foreman-Wernet, and Eric Lauterbach (Cresskill, NJ: Hampton Press, 2003), 61–73; Foreman-Wernet, "Rethinking Communication," 3–16; Karen E. Fisher, Sandra Erdelez, and Lynne (E. F.) McKechnie, *Theories of Information Behavior* (Medford, NJ: Information Today, 2005); Tonyia Tidline, "Dervin's Sense-Making," in *Theories of Information Behavior*, ed. Karen E. Fisher, Sandra Erdelez, and Lynne (E. F.) McKechnie (Medford, NJ: Information Today, 2005), 113–14.

5. Dervin, "From the Mind's Eye of the User"; Brenda Dervin, "Sense-Making's Journey from Metatheory to Methodology to Method," in *Sense-Making Methodology Reader: Selected Writings of Brenda Dervin*, ed. Brenda Dervin, Lois Foreman-Wernet, and Eric Lauterbach (Cresskill, NJ: Hampton Press, 2003), 133–65.

6. Foreman-Wernet, "Rethinking Communication," 7.

7. Dervin, "From the Mind's Eye of the User"; Dervin, "Sense-Making's Journey."

8. Dervin, "From the Mind's Eye of the User."

9. Dervin, "Sense-Making's Journey."

10. Brenda Dervin and CarrieLynn D. Reinhard, "How Emotional Dimensions of Situated Information Seeking Relate to User Evaluations of Help from Sources: An Exemplar Study Informed by Sense-Making Methodology," in *Information and Emotion: The Emergent Affective Paradigm in Information Behavior Research and Theory*, ed. Diane Nahl & Dania Bilal (Medford, NJ: Information Today, 2007), 56.

CHAPTER TWENTY-TWO

Nahl's Affective Load

Diane Nahl walks right up to the feeling of knowing and dances all around it without quite connecting to it. Her *affective load theory* was a response to the behavioral-dominant approach taken by information science theorists. This "social-behavioral perspective" connects behaviors to both thinking and feeling with information behavior. Importantly, Nahl recognizes *both* habits of thinking and habits of feeling that impact information behavior. Like other theories, she still focuses on disruptions to thinking. Her goal is to have individuals recognize when affective states disrupt the process and then seek "coping assistance services" as a means to lessen the disruption.[1] Her use of the terms *cognition* and *affect* move closer to the uses outlined by current neuroscience.

Nahl defines three key components that underpin her approach. She outlines cognitive factors that impact behavior. By *cognitive*, she is referring to decision-making capabilities or our capacity for planning and making deductions based on the world around us. The cognitive abilities are treated almost as tools that do not have direction or goals. For her, the direction is provided by the *affective* factors, which are the second component. Affect draws on emotions to build feelings, putting into place a range of factors such as motivation, optimism, uncertainty, and others. Affect sets the goals and pushes decisions forward. She does not recognize that knowing requires feeling, but her approach steps closer to the feeling of knowing. The final component for Nahl is the sensorimotor or psychomotor abilities, which allow individuals to act in their world. This is the performative nature of behavior where ideas manifest as actions once decisions are made. This is the connection between the brain (i.e., the mind/thinking) and the body through the nervous system.[2] The sensorimotor component moves us closer to embodied knowing and the felt sense, even though she does not reference these ideas.

In terms of information behaviors, Nahl argues that affect (as she defines it) is vital to information processing and decision making. It is the affective side of the mind that brings motivation to the process, sets goals based upon criteria and feelings, and recognizes when those goals have been met. As she writes,

> Affective control theory insists that cognitive processes cannot be understood without recognizing the mechanism by which feelings and emotions control the parameters of every cognitive operation. . . . The affective filter outlines which information will be included or excluded. It impacts what is ignored and what is noticed. . . . The affective system is clearly in charge of all aspects of information processing and use.[3]

Nahl's view of affect is fairly close to the feeling of knowing, but her approach is more akin to emotions and not related to unconscious processing. Nahl sees two basic biological functions of the affective system for information usage. First, the affective system plays a role in information reception. This involves noticing a signal as information (delineating meaning from noise). Once information is recognized, the affective system plays a role in evaluating that meaning and giving it value. Second, the affective system is involved in information usage. As one works with information and explores its meanings, the affective system emphasizes meaning and offers context around those meanings. She notes that the process of information usage is intertwined with the cognitive and the sensorimotor. "This dynamic flow involving noticing the information, appraising it, and attaching value to it is continuous throughout information reception, both at the micro and macro levels of information behavior."[4]

Nahl emphasizes that it is the affective system that establishes the "criterial feeling," which is the sense one gets around the completion of a goal. Affect is a recognition along the lines of motivation. She notes that a feeling of optimism may help expand a search while a feeling of pessimism may limit choices and reduce flexibility. One skill set that she clearly connects with affective systems is *coping skills*. Coping skills allow the individual to deal with unforeseen challenges as they arise and maintain a positively oriented affective stance. Nahl works to operationalize potential affective measures.[5] Nahl outlines the following:

- Task completion motivation: affective component connecting to the intensity of the motivation.
- Uncertainty feelings in information seeking: affective component that is generally negative and intensifies. Levels of uncertainty are irritation, anxiety, frustration, rage.
- Time pressure: affective component that increases in certainty. When time pressure is low, the uncertainty factor will be at a lower level.
- Affective load in searching: uncertainty multiplied by time pressures.
- Self-efficacy feeling as a searcher: affective component that gauges the searchers' trust in their ability to succeed. Individuals who have higher self-efficacy scores have coping mechanisms that allow them to succeed or allow them to believe that they will succeed.
- Search optimism feeling: affective component that gauges the motivation to put off quitting despite the time pressure and uncertainty.
- User coping skills: affective component that is defined by self-efficacy and search optimism.
- Evaluation of search episodes: affective component that measures the degree that a user feels they have met their search goal.
- Acceptance of search environment: affective component measures the degree that a user feels supports for the search environment.[6]

Nahl defines many different areas where feelings enter the search process. She thinks broadly about how this might work and helps counter the purely rational approach that we often assume. But Nahl does not connect knowing directly to feelings, and because of this, she misses the potential metacognitive aspects of the process. Reflecting on the sources of our own beliefs seems to an important aspect of the feeling of knowing that is entirely absent from her approach.

Nahl worked with college students using a talk-out-loud protocol to construct a qualitatively derived model. Even though the cognitive, affective, and sensorimotor systems are intertwined in the information search process, Nahl's model pulls apart these systems to make them more apparent. The larger goal of this process is to give intention and purpose to information. This is a feeling of wanting or needing to act. It is intentionality put into action.[7] She defines the following:

- Step 1: noticing practices (sensorimotor satisficing): identifying, ignoring, locating, etc.
- Step 2: appraising practices (cognitive satisficing): interpreting, categorizing, justifying, giving reasons.

- Step 3: evaluating practices (affective satisficing): giving value, applying norms, accepting, prioritizing.
- Step 4: performing practices (sensorimotor optimizing): acting, verbalizing, clicking, etc.
- Step 5: planning practices (cognitive optimizing): problem solving, predicting, extending, etc.
- Step 6: intending practices (affective optimizing): goal setting, regulating, implementing.[8]

We may debate the accuracy of these steps, but their importance does not necessarily revolve around their exactness. Nahl's argument emphasizing the central role of emotions and feelings in determining value and setting priorities is key for us. Information usage is not the rational, logical computation of data that we often assume. It is a process laden with value judgments. For Nahl, the ways that individuals make these judgments originates within the groups to which they belong. Individuals reflect the values derived from the environment around them. She uses the term *ecological constructionism framework* to describe this process.[9]

The importance of Nahl's approach is that she gives feeling (and emotion) a central role in her process. She goes further than any other theoretician within information behavior research. She emphasizes that feelings signal value and offer meaning when it comes to interpreting information. Her work has strong connections to the feeling of knowing.

Notes

1. Diane Nahl, "A Conceptual Framework for Defining Information Behavior," *Studies in Multimedia Information Literacy Education* 1, no. 2 (2001): 1–16; Diane Nahl, "Affective Load," in *Theories of Information Behavior*, ed. Karen E. Fisher, Sandra Erdelez, and Lynne (E. F.) McKechnie (Medford, NJ: Information Today, 2005), 39–43.

2. Nahl, "Conceptual Framework"; Diane Nahl, "Measuring the Affective Information Environment of Web Searchers," *Proceedings of the 67th Annual Meeting of the American Society for Information Science & Technology* 41 (Medford, NJ: Information Today, 2004); Nahl, "Affective Load"; Reijo Savolainen, "The Interplay of Affective and Cognitive Factors in Information Seeking and Use," *Journal of Documentation* 71, no. 1 (12 January 2015): 175–97.

3. Diane Nahl, "The Centrality of the Affective in Information Behavior," in *Information and Emotion: The Emergent Affective Paradigm in Information Behavior Research and Theory*, ed. Diane Nahl & Dania Bilal (Medford, NJ: Information Today, 2007), 24.

4. Nahl, "Centrality of the Affective," 5.
5. Nahl, "Measuring the Affective Information Environment."
6. Nahl, "Measuring the Affective Information Environment."
7. Nahl, "Centrality of the Affective."
8. Nahl, "Centrality of the Affective."
9. Savolainen, "Interplay of Affective and Cognitive Factors."

CHAPTER TWENTY-THREE

Everyday Life Information Seeking and Other Theories

While much of the information behavior theory has focused on formal research processes especially coming out of academic settings, there has also been much work done looking at "everyday" information use. This shifts from focusing on information systems to focusing on the experiences and lives of users. Theorists recognize that a great deal of information acquisition occurs incidentally over the daily lives of individuals.[1] For instance, Savolainen defines everyday life information seeking as a "way of life" where individuals need to build a "cognitive order" that defines their perception as to what counts as normal. Thus, people seek an internal order that helps to guide choices and decisions. This order directly impacts how they acquire information from the external environment around them.[2] Savolainen used this model to study teachers and industrial workers. This study showed that the way of life directly impacts information seeking. This impacted media interactions and other information sources. The literature around everyday information use offers avenues for psychology to enter information science discourse. Specifically, many of these discussions have connections to the role of experience, schemas, and mind's simulation in how we see the world and interpret information.

Savolainen emphasizes the idea of *habitus*,[3] which attempts to account for the social and cultural factors that impact information usage in everyday life. Information usage is conditioned within a particular moment that connects the environment (history, society, and culture) with the psychological.[4] He writes,

> Habitus can be defined as a socially and culturally determined system of thinking, perception, and evaluation, internalized by the individual. Habitus is a relatively stable system of dispositions by which individuals integrate their experiences and evaluate the importance of different choices, for example, the preference of information sources and channels.[5]

This is a kind of sense-making endeavor that attempts to account for the many factors in everyday information use.

Similarly, the *theory of information intents* connects with everyday information utilization by setting purposeful information usage into the larger context of everyday life. Todd developed this theory looking at the drivers that motivate information use and influence the cognitive side of information behavior. Todd defines this theory:

> The Theory of Information Intents posits that people engage with information in purposeful, deliberate, and selective ways to get expanded, and/or change, and/or clearer and/or verified pictures, and/or by being able to state positions. As drivers and outcomes of information utilization, information intents enable people to move forward in their information endeavors, constructing new pictures that represent new understandings. This is not random acquisition, but one shaped by a desired cognitive intent in the context of individual frames of reference such as personal experience, existing knowledge, and current stage of life cycle.[6]

This theory's focus on experience puts the self and the schemas we build in the center of information utilization. For Todd, the process of information construction is important. He argues that information interactions help individuals build new understandings and therefore puts experiences in the center of shaping our worldview. We are not passive in our information acquisition, but we actively construct the world based on our intents.

Miwa directly pulls psychological theory into information science when she outlines how Albert Bandura's *social cognitive theory* can be applied to information behavior and information usage. This theory stresses the social origins of thought as well as how social interactions impact cognition, actions, and motivation.[7] This is an entry point of the social mind and social learning into information behavior theory. Miwa outlines three premises:

1. "Triadic reciprocal causation posits that behavioral, cognitive, and other environmental influences all operate interactively as determinants of each other."[8]

2. "Multiple levels of goals assumes that goals are cognitively generated future events which motivate present human behavior"[9] (i.e., different levels of goals exist within different contexts).
3. "Self-efficacy proposes that people generate their thoughts, behavior, and affective states, and that these, in turn, affect the course of action people choose to take, the amount of effort they put forth, their resistance to failure, and the level of accomplishment they achieve."[10]

Miwa attempts to account for the ways that internal and external social constraints shape how we interact with information. Individuals are not simply lone actors analyzing the world, but are instead members of communities and are in countless relationships where the expectations of others impact our decisions. Social dynamics shape how we see ourselves and how we view information around us, which we have seen in our discussions of the social nature of knowing.

Chatman further elaborated on these social connections with her *life in the round*, which is a "public form of life in which things are implicitly understood."[11] by a small group of members who recognize and create social roles within this group. Chatman studied female prison inmates to build this theory. Chatman's work connects to how the mind constructs our simulation of reality along with Foucault's discussions on the role of norms within our understanding of how the world works. A life in the round has four key concepts:

1. *Small world*: small grouping of people where members share a worldview. "Living in the round has a particular effect upon information behavior: since 'life in the round' is routine, information seeking beyond that world is neither needed nor wanted."[12]
2. *Social norms*: accepted behavior within groups given a specific context. Information is gathered to shape this behavior.[13]
3. *Social types*: this is the way people classify other people given different contexts. Individuals are given social roles.[14]
4. *Worldview*: "the collective of common beliefs, customs, and the language of small world members, by which they evaluate behavior and interpret the world."[15]

The *life in the round* helps us understand how small groups operate, especially when they have some degree of isolation from the "outside" world. There is a kind of socialization process through which members interpret their world, including interpreting and utilizing information. For information to be relevant, it must connect with the *small world*. Information sources (whether human or otherwise) are credible to the extent that they can be trusted with the small world context and within the established social norms. External information that does not bring value within the community is ignored or can even be viewed as harmful. Chatman notes that many of the inmates she interviewed purposefully limited their contact with outside family and friends because it distracted from their lives inside. Chatman's work illustrates our mind's natural tendency for socially constructed knowing.[16]

McKenzie explored everyday life information behavior by interviewing pregnant women who have a range of information needs, consult with medical experts, share information with friends, and often read a range of sources on pregnancy and parenting as they prepare. She outlines a series of "information practices"[17] that factor into their information utilization:

- "identification of potentially helpful sources";
- "serendipitous encounters";
- "being given information without active seeking";
- "planned encounters with potentially helpful sources";
- "referrals to potentially helpful sources";
- "proxy searchers" (someone else searches and retrieves info for person);
- "barriers to seeking connections";
- "making connections with potentially helpful sources";
- "connection failures: unsuccessful attempts to make connections with potentially helpful sources";
- "barriers to interaction with identified sources"; and
- "patterns of interaction with identified sources" (seeing a source/person but not following up due to hints, etc.).

These practices are context bound and are broken down into four broad categories: (1) actively seeking information, (2) actively scanning and browsing over sources, (3) accidental encounters, and (4) third-party interventions.[18] This work is very useful as an example of the messy and serendipitous nature of everyday life information gathering, but this approach does not delve very far into how we make decisions around this information encounters. What processes are at work that make some sources trustworthy and others not?

One interesting exploration of information processing in action is the work of Parker and Berryman, who try to understand the idea of *enough*.[19] They don't use the term, but this is really a way to explore the feeling of knowing. When do we judge that we have enough information? This seems especially relevant in an environment where information overload is the norm. They did a qualitative study of graduate students who were engaging in individual research. They found different ways in which their participants discussed *enough*:

- **Control**: feeling of enough that they had the right amount to keep control and finish.
- **Optimal**: feeling of enough that they had the optimal amount to finish the task at hand.
- **Understanding**: feeling of enough that they understood enough to produce. Engagement in the process.
- **Completion and satisfaction**: feeling of enough that they had a sense of completeness. Enough to make sense.
- **Generation and creation**: feeling of enough that they drive the development or creation process.[20]

Parker and Berryman's work is a novel way to connect mental sensations—feelings—to the information search and utilization process. They focus on feelings and target the realities of information acquisition and everyday use. Information scientists would love a world where a formulaic answer exists to how much information is *enough*, but in the end, individuals do not rely upon exact measurements. How do we know when we have enough? The feeling of knowing tells us that we have enough. The mind *feels* it.

Another information science exploration that verges into the psychological realms is that of *tacit knowledge*. This area of information science explores the mind's unconscious processing, but theoreticians writing in this area do not use the phrase *unconscious processing*. The goal of tacit knowing is to look at unstated knowledge that cannot be put in words. Crowley argues that tacit knowledge is deeply personal, set within a specific context, partly known but also partly "difficult to articulate."[21] Many times tacit knowledge exists within social contexts where individuals are not even aware that this knowledge exists. It is not recognized. Crowley emphasizes that tacit knowledge emerges connected to *if-then* rules. *If this condition presents itself, then act this way*. Day has used tacit knowledge as a kind of expertise where the individual recognizes unwritten rules. Too often, we view "knowledge" to be akin to holding content in our minds as if we were a type of book or information tool. But Day emphasizes that *knowing* requires the ability to recognize unwritten rules and act accordingly. For him, tacit knowledge is the "process of creating general understandings from particular entities."[22] Bratianu and Orzea connect tacit knowledge to what they term "emotional knowledge," where they emphasize the connection between thoughts and feelings. They note that "cognitive knowledge" and "emotional knowledge" hand off ideas as if energy is moving between them.[23]

Another effort that attempts to make tacit knowledge explicit within higher education is the work at *Decoding the Disciplines*.[24] This work aims to improve learning by challenging instructors with disciplinary expertise to consider the unwritten ways of knowing that exist within each discipline and how this results in different structures around knowledge within the disciplinary context. They outline the following steps in decoding these unwritten rules:

- Identify a bottleneck hampering learning.
- Outline the mental tasks that can address the bottleneck.
- Model ways for students that disciplinary experts address these tasks.
- Set up opportunities for students to practice.
- Design a learning environment that motivates students.
- Assess student progress and mastery.
- Work within the discipline to share what has been learned.

Decoding the Disciplines is a useful example of how we can be locked into ways of knowing that get subsumed into our unconscious processing to the level that we cannot step away from our disciplines. Each discipline has its own unique history and built-in assumptions about how this knowledge reveals truth about the world.

The larger discussions around *tacit knowledge* have really tried to capture the dynamic between the conscious and unconscious mind. As practices and ways of knowing biome routine, they get built into our schemas and become part of our unconscious processing. The authors who write about tacit knowledge have not often cast their discussions in terms of neuroscience or psychology. They essentially acknowledge that decision making has deeper components than the explicitly "rational" discussions we assume. They focus on the content—what ideas are hidden in tacit knowledge—and less on how that knowledge becomes tacit.

In all of these discussions there is a very tricky concept. I discussed it in chapter 18 in talking about defining information, and it pops up across the information science literature. It is the concept of *context*. Information, decision making, understanding, and worldview are all contextualized. They are not abstractions but live within a moment. This is widely acknowledged, but pinning down the meaning of context has its own challenges. Johnson notes that to really understand information behavior, we must *at least* acknowledge context, but this is difficult because context is always tied to a changing environment. Accounting for the fluidity of the moment is difficult and oftentimes impossible, so many researchers end up ignoring the effects of context. Another issue with context is that it is very open to interpretation and therefore also difficult to define. Context may not even be apparent unless we compare across different situations. Moreover, context itself may be defined in innumerable ways such as societal trends, local trends, individual interpersonal quirks, and more.[25] Komlodi acknowledges the decades of work done in anthropology and sociology exploring culture, and in so doing, makes note of "high context" cultures that emphasize unspoken symbols in information exchanges and "low context" cultures that emphasize the content of the message. This is an example of the role of context, which encompasses the *unspoken* or even *unrecognized* environment surrounding information behavior. This environment holds many dimensions such as speed of messages, information flow, power distance, individualism versus collectivism, and others.[26] Like tacit knowledge, the study of context is another avenue in understanding the unconscious ways that we process the world. The mind is influenced by context, it reacts to unstated environmental factors, and it acts on assumptions that are not always apparent.

Goffman's classic work on *frame analysis* seems relevant to the discussion of context.[27] Goffman's work has been referenced in information behavior theories.[28] For Goffman, individuals are part of a framework that is used to make sense of the world around them. This framework is culturally bound. Individuals may move across and between frames as they move across and between different groups of people. Goffman recognizes that the work of frames is both visible in the interactions between people but also invisible occurring "behind-the-scenes" within the mind. Individuals work to manage a kind of "impression management" with the goal of revealing or hiding information in order to save face or reach other social goals.[29] Goffman recognizes that errors occur within frameworks when individuals do not recognize a particular frame (for example when a statement that is intended as a joke is not taken as a joke), when a situation's frame is ambiguous, where individuals are not sure how to address the moment, or even when deception is introduced. The use of frame analysis is one avenue to defining contexts and the larger meanings that individuals may bring to a situation.

One of the challenges with understanding *context* is that the word is used in different ways. Johnson defines three general ways that the term *context* is used, which I discussed in chapter 18: (1) "context as equivalent to situation," (2) "context as contingency," and (3) "context as framework."[30] In thinking about these different uses, we need to keep in mind the contextual nature of memory. Memory is stored in pieces across the brain and context activates the relevant components, but not always all components. Context is often approached as an invisible hand guiding decisions and molding the past to meet the present moment. Stonebreaker and Howard take efforts to make context more apparent around decision making. They work with students on a reflective approach that centers on processes. The primary goal is to recognize the decision-making context and have students recognize the process given that there is more information than any one individual can process on their own. By making students aware of evidence-based decision making, they engage in a more thoughtful process.[31]

Everyday life information seeking as well as the theories discussed in the preceding three chapters—Nahl's affective load theory, Kuhlthau's information search process, and Dervin's sense making—are foundational information science theories that offer different approaches to how we utilize information. They each make their own assumptions about conscious versus unconscious processing. All of them offer entry points for bringing ideas around the feeling of knowing into information science and educational discourses.

Notes

1. Kristy Williamson, "Ecological Theory of Human Information Behavior," in *Theories of Information Behavior*, ed. Karen E. Fisher, Sandra Erdelez, and Lynne (E. F.) McKechnie (Medford, NJ: Information Today, 2005), 128–32.

2. Reijo Savolainen, "Everyday Life Information Seeking," in *Encyclopedia of Library and Information Sciences*, third edition, ed. Marcia J. Bates and Mary Niles Maack (Boca Raton, FL: CRC Press, 2010): 1780–89.

3. I discussed Bordieu's concept of *habitus* in chapter 3.

4. Reijo Savolainen, "Everyday Life Information Seeking," in *Theories of Information Behavior*, ed. Karen E. Fisher, Sandra Erdelez, and Lynne (E. F.) McKechnie (Medford, NJ: Information Today, 2005), 143–48.

5. Savolainen, "Everyday Life Information Seeking," 143.

6. Ross J. Todd, "Information Intents," in *Theories of Information Behavior*, ed. Karen E. Fisher, Sandra Erdelez, and Lynne (E. F.) McKechnie (Medford, NJ: Information Today, 2005), 200.

7. Makiko Miwa, "Bandura's Social Cognition," in *Theories of Information Behavior*, ed. Karen E. Fisher, Sandra Erdelez, and Lynne (E. F.) McKechnie (Medford, NJ: Information Today, 2005), 54–57.

8. Miwa, "Bandura's Social Cognition," 54.

9. Miwa, "Bandura's Social Cognition," 54.

10. Miwa, "Bandura's Social Cognition," 54.

11. Elfreda A. Chatman, "A Theory of Life in the Round," *Journal of the American Society for Information Science* 50, no. 3 (1999): 212.

12. Crystal Fulton, "Chatman's Life in the Round," in *Theories of Information Behavior*, ed. Karen E. Fisher, Sandra Erdelez, and Lynne (E. F.) McKechnie (Medford, NJ: Information Today, 2005), 80.

13. Fulton, "Chatman's Life in the Round."

14. Fulton, "Chatman's Life in the Round."

15. Fulton, "Chatman's Life in the Round," 80.

16. Fulton, "A Theory of Life in the Round."

17. Pamela J. McKenzie, "A Model of Information Practice in Accounts of Everyday Life Information Seeking," *Journal of Documentation* 59, no. 1 (2003): 19–40.

18. McKenzie, "Model of Information Practice."

19. Nicola Parker and Jennifer Berryman, "The Role of Affect in Judging 'What is Enough,'" in *Information and Emotion: The Emergent Affective Paradigm in Information Behavior Research and Theory*, ed. Diane Nahl and Dania Bilal (Medford, NJ: Information Today, 2007), 85–95.

20. Parker and Berryman, "Judging 'What is Enough.'"

21. Bill Crowley, "Tacit Knowledge, Tacit Ignorance, and the Future of Academic Librarianship," *College & Research Libraries* 62, no. 6 (2001): 566–84.

22. Ronald E. Day, "Clearing Up 'Implicit Knowledge': Implications for Knowledge Management, Information Science, Psychology, and Social Epistemology," *Journal of the American Society for Information Science and Technology* 56, no. 6 (2005): 632.

23. Constantin Bratianu and Ivona Orzea, "Emotional Knowledge: The Hidden Part of the Knowledge Iceberg," *Management Dynamics in the Knowledge Economy* 2, no. 1 (2014): 41–56.

24. David Pace and Peter Reigler, "Decoding the Disciplines: Improving Student Learning," http://decodingthedisciplines.org/ (13 Dec 2023); Joan Middendorf and David Pace, "Decoding the Disciplines: A Model for Helping Students Learn Disciplinary Ways of Thinking," *New Directions for Teaching and Learning* 98 (2004): 1–12.

25. David J. Johnson, "On Contexts of Information Seeking," *Information Processing and Management* 39, no. 5 (2003): 735–60.

26. Anita Komlodi, "Cultural Models of Hall and Hofstede," in *Theories of Information Behavior*, ed. Karen E. Fisher, Sandra Erdelez, and Lynne (E. F.) McKechnie (Medford, NJ: Information Today, 2005), 108–12.

27. Erving Goffman, *Frame Analysis: An Essay on the Organization of Experience* (Cambridge, MA: Harvard University Press, 1974).

28. Lorri Mon, "Face Threat," in *Theories of Information Behavior*, ed. Karen E. Fisher, Sandra Erdelez, and Lynne (E. F.) McKechnie (Medford, NJ: Information Today, 2005), 149–53.

29. Goffman, *Frame Analysis*; Mon, "Face Threat."

30. Johnson, "On Contexts of Information Seeking."

31. Ileana Stonebreaker and Heather A. Howard, "Evidence-Based Decision-Making: Awareness, Process, and Practice in the Management Classroom," *Journal of Academic Librarianship* 44, no. 1 (2018): 113–17.

PART V

METACOGNITION AND THE FEELING OF KNOWING

This section takes the feeling of knowing and uses it to reconsider how we define information, knowledge, and information seeking. We can broaden our own epistemologies as a profession by broadening the Framework for Information Literacy.

CHAPTER TWENTY-FOUR

Content Wrapped around a Feeling

Information science theoreticians or those of us in libraries or classrooms need to be able to take what the neuroscientists and psychologists are teaching us and put it into use. We need to understand *how* the mind takes experience (or takes an information source or a lesson in a classroom), breaks it apart, generates a feeling of knowing, and builds the simulation from this. We need to take the *how* and put it into use. Unfortunately for us, the neuroscientists and psychologists cannot really answer the "how" question with great precision. I am sorry to say that you've made it this far into this book, but I don't *really* know the answer and neither do the brain-imaging researchers. The science has not yet been able to understand how groupings of neurons form networks to preserve memory. We know that this is what happens, but not exactly how it happens. Where does that poem we memorized go? How do we call it back? What mechanisms trigger that poem when we hear something that reminds us of it? We may have some rough ideas, but we don't really know. Not yet. But just because we have not yet cracked the code, that does not mean that we do not know *some* things. Actually, there are many things that we *do* know, and some of those things run counter to theories in information science, librarianship, and education while some expand upon existing ideas. We should do our best to tease out the difference.

So, what can we say? We start by thinking about *information* itself. Librarians like to think that we are information experts. If this is so, it seems particularly important that we have a definition of *information* that is in line with the things we know about the mind. Luckily, we already have a definition that seems to work, which is the definition that Case offers: "*Information* can be any difference you perceive, in your environment or within yourself. It is any aspect that you notice in the pattern of reality."[1] Thinking of information as our ability to notice a pattern in reality makes sense when we consider Dewey's reflective thinking[2] and Pagel's algorithmic thinking.[3] Generally, the mind builds its simulation of the world based on what it expects, drawing on past experience. When our mind's simulation aligns with the world around it, then it does not take note, but when the mind comes across something unexpected, it takes note. Unconscious processing halts and consciousness steps in to take measure. Patterns exist all around us, but it is the thing that falls outside of the expected pattern that becomes information. This is what we use to change and update expectations, to alter our schemas, or—to put it simply—to be informed.

Our patterns of reality are at the heart of our worldview. The way that we expect the world to work is built upon the way that we experience the world. The things that are "normal," the way that things operate, the way that we understand others, are all part of these patterns. We recognize information within these patterns. Our intuitive beliefs are a result of this.[4] And relatedly, our patterns, then, open up the gateway for the social mind and reasoning as an aspect of social knowing. When we reason in groups and we argue from our *myside bias*;[5] we are arguing based on our expectations and understandings. Our arguments are biased because we have no other avenue. There is no way to reach a purely objective perspective. We may try to compensate for our worldview, and we may try to broaden our perspective, but there are always going to be limits to what we recognize as information in our world. The things we value, the solutions we seek out, and the things that make us stop and take note are related to our unique stance. Thus, information can only be based on the mind's simulation of the world.

At this point, it is important to draw a distinction between information and knowledge. Information science, librarianship, and education in general use these terms interchangeably. Interestingly, neuroscientists or psychologists do not really use the term *knowledge*. They focus more on memory and schemas. They typically do not have an operational definition for knowledge. Information science theoreticians, and librarians regularly think about knowledge. As I discussed in chapter 18, Case chooses to sidestep the debate around *data*, *information*, and *knowledge*. He ignores the traditional hierarchy using these terms "synonymously" because

> they are usually not clearly delineated in studies of information behavior. Knowledge, however, is strictly a phenomenon of the human mind, whereas

> data and information are often represented by tangible, physical objects. That information usually has a physical manifestation has often been the key consideration in past studies of information seeking. The way that information seeking is typically approached under the new paradigm, though, is in the sense of knowledge—something in someone's mind—not primarily as a physical object.[6]

But to me, it seems clear that information and knowledge are not the same thing. If information is that pattern of reality, then processing that information into our simulation changes that information into something else. It becomes *knowledge*. And even though neuroscience and psychology tend not to use the term *knowledge*, I think that the term remains valuable for information science. First off, the word is not going away anytime soon, so we might as well have a more nuanced way to think about it that draws distinction from information. Second off, if we think about knowledge in relation to the feeling of knowing, it may become more useful as we build future theory.

So, what is knowledge? I think of knowledge as a process within the mind that brings together schemas, the feeling of knowing, and consciousness. When information becomes part of our schemas or our simulation of the world, we can call forth knowledge that draws on the multiple processes of the mind. Too often, information science treats knowledge as information that someone filed away in the mind. It is just content. But we need to see it as more. It is content, but content wrapped around a feeling that comes from the mind's modules processing that content. There are three important subpoints to make this with this. First, the inclusion of consciousness as a part of knowledge brings in aspects of the self. Knowing is tied to who we are, the tribes we join, and the self-schemas we have built. Second, the moment matters with knowing. This is the context problem.[7] The study of memory has shown that context matters and that the current context activates some aspects of memory while other aspects remain hidden away in the mind. This momentary activation means that we cannot treat knowledge like simple information filed away like books on shelves. Knowledge is not a complete work that is just waiting to be called forth once we have the right call number. Knowledge is momentary and personal. Third, given the role of consciousness in knowing and the role of context, we must view knowledge as something dynamic. It is more fluid that we realize. *What* we know and *how* we know will vary in different situations and at different times.

All of this is to say that when we use the terms *information* and *knowledge* interchangeably, we lose the dynamic nature of knowledge. We lose the multiple processes that are at work within the unconscious mind. We lose the self that is part of the conscious mind. This view of knowledge also means that *your* knowledge cannot possibly be *my* knowledge and vice versa. This dynamic view of knowledge makes sense when we consider how power structures are embedded within knowledge. Given the Foucauldian view of norms—that each person is "the principle of his own subjection"[8]—we apply norms within our knowledge systems because these norms are built into the schemas we hold about the world. Our assumptions of normalcy include assumptions about how power is distributed and who is privileged by this power. Recognizing knowledge's relationship to power is also a part of recognizing our own contribution to structures of power. As Clara Chu states in an interview with Todd Honma,

> "Information is power" tends to be regarded as a statement, often a statement of some type of universal truth—if one possesses information, one possesses power. Implicit within that formulation is, again, the emphasis on the individual, as the individual is the one who can possess information and thereby possess power. But such a statement doesn't ask you to rethink the overall system within which information functions, a system (as we've been discussing) that is steeped in privilege and oppression. "Information as power" asks that we take a more active and critical approach to how we understand information and its dynamic role in society.[9]

Within the education literature, we often use the term *construction* to describe how knowledge is created or the theory of *constructivism* drawing from Jean Piaget and inquiry-based learning.[10] The use of construction as a metaphor describing how knowledge is acquired does not really arise within the neuroscience or psychology literature. The term mostly lives within education theory. As an education theory, there are aspects of this idea that make sense. Construction may be a useful metaphor, but often when we use it, we use it in a way that does not include the feeling of knowing. We neglect the role of schemas, the self, and social knowing. We act as if the mind takes information and welds it with other pieces of information to create a new knowledge structure. To extend the metaphor, information sources are not girders holding up knowledge structures. We often do not consider the mix of unconscious processes that are at work within the construction process. If I were going to define what construction means, to me it would mean taking new information and connecting it to the schemas we hold in our minds. I am not so sure that we are actually constructing as much as we are absorbing, molding, and melding experience around our existing schemas. This may seem like a matter of semantics or preference of metaphor, but it is more than this. We cannot take learning to be a direct assembly process. Learning is personal, building on experience by adjusting neural pathways. New ideas are broken down and distributed across the mind for later retrieval or they are melded into schemas we already hold, and those existing structures are tough to entirely change.

Our dynamic view of knowing also helps us see *uncertainty* and *relevance*—two important ideas in information science—in new ways. Both can be seen as aspects of the feeling of knowing. Uncertainty is a feeling. It is the absence of the feeling of certainty or part of the spectrum of the feeling of knowing. As we explore the feeling of knowing, we have different levels of certainty. In terms of information science, this is important because uncertainty can keep us moving forward if we are searching for information. Uncertainty can also be a source of creativity as we are driving toward something new. When we face a challenge to know something or discover a new idea, uncertainty keeps our drive alive. When we talk about uncertainty, we need to understand it as a feeling. And, moreover, that feeling is, like all mental sensations, the result of the mind as democracy. The mind's multiple processes are at work, battling and evaluating and arguing. The result of this mental struggle generates a feeling that is inconclusive. We do not know, so we drive forward.

Recognizing uncertainty as it relates to the feeling of knowing is very important for information science and those of us in libraries, because, often, when we talk about decision making or the research process, we do not have a means to talk about how we make decisions. We may read twenty-five articles for a journal article we are authoring or we may read four hundred sources for a dissertation, but how do we know when we have enough? At some point, we satisfy our uncertainty. We make a recognition that we have enough. That recognition is a feeling. We feel it. There is no definitive mechanism in the mind that switches on or off as we cross some information boundary. No. We know we have enough when we feel that we have enough.

So much of what we do when we are utilizing information is context dependent. As I mentioned, the difference between writing an article or writing a dissertation sets a different context. Creating fiction, reading a political argument, or joining a religious dialog are all different contexts. These contexts all produce different kinds of needs and, relatedly, different levels of uncertainty. The only way that I can possibly think about to manage these differences is the feeling of knowing. Our unconscious processes are built to work within the countless variables and produce the feelings that guide us as we interpret, analyze, and weigh our stance within each situation.

Relevance, as a concept in information science, is also connected to the feeling of knowing. Relevance is generally focused on topicality or aboutness. How does one idea relate to another idea? At what point are two ideas not related at all? For us to recognize that an idea is relevant, we must have a feeling around that idea. We generate a feeling of knowing that helps us understand how ideas are related. When we do not generate that feeling, we do not see connections and do recognize relevance. For this book, I have spent several years reading neuroscience and psychology articles, but I didn't *feel* like this was enough. I knew that different branches of philosophy and feminist theory spoke to identity and how we understand our world, so I expanded my reading. I found areas and topics that *felt* connected to what I saw in scientific literature. These connections utilized reason and rationality at some level, but the connections that I found were expressed as a feeling of knowing. When I saw their relevance, I felt it. It is easy for librarians to think of relevance as a measure of subject headings, subheadings, and classification, but that is not how it works in practice. To recognize relevance, we must feel it.

This brings us to information seeking and information behavior, which are ideas that take up a lot of space within the information science literature. We can start with Case's definition: "Information seeking is a conscious effort to acquire information in response to a need or gap in your knowledge."[11] This definition largely makes sense. My interpretation of his definition is that by *conscious* he is not referencing the mind's conscious processing but that he is referring to a purposeful, goal-directed process. We recognize some sort of need or decision that we must make where additional information beyond our own knowledge will be helpful. But of course, the issue I may take with this definition is that we need to recognize that how the mind operates in information seeking involves both conscious processing and unconscious processes, including shortcuts. Information seeking is not just rationality and reason but also draws on other mental processes such as intuitions built on experience. We may consciously seek out information to make a decision, solve a problem, or complete an assignment for a project, but through all of these, we are guided by the feeling of knowing. As discussed above, with uncertainty and relevance, our feeling of knowing is important within information seeking. Our feeling of knowing is the result of unconscious processes dealing with the information we encounter.

When we think of information seeking as a process infused with the feeling of knowing, we can get a more complete picture of this process. We are not just adding up information into new ideas. We are strategically negotiating with information within the limits of how we know the world. We are set within historical limitations such as inherited knowledge, the limits of our experience, and the power structures that we are part of. To understand information seeking, we must turn inward. It is not just about adding up outside sources but also understanding how those outside sources interface with our schemas. It is understanding that information is shaped by group interactions and lives within a social context. We shape information as we interact with it, and it shapes us in a kind of Möbius strip, folding back on itself.[12]

While information seeking is a concept that I think we can explore and grow as we better understand the feeling of knowing, *information behavior* is an idea that I have come to struggle with. It is a body of work and foundational theory within information science, which is why the term ended up as a subtitle of this book. But I find it less and less useful. Here is Case's definition:

> *Information behavior* encompasses information seeking as well as the totality of other *unintentional* or *passive* behaviors (such as glimpsing or encountering information), as well as purposive behaviors that do not involve seeking, such as actively avoiding information.[13] (italics in the original)

The neuroscience and psychological literature have brought me to the point where I see all behavior is information behavior. I don't know what kind of behaviors could possibly count as non-information behaviors. The idea of information behavior originates from a time where information was stored in a physical object, and we could watch how people interacted with those objects. But I don't see how this holds up around the ways that neuroscientists are explaining the ways that our minds process our world. If we wanted to outline specific situations of information seeking—like writing a paper, searching a database, taking notes from a book, or countless other examples—these all make sense as information seeking. But it makes more sense to me to not use *information behavior* as a term and just talk about how the mind builds the simulation of the world. Information science theorists treat information behavior as a broader term that subsumes information seeking but also includes "unintentional or passive behaviors." I don't think that the unintentional or passive behaviors are actually behaviors. They are just mental processes. We can still talk about things like information avoidance and incidental exposure to ideas, but I think that information science needs to step away from information behavior as a grand theory. We should follow the neuroscience and focus on how the mind processes the world.

In this book, I have highlighted several information science theoreticians, but I have given three of them a particular spotlight. Those are Nahl's affective load theory, Kuhlthau's information search process, and Dervin's sense making. I am not exactly sure where information science is going to go in the future, but I do believe that these theories help to build a foundation. The corollaries that Kuhlthau provides to her ISP offer interesting avenues for future research, especially using the feeling of knowing as a lens to see them. The process corollary, formulation corollary, redundancy corollary, mood corollary, prediction corollary, and interest corollary attempt to peek into the mind during information seeking. Dervin's sense making opens up an avenue for unconscious processing within information science. She doesn't use the terms, but her focus is on how our schemas come together to build the simulation around us. Finally, Nahl's affective load may be information science's best formulation on how the mind processes information. Her work almost captures the feeling of knowing by recognizing that feeling helps us notice or receive information from the environment around us and that the feeling is vital in information usage.

As I discussed at the opening of this book, I am an instruction librarian, and for more than two decades, I have thought about students' use of information. I helped them evaluate sources as they completed projects. My questions about authority and credibility were the early kernel that led to this book. Why do we trust some sources and not others? What compels us to give away trust? If we know this, can we help students better develop their information literacy skills? Throughout this book, I have stated that too often our underlying assumption when we teach research is rationality. All of us are rational, and if only we had the same information, we'd make the same choices. If we only had better information, we'd make better choices. If we all could just define authority and credibility the same way, then we'd trust the right sources, and we'd all get along so much better. But the neuroscience and psychology show us something different. Our underlying assumption should not be pure rationality. Using information cannot be based on a formula.

But if we cannot assume rationality, what can we assume? What does it look like to *not* assume rationality? Reassessing our assumptions about how students—and people—use information is a tricky business, but I keep coming back to Goldberger's idea of *knowing as strategy*.[14] When we work with students, it is not enough to have a credibility checklist or to focus on source quality, because our schemas, myside bias, and intuitions give a unique positionality to how our simulation of the world interfaces with sources. To put it another way, our own perspectives on how the world operates will influence how we understand information sources and which outside sources we trust. It is not so much that we are each purely relativistic in how we see "truth," but that our experiences and social connections weave a gossamer web of understanding influencing where we stand. And for each of us to really understand where we stand, we need to better understand how we *feel* about the topics driving our information needs. When we think about knowing as strategy, it is not enough just to know the content; we need to examine and challenge the way that we feel about the content of those things we know.

Ironically, I think that our goal should be to follow Goldman's goal of correspondence theory.[15] We should try to judge whether our beliefs correspond to what we are seeing in our external world, no matter how fraught that endeavor may be. But if we are to do this, we must see knowing as strategy and take a metacognitive approach to knowing. It is our deliberative cognition[16] that makes metacognition possible. Humans, unlike any other species, are able to build mental models of our thought processes. Through metacognition, we can recognize the feeling of knowing, pulling it apart from what we know. Our own internal awareness can separate the feeling from the schemas we hold. As Zull writes, "The goal is to become aware of what we assume, think, and believe, and how we use that awareness in our mental activities."[17] Being aware means recognizing the feeling of knowing. This is important in our metacognition because this feeling is a summation of the inferential judgments coming out of unconscious processing. Metacognition is not just a set of ideas about how we think but a feeling drawing on the multiple processes at work within the mind. Using tools like reflection and the felt sense, we can try to recognize the origins of knowledge.

As we recognize the value of metacognition, we can consider how this can be applied to our classrooms and libraries. We can create learning opportunities for students that explicitly build metacognitive skills. Brookfield's approach to critically reflective teaching presents us with a possible metacognitive strategy. He challenges us to recognize embedded power relationships permeating our classrooms:

> An awareness of how the dynamics of power permeate all educational processes helps us realize that forces present in the wider society always intrude into the classroom. Classrooms are not limpid, tranquil ponds, cut off from the river of social, cultural, and political life. They are contested spaces—whirlpools, containing the contradictory crosscurrents of struggles for material superiority and ideological legitimacy that exist in the world outside. When we become aware of the pervasiveness of power, we start to notice the oppressive dimensions to practice that we had thought were neutral or even benevolent.[18]

He defines four critically reflective lenses. The first is our own autobiographies as learners and teachers. We often teach based on how we have learned. This can help us explain why we gravitate in one direction or another in terms of how the classroom should work. The second is to try our best to view learning through our students' eyes. When we put ourselves in the perspective of our students, we learn new things about how our own classroom works. Unfortunately, students are often reluctant to be honest with us because of power dynamics. The third lens is that of our colleagues' experiences. Having conversations with peers opens our eyes to different versions of events and experiences. The final lens is through the theoretical literature. Using theory can help us "name" our own practices by highlighting elements that we may not recognize in our day-to-day experience. Brookfield's four lenses are a starting point for reflection.

If neuroscience and psychology teach us anything, they teach us that we are not very good at seeing our own schemas. Our reflective practice will have its own failings. The malleability of memory, the inaccessibility of how memories are stored away in the mind, or the impact of context on what we recall should make us skeptical of our own understanding of the world. We may feel that we are correct, but if we can recognize that feeling and step back, this is an important type of reflection. Recognizing the feeling of knowing and exploring its origins seems particularly vital. Source monitoring is one metacognitive tool that helps us manage our mental lives. Source monitoring is the effort we take to keep track of the sources of memories. We can extend this to understanding our schemas. What are the building blocks for what we know? Conflict monitoring is another metacognitive tool where our mental processes are in conflict as they deal with new or challenging experiences. This happens when we read an article that causes us to pause and think things over. Our feeling of knowing is weak as we work through new ideas. Using source monitoring to track down the origins of our schemas and conflict monitoring in the moment to pause and recognize how we are processing are two possibilities to strengthen our metacognitive arsenal. Knowing as strategy means deeply deconstructing our beliefs and getting to their origins. It also means living within the modularity of the mind. When we struggle to process and achieve the feeling of knowing, we must take note. To know that we have learned is a feeling. To know that we have not quite captured a concept is also a feeling.

For librarians and other educators, we must remain focused on the needs of our patrons and our students. This is the thing that differentiates us from other disciplines. We should not try to be psychologists or neuroscientists. But we should try to learn from them. Information literacy is especially focused on the needs and success of those utilizing information. When I say that we often assume rationality, this is another way of saying that our past approaches to information literacy have lacked a metacognitive focus. Our underlying assumption is that with the right information our students will reach similar conclusions. We do not adequately challenge them to reflect.

An obvious example of this can be seen with teaching evaluation of sources. We can focus on checklists and source quality. We can conduct background reading and lateral reading across sources. But if we are going to think about knowing as strategy and the relationship of our knowledge to the feeling of knowing, then we need to think reflectively. We cannot consider why a source is authoritative *to us* without metacognitive thinking. What are our schemas that make a course compelling? What is it about our beliefs that pushes us to trust one source over the millions of other sources that are out there?

If we look at *The Framework for Information Literacy for Higher Education from the Association of College and Research Libraries*,[19] which is the guiding document on information literacy for the profession, we can see glimpses of metacognitive references, but we will largely find missed opportunities. For those who are unfamiliar, *The Framework* defines six "frames" that represent threshold concepts at the heart of information literacy. I want to look at the four frames that most directly address knowing: Authority Is Constructed and Contextual, Information Has Value, Research as Inquiry, and Scholarship as Conversation. Looking at each of these frames is a way to view how instruction librarians think about what we do and how we approach our students. It also presents a kind of discourse for how we define information and our interactions with information.

The frame that is most aligned with the feeling of knowing is Authority is Constructed and Contextual. It states that

> Information resources reflect their creators' expertise and credibility and are evaluated based on the information need and the context in which the information will be used. Authority is constructed in that various communities may recognize different types of authority. It is contextual in that the information need may help to determine the level of authority required. Experts understand that authority is a type of influence recognized or exerted within a community. Experts view authority with an attitude of informed skepticism and an openness to new perspectives, additional voices, and changes in schools of thought. Experts understand the need to determine the validity of the information created by different authorities and to acknowledge biases that privilege some sources of authority over others, especially in terms of others' worldviews, gender, sexual orientation, and cultural orientations.[20]

At first glance, this frame looks to rely on the construction metaphor of learning, but it doesn't exactly say how the mind performs this construction. It takes pains to emphasize that authority results from communities and that authority is somewhat relativistic in nature, shifting based on need.

It acknowledges worldview and power structures. This seems to really make sense with knowing as strategy. But this frame does not push us to look inward. It may emphasize community, but it does not challenge us to consider how our community membership influences us and in what ways this could be positive or ways it may be detrimental. It emphasizes the contextual nature of knowing, but it does not acknowledge how contexts may limit the ways that we access memory or utilize our schemas. From a metacognitive vantage, if we are to understand how we—as individuals—judge authority, we must look inward. We must be reflective. *What do I count as authoritative? Who do I view as an authority?* In order to answer these questions, I have to turn inward. I have to examine my feeling of knowing.

The frame Information Has Value connects value judgments to how we negotiate meaning and how different interests influence value. It states that

> Information possesses several dimensions of value, including as a commodity, as a means of education, as a means to influence, and as a means of negotiating and understanding the world. Legal and socioeconomic interests influence information production and dissemination. . . . Experts understand that value may be wielded by powerful interests in ways that marginalize certain voices. However, value may also be leveraged by individuals and organizations to effect change and for civic, economic, social, or personal gains.[21]

The frame does a decent job placing information within the cultural and power dynamics that can shape it. This frame could almost be called *information is power*. There are many ways to measure value and many factors that go into making information valuable. This frame casts a wide net in an effort to capture many of them. But, of course, this frame does not address how these different factors come together and operate as we process information. Many of these factors will be explicit, but many of them will not be so clear because they are embedded in cultural understandings. Examining the ways that our mind manages overlapping or conflicting value measures would be a nice avenue for future exploration. Heuristics, power structures, rationality, the feeling of knowing, and other processes are all possible avenues to better understand how we value information. Judging the value of information is the ultimate exercise in contextualization. Societal, power, and personal context push our judgments.

The frame Research as Inquiry is a missed opportunity. This frame talks about conversation and knowledge but not reflection:

> Research is iterative and depends upon asking increasingly complex or new questions whose answers in turn develop additional questions or lines of

> inquiry in any field. . . . Many times, this process includes points of disagreement where debate and dialogue work to deepen the conversations around knowledge. This process of inquiry extends beyond the academic world to the community at large, and the process of inquiry may focus upon personal, professional, or societal needs. The spectrum of inquiry ranges from asking simple questions that depend upon basic recapitulation of knowledge to increasingly sophisticated abilities to refine research questions, use more advanced research methods, and explore more diverse disciplinary perspectives.[22]

The inquiry metaphor is different from the construction metaphor—used to describe authority above—in that it sets research into a mode of seeking answers to questions, a discovery process. This is a more useful representation than thinking of research as a formula or as a compilation of facts. Research is a process that seeks truth as opposed to setting out to find evidence for preexisting beliefs. However, this is the missed opportunity. By not addressing preexisting beliefs and by not turning inward, this frame does not actually address how research brings us to answers. It sets up research as a question for knowledge, but never delves into how we use research to make decisions. It says that research is iterative because questions become more complex, which is probably true. But it may also be iterative because our schemas may change and evolve. We may process the world differently. Our feeling of knowledge may shift. The missed opportunity here is that it does not address how the mind works through challenging ideas within the research process. How does experience with research change our unconscious processing? Or does it? Can formal methodologies be utilized to address our shortcuts and heuristics?

The next frame, Scholarship as Conversation, offers some interesting potential. It states that

> Communities of scholars, researchers, or professionals engage in sustained discourse with new insights and discoveries occurring over time as a result of varied perspectives and interpretations. Research in scholarly and professional fields is a discursive practice in which ideas are formulated, debated, and weighed against one another over extended periods of time. Instead of seeking discrete answers to complex problems, experts understand that a given issue may be characterized by several competing perspectives as part of an ongoing conversation in which information users and creators come together and negotiate meaning.[23]

This frame's focus on negotiating meaning makes sense with what we are learning about the mind. The idea of competing perspectives aligns with our evolutionary view of culture and competing ideas within the social mind. The use of the metaphor of conversation really connects with Mercier and Sperber's perspective on how reason evolved to function within groups.[24] But as we have seen in other frames, this frame misses out on the chance to really explore what this means. Yes, scholarship may be a conversation where we negotiate meaning, but the social nature of knowing and the way that groups make knowledge are not addressed. It does not address how intuitions that are based in unconscious processing and rationality that involves both conscious and unconscious processing may grow more complex over time.

Taken as a whole, *The Framework* demonstrates where instruction librarians are in understanding how the mind processes information. It seems fair to say that this document does not delve deeply into how the mind processes information or the world more broadly. *The Framework*'s focus on moving from novice to expert could become an avenue for understanding how processing changes over time—assuming that we can consistently move students toward expert practice and understandings. The move from novice to expert may be a path toward complexity, self-awareness (reflection), and better utilization of different kinds of processing.

For librarians and educators—and especially for instructional librarians like me—we need to recognize that individuals who use information at a complex level are reflective. They see knowing as a strategy and employ metacognitive skills to challenge the source of their own knowing, the structures—societal and cultural—that underpin knowing, and the content—memory and experience—that is known. To accomplish this, the existing *Framework* needs a significant revision, and along with this, I believe we need an additional frame that draws out how the mind interacts with information to build knowledge. This would fill an epistemological gap in *The Framework* and our profession's underlying theory.

I propose the following additional frame as a draft. This should be vetted and worked on by our community, but it is my intention that this advance our discourse:

Knowledge as a Feeling

Understanding and using information to make a decision is a complex process that involves conscious and unconscious mental processing. The feeling of knowing is a metacognitive result that comes into consciousness from unconscious processing. This feeling drives us forward when we have a specific information need, but also more generally it captures memories and builds schemas from these memories. Therefore, it is not enough to know what we are thinking. We must also know how we are feeling about the things we are thinking.

The feeling of knowing is a mental sensation that is situational and highly social. Cultural norms, identity, and power structures deeply impact this feeling. Novice learners view their interactions with information sources as purely rational and, often, formulaic. They do not recognize their own biases or the influences of norms on their knowing. Experts take a metacognitive stance toward knowing, accepting that knowing is built into a larger fabric to which they contribute. Experts understand that having a feeling of knowing does not necessarily mean that this feeling reflects external reality. Experts find ways to interrogate the feeling of knowing to better recognize the sources of knowing.

Knowledge Practices

Learners who are developing their information literate abilities

- recognize the feeling of knowing around the content that is to be known,
- notice emotional responses to information sources and debates and try to understand the causes of these responses,
- reflect on the experiences that build their schemas and how these experiences influence what they know,
- evaluate information utilizing reflective practices,
- recognize the influence of group membership in knowing, and
- understand power structures and how they influence knowing.

Dispositions

- Knowing is a result of the modular nature of the mind.
- Critical thinking requires reflection on the sources of knowing.
- Reason operates best in groups of trusted individuals.
- Knowledge is judged as a product of groups.

As I have stated from the start, the goal of this book is not to be definitive but to push forward the conversation. Broadly, I hope that I have demonstrated the value in connecting information science, librarianship, information literacy, and education theory to the neuroscience and psychology. Clearly, from the citations throughout this book, I am not the first person to come up with this idea, but I hope that I have taken the past work and moved it forward. There are many avenues to explore and much to rethink. More specifically, I hope that my arguments about the feeling of knowing deepen our understandings of the relationship between knowledge and information. We must reexamine our foundational knowledge about knowledge itself. When we work with students, we must recognize that knowing is not about rationality, facts, or data. It is about feeling. Strong feelings, weak feelings, and lukewarm feelings not only impact learning, but determine the success of learning.

I end this chapter with the quote that I used in the introductory chapter from screenwriter Charlie Kaufman, who captured this so perfectly:

> To me, when I relate to a piece of fiction, you know, or a novel or something, it isn't that it makes me step outside myself, although sometimes there are those kinds of books. *But I mean, the things that I really relate to is when I read something that has articulated something that I felt but haven't been able to articulate.* And I find that incredibly moving. And I find an incredible sense of community in that.[25] (italics added)

The most powerful moments of learning come "*when I read something that has articulated something that I felt but haven't been able to articulate.*"

Notes

1. Donald Case, *Looking for Information: A Survey of Research on Information Seeking, Needs, and Behavior*, second edition (Amsterdam: Elsevier, 2007), 5.
2. John Dewey, *How We Think* (CreateSpace Independent Publishing, 2014).
3. Mark D. Pagel, *Wired for Culture: Origins of the Human Social Mind* (New York: Norton, 2013).
4. Hugo Mercier and Dan Sperber, "Why Do Humans Reason? Arguments for an Argumentative Theory," *Behavioral and Brain Sciences*, 34, no. 2 (2011): 57–111.
5. Hugo Mercier and Dan Sperber, *The Enigma of Reason: A New Theory of Human Understanding* (London: Penguin, 2018).
6. Case, *Looking for Information*, 65.
7. J. David Johnson, "On Contexts of Information Seeking," *Information Processing and Management* 39, no. 4 (2003): 735–60; Case, *Looking for Information.*
8. Michel Foucault, *Discipline and Punish: The Birth of the Prison* (New York: Vintage Books, 1977), 108.
9. Todd Honma and Clara Chu, "Positionality, Epistemology, and New Paradigms for LIS: A Critical Dialog with Clara M. Chu," in *Pushing the Margins: Women of Color and Intersectionality in LIS*, ed. Rose L. Chou and Annie Pho (Sacramento, CA: Library Juice Press, 2018), 455–56.

10. Alison Gopnik, *The Gardener and the Carpenter: What the New Science of Child Development Tells Us About the Relationship Between Parents and Children* (New York: Farrar, Straus, and Giroux, 2016); Joshua R. Eyler, *How Humans Learn: The Science and Stories Behind Effective College Teaching* (Morgantown: West Virginia University Press, 2018).

11. Case, *Looking for Information*, 5.

12. Thanks to Margy MacMillan for this great metaphor.

13. Case, *Looking for Information*, 5.

14. Nancy Rule Goldberger, "Cultural Imperatives and Diversity in Ways of Knowing," in *Knowledge, Differences, and Power: Essays Inspired by* Women's Ways of Knowing, ed. Nancy Rule Goldberger, Jill Mattuck Tarule, Blythe Clinchy McVicker, and Mary Field Belenky (New York: Basic Books, 1996), 335–71.

15. Alvin I. Goldman, *Knowledge in a Social World* (Oxford, UK: Clarendon Press, 1999).

16. Joseph LeDoux, *The Deep History of Ourselves: The Four-Billion-Year Story of How We Got Conscious Brains* (New York: Viking, 2019).

17. James E. Zull, *From Brain to Mind: Using Neuroscience to Guide Change in Education* (Sterling, VA: Stylus Publishing, 2011), 259.

18. Stephen Brookfield, *Becoming a Critically Reflective Teacher* (San Francisco: Jossey-Bass, 1995), 9.

19. Association of College and Research Libraries, "Framework for Information Literacy for Higher Education," *American Library Association*, 2015, https://www.ala.org/acrl/standards/ilframework (12 Jan 2023).

20. Association of College and Research Libraries, "Framework for Information Literacy."

21. Association of College and Research Libraries, "Framework for Information Literacy."

22. Association of College and Research Libraries, "Framework for Information Literacy."

23. Association of College and Research Libraries, "Framework for Information Literacy."

24. Mercier and Sperber, *Enigma of Reason*.

25. Charlie Kaufman, "Charlie Kaufman On Being—And Directing," *Fresh Air*, October 23, 2008, https://www.npr.org/transcripts/96023004 (13 Jan 2023).

Epilogue

This Moment

As I have been working on this book over the past few years, I cannot help but think about how situated my thinking is within this moment of history. We cannot ignore or downplay the fact that we, as a society, are working through something. The arrival of the internet in our recent past has continually recrafted our information landscape, and those of us who teach research skills and work to provide information to communities have been in a state of constant flux around its ever-changing nature. We have been optimistic at the Arab Spring and #Blacklivesmatter movement and flabbergasted by misinformation-driven events such as the January 6th insurrection in the United States. Our society is being molded by the changes in how we know our world.

Clearly, our world is more interconnected than ever before, and this interconnection produces a flow of information that we shape and that shapes us. So, how do we participate in this flow? We are guided by the feeling of knowing. At the outset of this book, I described my early years in the classroom, teaching students about credibility and authority drawing a contrast between the research databases my library provided and the early days of the open World Wide Web. The thing that interested me most—how the mind processes information—is not itself a technology problem, but it was made apparent by technological changes that we were facing. The advance of the web and its acceleration through social media and mobile devices did not necessarily change our brains, per se, and have not necessarily changed how we process information. But it did unleash a torrent of content that was more readily available than ever, and it was up to our neural networks to manage this torrent. Ultimately, this book is a consideration as to how the feeling of knowing interacts with a constantly evolving information landscape.

So stepping back and taking a historical perspective on the changes happening around us is useful. In some ways, the changes we face are new, but dealing with changes to information technologies is not new. In fact, it is common. In the 1970s, the famous psychologist Abraham Maslow wrestled with the impact of new information technology:

> I have a very strong feeling of a change of pace in history. It seems to me that we are at a point in history unlike anything that has ever been before. Life moves far more rapidly now than it ever did before. Think, for instance, of the huge acceleration in the rate of growth of facts, of knowledge, of techniques, of advances in technology. It seems very obvious to me that this requires a change in our attitude toward the human being, and toward his relationships in the world.[1]

As you probably know, Maslow saw education as the path to self-actualization. Almost six decades ago, in this pre-internet age, he outlined the need to change education to emphasize creativity. He noticed that it is no longer enough to teach students a list of facts about the past. He emphasizes the need for improvisational thinking in students. He noted in the 1970s that society was in the midst of rapidly changing technology and that the "techniques in fact" that teachers learn are not enough for students. He noted that teachers (especially in higher education) were "buggy whip makers." His argument for change feels quite familiar to us today.

Similarly, and also famously, Marshall McLuhan struggled with changes that he saw in the "electronic age" in the 1960s.[2]

> Print technology created the public. Electric technology created the mass. The public consists of separate individuals walking around with separate fixed points of view. The new technology demands that we abandon the luxury of this posture, this fragmentary outlook.[3]

His famous idea, *the medium is the message*, is a statement that *how* we communicate shapes us as much as or even more than *what* we communicate. McLuhan was theorizing during a time that television had been embraced in living rooms around the world and media was shifting from a print-dominant world to a broadcast-dominant world. The changes we lament today assume that the broadcast-dominant world—in which many of us grew up—was the norm. McLuhan saw that media are extensions of the mind, and he believed that in the print world people were "fragmented" with a kind of limited and disconnected view of the world. In contrast, the electronic world connected people in the moment as never before.[4]

> Men are suddenly nomadic gatherers of knowledge, nomadic as never before, informed as never before, free from fragmentary specialism as never before; since with electricity we extend our central nervous system globally, instantly interrelating every human experience.[5]

During this same time, communications scholar Wilbur Schramm was also trying to make sense of mass communication. He emphasized that people built their understanding of the world based upon the information they consume, and, importantly, individuals then molded the ways they participated in the world on this understanding. He notes that it was Gutenberg who really introduced the machine into the communication process in a significant way, providing individuals with a kind of "radar" for the world around them. With each step in the growth of mass communications, our mental maps of where we fit in the world extend.[6] He explains,

> It is no accident that we have use the word revolution in talking about social interactions with mass communication. The media have been involved in every significant social change since they came into existence—intellectual revolutions, political revolutions, industrial revolution, and revolution in taste, aspirations, and values. They have taught us a basic precept: Because communication is the fundamental social process, because man is above all an information-processing animal, a major change in the state of information, a major involvement of communication, always accompanies any major social change.[7]

John D. Steinbrenner in his 1974 book *The Cybernetic Theory of Decision* reacted to what he saw as the growing complexity of society stemming from increased access to information and the growing size of organizations across all sectors of the economy. Individuals could not command a broad enough perspective to make decisions, and in addition to this, many decisions were distributed across groups of people within organizations whether it be government agencies, corporations, or educational institutions, to just name a few examples. Steinbrenner makes an argument that complex situations should lead to "indecisiveness." Most situations in organizations, governments, healthcare, etc., are too complicated for any single person to gather enough information to make an informed decision. But somehow we still decide.[8] We do not see indecision. Steinbrenner writes,

> The mind constantly struggles to impose clear, coherent meaning on events, uses categorical rather than probabilistic judgments in doing so, and thus expects to anticipate outcomes exactly rather than having to assign probabilities to a range of outcomes. This tendency is the natural result of built-in, unconsciously operating inference mechanisms which are highly functional in everyday life. Under complexity, where the decision maker does not encounter highly structured and obviously random processes, the tendency is even stronger. This process of resolving uncertainty by imposing an inferential structure is a critical assumption of cognitive theory.[9]

The structures we impose are built upon our beliefs of how the world works. Beliefs simplify decisions, reduce information overload, and ultimately, reduce uncertainty.

Again, the comments of Steinbrenner, Schramm, and Maslow in the early 1970s as well as the feelings of McLuhan in the 1960s feel quite familiar to us. Their specific arguments are less important for us here than the feelings of information overload, the fear of rapid change, the struggle of the mind to manage the information ecosystem, and the reconstitution of the relationship between the individual and society. All of this boils down to how our feeling of knowing negotiates technological changes.

We can jump back five hundred years to one example of these negotiations at work. The English felt the shocks of the newly available print technology at the end of the sixeenth and throughout the seventeenth century. During Henry VIII's reign, England saw roughly eighty publications regularly in print over the year, but a century later, at the start of the English Civil War, it had around two thousand. A figure that would more than double over the course of the conflict. As the war approached, print helped to build a consciousness within society tying to personal religious identity as never before. English citizens followed conflicts between Roman Catholics and Protestants in France and Spain. When the English Civil War erupted, arguments in print exacerbated political division. Communities of believers formed across geographies based on ideas shared in print. This may be one of the first examples of an information war. The birth of pseudo-newspapers, regularly published, providing news and arguments, proliferated across communities. News became a tool of war.[10]

Prior to the English Civil War, the government of Charles I did not produce an official paper. This was beneath the king, and therefore, he relied on others to advocate for him in print. After the war, Charles II could no longer ignore this technology. Print had become a tool of governing. His official paper dominated debates and marked the start of papers that were carried around the world.[11]

The use of print elbowed its way into existing information structures. At first, print was read aloud to groups of people—think town crier. Oral news networks dominated, so print interjected itself, enhancing what already existed. But over time, information ecosystems molded themselves into a mostly print-dominant system. By current standards, literacy rates remained comparably low, but as literacy spread, especially among elites, new forms of print shaped economics, politics, and culture.[12]

I want to be clear that information technology alone does not foretell catastrophe or war. Social, economic, political, and cultural forces are at work with information technology acting as a catalyst. But history does seem clear that technological change brings about negotiations and renegotiations within social structures.

For us today, our information crisis is partly a result of the *disintermediation* of the mass media channels that coalesced in the middle of the twentieth century. The sources of authority in print and broadcast media have been bypassed in the online information environment. Media organizations sought to adapt as their business models disintegrated. Notions of credibility and trust eroded as the foundations of information distribution have shifted.[13]

Our most acute information crisis today revolves around our ever-increasing political polarization. This takes disintermediation and weaponizes it for political gain. Of course, it has been noted that the invention of social media and the impact on online communications more broadly did not bring about polarization, but, like all moments in history, the information technology is an enabler. The manipulation by political elites, the interference of outside actors such as Russian hackers, and the propensity of the American system to emphasize free speech and free markets while resisting the regulation of speech open the United States to significant attacks. The United States—and perhaps countries globally—has sorted itself into like-minded communities with competing understandings of how the world operates—competing cultures, schemas, and simulations. The changing nature of information technology is part of the underlying issue, but only a portion.[14] Our state of polarization is a direct symptom of the feeling of knowing—the application of schema that we hold, the way the world works, the identities we hold, and the grievances built there within. Given all of these factors, addressing polarization will not be accomplished by making technological changes alone. We do not need a better social media platform or a more authoritative journalism. We do not need more fact checkers.

As media researcher danah boyd notes, everyone believes that they are employing "critical thinking" as they seek to understand the information being transmitted all around them. "Media literacy" is a standard that everybody believes they achieve. As people segment themselves based on worldview, the very filters that individuals use to understand the world are the things that lock our worldview into place. The worldview we hold is part of the weaponization of information.[15] boyd goes on to say,

> It's one thing to talk about interrogating assumptions when a person can keep emotional distance from the object of study. It's an entirely different thing to talk about these issues when the very act of asking questions is what's being weaponized. This isn't historical propaganda distributed through mass media. Or an exercise in understanding state power. This is about making sense of an information landscape where the very tools that people use to make sense of the world around them have been strategically perverted by other people who believe themselves to be resisting the same powerful actors that we normally seek to critique.[16]

In echoes of McLuhan and Maslow, education scholar Maryanne Wolf outlines a different kind of technology-driven problem. She asks if we are losing the quality of attention for deep reading. She defines a tension between evolutionary pressures and modern culture:

1. Novelty bias: The brain is attuned to seek and focus on new things in environment.
2. Hyperattention: The constantly shifting, partial attention due to switching tasks within the digital environment. This is fed by massive amounts of information coming at each of us.
3. The lack of time for quiet, nurturing thinking.[17]

To handle the overload, we simplify as much as possible, process information rapidly (consume in small bursts and not deeply) and ignore much. She worries that we often let others think for us when we do not process ourselves. Wolf worries that we no longer have the *cognitive patience* for deep processing of information.

> The time needed to process what we perceive and what we read is profoundly important, whether in building memory, in storing background knowledge, or in every other deep-reading process.[18]

She argues for a "biliterate brain" that can utilize print for deep processing while moving to digital to connect with others and create. Wolf's work is impressive, and it is an important part of the conversion around how we take our next steps. But I am not entirely convinced that she has it entirely in place.

boyd offers a different kind of biliterate brain, not just one that can move between different types of thought—deep processing versus online skimming—but, instead, the ability to recognize and move between worldviews while still seeing where you stand in your own worldview.

> From an educational point of view, this means building the capacity to truly hear and embrace someone else's perspective and teaching people to understand another's view while also holding their view firm. It's hard work, an extension of empathy into a practice that is common among ethnographers. It's also a skill that is honed in many debate clubs. The goal is to understand the multiple ways of making sense of the world and use that to interpret media. Of course, appreciating the view of someone who is deeply toxic isn't always psychologically stabilizing.[19]

boyd's description here really feels like *knowing as strategy*.

To me, the one thing that seems quite clear is that we are in the midst of significant change and disruption. This is probably not a shock to you. If McLuhan was correct and the way society communicates warps itself to what a particular medium allows—*the medium is the message*[20]—then we are still in the throes of change, and it is not at all clear how we will come out the other side. As media scholar Clay Shirky noted when considering how the disruption caused by online technologies compares to the disruptions caused by the printing press one thousand years ago,

> As with the printing press, it doesn't take us from point A to point B. *It takes us from point A to chaos*. The printing press precipitated 200 years of chaos moving from a world where the Catholic church was the sort of organizing political force to the Treaty of Westphalia where we finally knew what the new unit [for political organization] was, the nation state.[21]

Chaos feels like an apt word for the moment.

The feeling of knowing and a better understanding how our mind processes information is surely not the final answer to the current moment. But technological solutions and better reading techniques—such as lateral reading—are not going to be enough to take us where we need to be. The neuroscientists and psychologists haven't figured it all out yet, but they offer a glimpse into how individuals and groups operate. They are not surprised by our propensity to fall for misinformation or by our polarized politics. They can directly connect our political disfunction to the ways that we form groups, build schemas, and process information. We are victims to the feeling of knowing. The neuroscientists and psychologists get it. The rest of us need to catch up. Ultimately, we need to reckon with the fact that information once absorbed into the mind as knowledge is not the same as the source itself. Information is different from knowledge, and the science is showing us why.

I started this book as a kind of exploration, because I was not happy with my understanding of authority and credibility. My exploration has taken me into neuroscience, psychology, philosophy, and several other directions. My assumption as I've been writing this book has been that my peers in librarianship and education will not take my arguments as anything definitive. And I hope that you don't. Clearly, there is much still to figure out. It is my hope that this opens a new line of conversation within our professions. I know that there is great opportunity ahead. And how do I know? . . . I just feel it.

Notes

1. Abraham H. Maslow, *The Farther Reaches of Human Nature* (New York: Arkana, 1993), 188.

2. Marshall McLuhan, *Understanding Media: The Extensions of Man* (New York: McGraw-Hill, 1964).

3. Marshall McLuhan and Quentin Fiore, *The Medium is the Massage: An Inventory of Effects* (New York: Random House, 1967), 68–69.

4. McLuhan, *Understanding Media*; Marshall McLuhan and Wilfred Watson, *From Cliché to Archetype* (New York: Viking, 1970); Wilbur Schramm, *Men, Messages, and Media: A Look at Human Communication* (New York: Harper & Row, 1973).

5. McLuhan, *Understanding Media*, 358.

6. Schramm, *Men, Messages, and Media.*

7. Schramm, *Men, Messages, and Media*, 16.

8. John D. Steinbrenner, *The Cybernetic Theory of Decision: New Dimensions of Political Analysis* (Princeton, NJ: Princeton University Press, 1974).

9. Steinbrenner, *Cybernetic Theory of Decision*, 112.

10. Ann Hughes, *The Causes of the English Civil War* (New York: Palgrave Macmillan, 1998); Kevin Sharpe, *Reading Revolutions: The Politics of Reading in Early Modern England* (New Haven, CT: Yale University Press, 2000).

11. Hughes, *Causes of the English Civil War*; Sharpe, *Reading Revolutions.*

12. Hughes, *Causes of the English Civil War*; Sharpe, *Reading Revolutions.*

13. Meriam Metzger and Andrew J. Flanagin, "Credibility and Trust of Information in Online Environments: The Use of Cognitive Heuristics," *Journal of Pragmatics* 59 (2013): 210–20.

14. Joshua A. Tucker, Andrew Guess, Pablo Barberá, Cristian Vaccari, Alexandra Siegel, Sergey Sanovich, Denis Stuka, and Brendan Nyhan, "Social Media, Political Polarization, and Political Disinformation: A Review of the Scientific Literature," *William and Flora Hewlett Foundation*, March 2018, https://ssrn.com/abstract=3144139; Kathleen Hall Jamieson, *Cyberwar: How Russian Hackers and Trolls Helped Elect a President* (Oxford, UK: Oxford University Press, 2018).

15. danah boyd, "You Think You Want Media Literacy . . . Do You?" *Points: Data & Society*, 2018, https://points.datasociety.net/you-think-you-want-media-literacy-do-you-7cad6af18ec2 (12 Jan 2023).

16. boyd, "You Think You Want Media Literacy . . . Do You?"

17. Maryanne Wolf, *Reader, Come Home: The Reading Brain in a Digital World* (New York: HarperCollins, 2018).

18. Wolf, *Reader, Come Home*, 121.

19. boyd, "You Think You Want Media Literacy . . . Do You?"

20. McLuhan, *Understanding Media.*

21. Clay Shirky, "Clay Shirky: Institutions vs. Collaboration," *TED* (2005), https://youtu.be/sPQViNNOAkw (14 Jan 2023).

Bibliography

Accardi, Marie T., Emily Drabinski, and Alana Kumbier. "Beginning and Extending the Conversation." *Communications in Information Literacy* 14, no. 1 (2020): 1–11. https://pdxscholar.library.pdx.edu/cgi/viewcontent.cgi?article=1409&context=comminfolit (12 Jan 2023).

Alcoff, Linda Martín. "How is Epistemology Political?" In *The Feminist Philosophy Reader*, edited by Alison Bailey and Chris Cuomo, 705–18. Boston: McGraw Hill, 2008.

Alston, William. "Belief-Forming Practices and the Social." In *Socializing Epistemology: The Social Dimensions of Knowledge*, edited by Frederick F. Schmitt, 29–52. Lanham, MD: Rowman & Littlefield, 1994.

André, Christophe. *Feelings and Moods*. Cambridge, UK: Polity Press, 2012.

Appelman, Alyssa, and S. Shyam Sundar. "Measuring Message Credibility: Construction and Validation of an Exclusive Scale." *Journalism and Mass Communication Quarterly* 93, no. 1 (2016): 59–79.

Arazy, Ofer, Rik Kopak, and Irit Hadar. "Heuristic Principles and Differential Judgements in the Assessment of Information Quality." *Journal of the Association for Information Systems* 18, no. 5 (2017): 403–32.

Association of College and Research Libraries. "Framework for Information Literacy for Higher Education." *American Library Association*, 2015. https://www.ala.org/acrl/standards/ilframework (12 Jan 2023).

———. "Information Literacy Competency Standards for Higher Education." *American Library Association*, 2000. http://www.ala.org/acrl/standards/informationliteracycompetency (12 Jan 2023).

Azevedo, Roger, and Vincent Aleven, eds. *International Handbook of Metacognition and Learning Technologies*. New York: Springer, 2013. https://link.springer.com/book/10.1007/978-1-4419-5546-3 (12 Jan 2023).

Ball, B. Hunter, Richard L. Marsh, J. Thadeus Meeks, and Jason L. Hicks. "The Reactivation of Associated Information Affects Source Monitoring." *Memory Cognition* 39, no. 5 (2011): 818–26.

Ball, Linden, and Edward Stupple. "Dual Reasoning Processes and the Resolution of Uncertainty: The Case of Belief Bias." In *Cognitive Unconscious and Human Rationality*, edited by Laura Macchi, Maria Bagassi, and Ricardo Viale. Cambridge, MA: MIT Press, 2016, 143–65.

Barrett, Lisa Feldman. *How Emotions Are Made: The Secret Life of the Brain*. Boston: Mariner Books, 2017.

Bates, Marcia J. "The Invisible Substrate of Information Science." *Journal of the American Society for Information Science* 50, no. 12 (1999): 1043–50.

———, "Toward an Integrated Model of Information Seeking and Searching. Keynote Address, Fourth International Conference on Information Needs, Seeking and Use in Different Contexts." *New Review of Information Behavior Research* 3 (2002): 1–15. https://pages.gseis.ucla.edu/faculty/bates/articles/info_SeekSearch-i-030329.html (12 Jan 2023).

Bateson, Gregory, and Mary Catherine Bateson. *Steps to an Ecology of Mind*. Chicago: University of Chicago Press, 2008.

Bilal, Dania. "Children's Use of Yahooligans! Web Search Engine. III. Cognitive and Physical Behaviors on Fully Self-Generated Search Tasks." *Journal of the American Society for Information Society and Technology* 53, no. 13 (2002): 1170–83.

Bordo, Susan. "Purification and Transcendence in Descartes's Mediations." In *The Feminist Philosophy Reader*, edited by Alison Bailey and Chris Cuomo, 672–87. Boston: McGraw Hill, 2008.

Bourdieu, Pierre. *Distinction: A Social Critique of the Judgment of Taste*. London: Routledge, 1984.

boyd, danah. "You Think You Want Media Literacy . . . Do You?" *Points: Data and Society*, 2018, https://points.datasociety.net/you-think-you-want-media-literacy-do-you-7cad6af18ec2 (12 Jan 2023).

Braasch, Jason L. G.iii, Jean-François Rouet, Nicolas Vibert, and M. Anne Britt. "Readers' Use of Source Information and Text Comprehension." *Memory Cognition* 40, no. 3 (2012): 450–65.

Bratianu, Constantin, and Ivona Orzea. "Emotional Knowledge: The Hidden Part of the Knowledge Iceberg." *Management Dynamics in the Knowledge Economy* 2, no. 1 (2014): 41–56.

Brisson, Janie, Walter Schaefer, Henry Markovits, and Wim De Neys. "Conflict Detection and Logical Complexity." *Psychologica Belgica* 58, no. 1 (2018): 318–32.

Brookes, Bertram C. "Measurement in Information Science." *Journal of the American Society for Information Science* 31, no. 4 (1980): 248–55.

Brookfield, Stephen. *Becoming a Critically Reflective Teacher*. San Francisco: Jossey-Bass, 1995.

Burton, Robert. A. *On Being Certain: Believing You Were Right Even When You're Not*. New York: St. Martin's Griffin, 2008.

———. *A Skeptic's Guide to the Mind: What Neuroscience Can and Cannot Tell Us about Ourselves*. New York: St. Martin's Griffin, 2014.

Cahoy, Ellysa Stern, and Robert Schroeder. "Embedding Affective Learning Outcomes in Library Instruction," *Communications in Information Literacy* 6, no. 1 (2012): 74–90.

Campbell, Virginia. *Are You Sure?: The Unconscious Origins of Certainty*. Hartford, CT: PYP Academy Press, 2020.

Carnes, Nate C., and Ronnie Janoff-Bulman. "Restraining Self-Interest or Enabling Altruism: Morality and Politics." In *Social Psychology of Political Polarization*, edited by Piercarlo Valdesolo and Jesse Graham, 123–42. New York: Routledge, Taylor and Francis Group, 2016.

Case, Donald. *Looking for Information: A Survey of Research on Information Seeking, Needs, and Behavior*, second edition (Amsterdam: Elsevier, 2007).

Caulfield, Mike. "Lesson 1: Introduction to SIFT," https://www.notion.so/Lesson-One-Introduction-to-SIFT-1609b8c742a94173a371db8e61d3a140 (12 Jan 2023).

———. "Web Literacy for Student Fact-Checkers." 2017. https://webliteracy.pressbooks.com/chapter/four-strategies/ (12 Jan 2023).

Chatman, Elfreda A. "A Theory of Life in the Round." *Journal of the American Society for Information Science* 50, no. 3 (1999): 207–17.

Coady, C. A. J. "Speaking of Ghosts." In *Socializing Epistemology: The Social Dimensions of Knowledge*, edited by Frederick F. Schmitt, 75–92. Lanham, MD: Rowman & Littlefield, 1994.

Code, Lorraine. "Taking Subjectivity Into Account." In *The Feminist Philosophy Reader*, edited by Alison Bailey and Chris Cuomo, 718–40. Boston: McGraw Hill, 2008.

Coleman, Jason, and L. Pankl. "Rethinking the Neoliberal University: Critical Library Pedagogy in an Age of Transition." *Communications in Information Literacy* 14, no 1 (2020): 66–74.

Compton, Josh. "Inoculation Theory and Metaliterate Learning." In *Metaliterate Learning for the Post-Truth World*, edited by Thomas P. Mackey and Trudie E. Jacobson, 63–79. Chicago: ALA Neal-Schuman, 2019.

Cooke, Nicole A. "Critical Library Instruction as a Pedagogical Tool." *Communications in Information Literacy* 14, no. 1 (2020): 86–96.

———. "Posttruth, Truthiness, and Alternative Facts: Information Behavior and Critical Information Consumption for a New Age." *Library Quarterly* 87, no. 3 (2017): 211–21.

Cope, Johnathan. "Information Literacy and Social Power." In *Critical Library Instruction: Theories & Methods*, edited by Maria T. Accardi, Emily Drabinski, and Alana Kumbier, 13–27. Duluth, MN: Library Juice Press, 2009.

Corrall, Sheila. "Crossing the Threshold: Reflective Practices in Information Literacy Development." *Journal of Information Literacy* 11, no. 1 (2017): 23–53.

Costa, Daniel Fonseca, Francisval de Melo Carvalho, Bruno César de Melo Moreira, and José Willer do Prado, "Bibliometric Analysis Includes the Association Between Behavioral Finance and Decision Making with Cognitive Biases such as Overconfidence, Anchoring Effect and Confirmation Bias." *Scientometrics* 111, no. 3 (2017): 1775–99.

Crowley, Bill. "Tacit Knowledge, Tacit Ignorance, and the Future of Academic Librarianship." *College and Research Libraries* 62, no. 6 (2001): 566–84.

Csikszentmihalyi, Mihaly. *Flow: The Psychology of Optimal Experience*. New York: Harper and Row, 2009.

Dalrymple, Prudence W. "A Quarter Century of User-Centered Study: The Impact of Zweizig and Dervin on LIS Research." *Library and Information Science Research* 23, no. 2 (2001): 155–65.

Day, Ronald E. "Clearing Up 'Implicit Knowledge': Implications for Knowledge Management, Information Science, Psychology, and Social Epistemology." *Journal of the American Society for Information Science and Technology* 56, no. 6 (2005): 630–35.

De Neys, Wim. "Bias and Conflict: A Case for Logical Intuitions." *Perspectives on Psychological Science* 7, no. 1 (2012): 28–38.

De Neys, Wim, and Michal Bialek. "Dual Processes and Conflict During Moral and Logical Reasoning: A Case for Utilitarian Intuitions?" In *Moral Inferences*, edited by Jean-Francois Bonnefon and Bastien Trémolière, 123–36. London: Taylor and Francis, 2017.

De Neys, Wim, and Samuel Franssens. "Belief Inhibition During Thinking: Not Always Winning but at Least Taking Part." *Cognition* 113, no. 1 (2009): 45–61.

De Neys, Wim, and Tamara Glumicic. "Conflict Monitoring in Dual Process Theories of Thinking." *Cognition* 106, no. 3 (2008): 1248–99.

De Neys, Wim, Elke Moyens, and Debora Vansteenwegen. "Feeling We're Biased: Autonomic Arousal and Reasoning Conflict." *Cognitive, Affective, & Behavioral Neuroscience* 10, no. 2 (2010): 208–16.

De Neys, Wim, Oshin Vartanian, and Vinod Goel. "Smarter Than We Think: When Our Brains Detect That We are Biased." *Psychological Science* 19, no 5 (2008): 483–89.

Depersio, Greg. "The Top 5 US Cities with the Highest Minimum Wage." *Investopedia*, 2022. https://www.investopedia.com/articles/investing/080515/top-5-us-cities-highest-minimum-wage.asp (12 Jan 2023).

Dervin, Brenda. "Comparative Theory Reconceptualized: From Entities and States to Processes and Dynamics." In *Sense-Making Methodology Reader: Selected Writings of Brenda Dervin*, edited by Brenda Dervin, Lois Foreman-Wernet, and Eric Lauterbach, 61–73. Cresskill, NJ: Hampton Press, 2003.

———. "From the Mind's Eye of the User: The Sense-Making Qualitative-Quantitative Methodology." In *Qualitative Research in Information Management*, edited by

Jack D. Glazier and Ronald R. Powell, 61–84. Englewood, CO: Libraries Unlimited, 1992.

———. "Sense-Making's Journey from Metatheory to Methodology to Method." In *Sense-Making Methodology Reader: Selected Writings of Brenda Dervin*, edited by Brenda Dervin, Lois Foreman-Wernet, Eric Lauterbach, 133–65. Cresskill, NJ: Hampton Press, 2003.

Dervin, Brenda, and CarrieLynn D. Reinhard. "How Emotional Dimensions of Situated Information Seeking Relate to User Evaluations of Help from Sources: An Exemplar Study Informed by Sense-Making Methodology." In *Information and Emotion: The Emergent Affective Paradigm in Information Behavior Research and Theory*, edited by Diane Nahl and Dania Bilal, 51–84. Medford, NJ: Information Today, 2007.

Dewey, John. *How We Think*. CreateSpace Independent Publishing, 2014.

Dillard, Cynthia B. "The Substance of Things Hoped for, the Evidence of Things Not Seen: Examining an Endarkened Feminist Epistemology in Educational Research and Leadership." *International Journal of Qualitative Studies in Education* 13, no. 6 (2000): 661–81.

Dodson, Chad S., Emma Powers, and Mariko Lytell. "Aging, Confidence, and Misinformation: Recalling Information with the Cognitive Interview." *Psychology and Aging* 30, no. 1 (2015): 46–61.

Douglas, Veronica Arellano. "Moving from Critical Assessment to Assessment as Care." *Communications in Information Literacy* 14, no. 1 (2020): 46–65.

Doyle, Terry, and Todd Zakrajsek. *The New Science of Learning: How to Learn in Harmony with Your Brain*. Sterling, VA: Stylus Publishing, 2019.

Evanston, Cara, and James Sponsel. "From Syndication to Misinformation: How Undergraduate Students Engage with and Evaluate Digital News." *Communications in Information Literacy* 13, no. 2 (2019): 228–50.

Eyler, Joshua R. *How Humans Learn: The Science and Stories Behind Effective College Teaching*. Morgantown: West Virginia University Press, 2018.

Farmer, Leslie. "The Role of Librarians in Supporting ICT Literacy." *Educause Review*, May 9, 2019. https://er.educause.edu/blogs/2019/5/the-role-of-librarians-in-supporting-ict-literacy (12 Jan 2023).

Fernyhough, Charles. *Pieces of Light: The New Science of Memory*. London: Profile Books, 2013.

Ferretti, Jennifer A. "Building a Critical Culture: How Critical Librarianship Falls Short in the Workplace." *Communications in Information Literacy* 14, no. 1 (2020): 134–52.

Fielding, Jennifer A. "Rethinking CRAAP: Getting Students Thinking Like Fact-Checkers in Evaluating Web Sources." *College and Research Libraries News*, December 2019.

Fisch, Audrey. "Trump, J. K. Rowling, and Confirmation Bias: An Experiential Lesson in Fake News." *Radical Teacher* 111 (Summer 2018): 103–8.

Fisher, Karen E., Sandra Erdelez, and Lynne (E. F.) McKechnie. *Theories of Information Behavior*. Medford, NJ: Information Today, 2005.

Fitzpatrick, Maureen L., and Yvonne Nalani Meulemans. "Assessing an Information Literacy Assignment and Workshop Using a Quasi-Experimental Design." *College Teaching* 59, no. 4 (2011): 142–49.

Foley, Richard. "Egoism in Epistemology." In *Socializing Epistemology: The Social Dimensions of Knowledge*, edited by Frederick F. Schmitt, 53–74. Lanham, MD: Rowman & Littlefield, 1994.

Folk, Amanda. "Drawing on Students' Funds of Knowledge: Using Identity and Lived Experience to Join the Conversation in Research Assignments." *Journal of Information Literacy* 12, no. 2 (2018): 44–59.

———. "Reframing Information Literacy as Academic and Equity-Based Foundation for Practice, Assessment, and Scholarship." *College and Research Libraries* 80, no. 5 (2019): 658–73.

Foreman-Wernet, Lois. "Rethinking Communication: Introducing the Sense-Making Methodology." In *Sense-Making Methodology Reader: Selected Writings of Brenda Dervin*, edited by Brenda Dervin, Lois Foreman-Wernet, and Eric Lauterbach, 3–16. Cresskill, NJ: Hampton Press, 2003.

Foucault, Michel. *Discipline and Punish: The Birth of the Prison*. New York: Vintage Books, 1977.

Fricker, Miranda. "Rational Authority and Social Power: Towards a Truly Social Epistemology." In *Social Epistemology: Essential Readings*, edited by Alvin I. Goldman and Dennis Whitcomb, 54–68. Oxford, UK: Oxford University Press, 2011.

Fulton, Crystal. "Chatman's Life in the Round." In *Theories of Information Behavior*, edited by Karen E. Fisher, Sandra Erdelez, and Lynne (E. F.) McKechnie, 79–82. Medford, NJ: Information Today, 2005.

Galambos, James, and John B. Black. "Using Knowledge of Activities to Understand and Answer Questions." In *The Psychology of Questions*, edited by Arthur C. Graesser and John B. Black, 157–89. Hillsdale, NJ: Routledge, 2017.

Gendlin, Eugene T. *Experiencing and the Creation of Meaning: A Philosophical and Psychological Approach to the Subjective*. Evanston, IL: Northwestern University Press, 1997.

———. *Focusing*. New York: Bantam Books, 2007.

———. *Focusing-Oriented Psychotherapy: A Manual of Experimental Method*. New York: Guilford Press, 1996.

Gibson, Craig, and Trudi Jacobson. "Habits of Mind in an Uncertain Information World." *Reference and User Services Quarterly* 57, no. 3 (Spring 2018): 183–92.

Gilhooly, Ken. "Incubation in Creative Thinking." In *Cognitive Unconscious and Human Rationality*, edited by Laura Macchi, Maria Bagassi, and Ricardo Viale, 301–13. Cambridge, MA: MIT Press, 2016.

Given, Lisa M. "Emotional Entanglements on the University Campus: The Role of Affect in Undergraduates' Information Behaviors." In *Information and Emotion:*

The Emergent Affective Paradigm in Information Behavior Research and Theory, edited by Diane Nahl and Dania Bilal, 161–76. Medford, NJ: Information Today, 2007.

Goffman, Erving. *Frame Analysis: An Essay on the Organization of Experience*. Cambridge, MA: Harvard University Press, 1974.

Goldberger, Nancy Rule. "Cultural Imperatives and Diversity in Ways of Knowing." In *Knowledge, Differences, and Power: Essays Inspired by* Women's Ways of Knowing, edited by Nancy Rule Goldberger, Jill Mattuck Tarule, Blythe Clinchy McVicker, and Mary Field Belenky, 335–71. New York: Basic Books, 1996.

Goldman, Alvin I. "A Guide to Social Epistemology." In *Social Epistemology: Essential Readings*, edited by Alvin I. Goldman and Dennis Whitcomb, 11–37. Oxford, UK: Oxford University Press, 2011.

———. *Knowledge in a Social World*. Oxford, UK: Clarendon Press, 1999.

Gopnik, Alison. *The Gardener and the Carpenter: What the New Science of Child Development Tells Us About the Relationship Between Parents and Children*. New York: Farrar, Straus, and Giroux, 2016.

Hall Jamieson, Kathleen. *Cyberwar: How Russian Hackers and Trolls Helped Elect a President*. Oxford, UK: Oxford University Press, 2018.

Halling, Steen, and Mical Goldfarb. "Grounding Truth in the Body: Therapy and Research Renewed." *Humanistic Psychologist* 19, no. 3 (Autumn 1991): 313–30.

Harada, Violet H. "Personalizing the Information Search Process: A Case Study of Journal Writing with Elementary-Age Students." *School Library Media Research* 5 (2002). http://hdl.handle.net/10125/40191 (13 Jan 2023).

Harding, Sandra. "'Strong Objectivity' and Socially Situated Knowledge." In *The Feminist Philosophy Reader*, edited by Alison Bailey and Chris Cuomo, 741–56. Boston: McGraw Hill, 2008.

Head, Alison J., Barbara Fister, Steven Geofrey, and Margy MacMillan, "The Project Information Literacy Retrospective: Insights from More Than a Decade of Information Literacy Research, 2008–2022." *Project Information Research Institute* (12 October 2022). https://projectinfolit.org/publications/retrospective (13 Jan 2023).

Heinström, Jannica. *From Fear to Flow: Personality and Information Interaction*. Oxford, UK: Chandos Publishing, 2010.

———. "Psychological Factors Behind Incidental Information Acquisition." *Library and Information Science Research* 28, no. 4 (2006): 579–94.

Hilligoss, Brian, and Soo Young Rieh. "Developing a Unifying Framework of Credibility Assessment: Construct, Heuristics, and Interaction in Context." *Information Processing and Management* 44, no. 4 (2008): 1467–84.

Hofer, Amy R., Silvia Lin Hanick, and Lori Townsend. *Transforming Information Literacy Instruction: Threshold Concepts in Theory and Practice*. Santa Barbara, CA: Libraries Unlimited, 2019.

Hoffman, Donald. *The Case Against Reality: Why Evolution Hid the Truth from Our Eyes*. New York: Norton, 2019.

Holiday, Wendy, and Qin Li. "Understanding the Millennials: Updating our Knowledge about Students." *Reference Services Review* 32, no. 4 (2004): 356–66.

Honma, Todd, and Clara Chu. "Positionality, Epistemology, and New Paradigms for LIS: A Critical Dialog with Clara M. Chu." In *Pushing the Margins: Women of Color and Intersectionality in LIS*, edited by Rose L. Chou and Annie Pho, 447–65. Sacramento, CA: Library Juice Press, 2018.

Hughes, Ann. *The Causes of the English Civil War*. New York: Palgrave Macmillan, 1998.

Isen, Alice M. "Positive Affect and Decision Making." In *Handbook of Emotion*, second edition, edited by Michael Lewis and Jeannette M. Haviland, 417–35. New York: Guilford Press, 2000.

Jagger, Alison M. "Love and Knowledge: Emotion in Feminist Epistemology." In *The Feminist Philosophy Reader*, edited by Alison Bailey and Chris Cuomo, 687–705. Boston: McGraw Hill, 2008.

James, William. *The Varieties of Religious Experience: A Study in Human Nature Being the Gifford Lectures on Natural Religion Delivered at Edinburgh in 1901–1902*. New York: Longmans, Green, and Co., 1917). https://www.gutenberg.org/ebooks/621 (Dec 2023).

Jasanoff, Alan. *The Biological Mind: How Brain, Body, and Environment Collaborate to Make Us Who We Are*. New York: Basic Books, 2018.

Johnson, J. David. *Cancer-Related Information Seeking*. Cresskill, NJ: Hampton Press, 1997.

———. *Information Seeking: An Organizational Dilemma*. Westport, CT: Quorum Books, 1996.

———. "On Contexts of Information Seeking." *Information Processing and Management* 39, no. 5 (2003): 735–60.

Johnson, Marcia K., Shahin Hashtroudi, and D. Stephen Lindsay. "Source Monitoring." *Psychological Bulletin* 114, no. 1 (1993): 3–28.

Kahneman, Daniel. *Thinking, Fast and Slow*. London: Penguin, 2012.

Kahneman, Daniel, and Amos Tversky. "Prospect Theory: An Analysis of Decision under Risk." *Econometrica* 47, no. 2 (1979): 263–91.

Kaufman, Charlie. "Charlie Kaufman On Being—And Directing." *Fresh Air*, October 23, 2008. https://www.npr.org/transcripts/96023004 (13 Jan 2023).

Kitcher, Philip. "Contrasting Conceptions of Social Epistemology." In *Socializing Epistemology: The Social Dimensions of Knowledge*, edited by Frederick F. Schmitt, 111–34. Lanham, MD: Rowman & Littlefield, 1994.

Klintman, Mikael. *Knowledge Resistance: How We Avoid Insight from Others*. Manchester, UK: Manchester University Press, 2019.

Komlodi, Anita. "Cultural Models of Hall and Hofstede." In *Theories of Information Behavior*, edited by Karen E. Fisher, Sandra Erdelez, and Lynne (E. F.) McKechnie, 108–12. Medford, NJ: Information Today, 2005.

Kornblith, Hilary. "A Conservative Approach to Social Epistemology." In *Socializing Epistemology: The Social Dimensions of Knowledge*, edited by Frederick F. Schmitt, 93–110. Lanham, MD: Rowman & Littlefield, 1994.

Kracker, Jacqueline, and Peiling Wang. "Research Anxiety and Students' Perceptions of Research: Part II. Content Analysis of Their Writings on Two Experiences." *Journal of the American Society for Information Science and Technology* 53, no. 4 (2002): 295–307.

Kruks, Sonia. "Women's 'Lived Experience': Feminism and Phenomenology from Simone de Beauvoir to the Present." In *The SAGE Handbook of Feminist Theory*, edited by Mary Evans, Clare Hemings, Marsha, Hazel Johnstone, Sami Machon, Ania Plomien, and Sadie Wearing, 75–92. Los Angeles: SAGE Reference, 2014.

Kuhlmann, Beatrice, Ute J. Bayen, Katharina Meuser, and Anna E. Kornadt. "The Impact of Age Stereotypes on Source Monitoring in Younger and Older Adults." *Psychology and Aging* 31, no. 8 (2016): 875–89.

Kuhlthau, Carol Collier. "Kulthau's Information Search Process." In *Theories of Information Behavior*, edited by Karen E. Fisher, Sandra Erdelez, and Lynne (E. F.) McKechnie, 230–34. Medford, NJ: Information Today, 2005.

———. "Rethinking the 2000 ACRL Standards: Some Things to Consider." *Communications in Information Literacy* 7, no. 2 (2013): 92–97.

———. *Seeking Meaning: A Process Approach to Library and Information Literacy Services*. Westport, CT: Libraries Unlimited, 2004.

Kuhlthau, Carol, Janice Heinstron, and Ross J. Todd. "The 'Information Search Process' Revisited: Is the Model Still Useful?" *Information Research* 13, no. 4 (December 2008): 45–59.

Kunda, Ziva. "The Case for Motivated Reasoning." *Psychological Bulletin* 108, no. 3 (1990): 480–98.

Land, Ray, and Jan H. F. Meyer. "Threshold Concepts and Troublesome Knowledge: Dynamics of Assessment." In *Overcoming Barriers to Student Understanding: Threshold Concepts and Troublesome Knowledge*, edited by Jan H. F. Meyer and Ray Land, 61–79. London: Routledge, 2006.

LeDoux, Joseph. *The Deep History of Ourselves: The Four-Billion-Year Story of How We Got Conscious Brains*. New York: Viking, 2019.

Letherby, Gayle "Feminist Auto/Biography." In *The SAGE Handbook of Feminist Theory*, edited by Mary Evans, Clare Hemings, Marsha, Hazel Johnstone, Sami Machon, Ania Plomien, and Sadie Wearing, 45–60. Los Angeles: SAGE Reference, 2014.

Leung, Sofia Y., and Jorge R. López-McKnight. "Dreaming Revolutionary Futures: Critical Race's Centrality to Ending White Supremacy." *Communications in Information Literacy* 14, no. 1 (2020): 12–27. https://pdxscholar.library.pdx.edu/cgi/viewcontent.cgi?article=1407&context=comminfolit (13 Jan 2023).

Linvill, Darren. "The Relationship Between Student Identity Development and the Perception of Political Bias in the College Classroom." *College Teaching* 59, no. 2 (2011): 49–55.

Lodge, Milton, and Charles S. Taber. "'Why People "Don't Trust the Evidence': Motivated Reasoning and Scientific Beliefs." *Annals of the American Academy of Political and Social Sciences*, March 2015, 121–33.

Longino, Helen E. "The Fate of Knowledge in Social Theories of Science." In *Socializing Epistemology: The Social Dimensions of Knowledge*, edited by Frederick F. Schmitt, 135–58. Lanham, MD: Rowman & Littlefield, 1994.

Luhtala, Michelle, and Jacquelyn Whiting. *News Literacy: The Keys to Combating Fake News*. Santa Barbara, CA: Libraries Unlimited, 2018.

Mackey, Thomas, and Trudi E. Jacobson. *Metaliteracy: Reinventing Information Literacy and Empowering Learners*. Chicago: ALA Neal-Schuman, 2014.

Mahoney, Michael. "Connected Knowing in Constructive Psychotherapy." In *Knowledge, Differences, and Power: Essays Inspired by Women's Ways of Knowing*, edited by Nancy Rule Goldberger, Jill Mattuck Tarule, Blythe Clinchy McVicker, and Mary Field Belenky, 126–43. New York: Basic Books, 1996.

Maslow, Abraham H. *The Farther Reaches of Human Nature*. New York: Arkana, 1993.

Materska, Katarzyna. "Information Heuristics of Information Literate People." *Communications in Computer and Information Science* 492 (2014): 59–69.

Mathiesen, Kay. "Informational Justice: A Conceptual Framework for Social Justice in Library and Information Services." *Library Trends* 64, no. 2 (Fall 2015): 198–225.

Matteson, Miriam Louise, and Beate Gersch. "Information Literacy Instruction in Public Libraries." *Journal of Information Literacy* 14, no. 2 (2020): 71–95.

McCann, Carole R., and Seung-Kyung Kim. "Introduction: Theorizing Feminist Times and Spaces." In *Feminist Theory Reader: Local and Global Perspectives*, edited by Carole R. McCann and Seung-Kyung Kim, 11–28. New York: Routledge, 2017.

McCann, Carole R., and Seung-Kyung Kim. "Introduction Section II: Theorizing Feminist Times and Spaces." In *Feminist Theory Reader: Local and Global Perspectives*, edited by Carole R. McCann and Seung-Kyung Kim, 165–79. New York: Routledge, 2017.

McCann, Carole R., and Seung-Kyung Kim. "Introduction Section III: Theorizing Feminist Knowledge and Agency." In *Feminist Theory Reader: Local and Global Perspectives*, edited by Carole R. McCann and Seung-Kyung Kim, 351–66. New York: Routledge, 2017.

McKenzie, Pamela J. "Justifying Cognitive Authority Decisions: Discursive Strategies of Information Seekers." *Library Quarterly* 73, no. 3 (2003): 261–88.

———. "A Model of Information Practice in Accounts of Everyday Life Information Seeking." *Journal of Documentation* 59, no 1 (2003): 19–40.

McLuhan, Marshall. *Understanding Media: The Extensions of Man*. New York: McGraw-Hill, 1964.

McLuhan, Marshall, and Quentin Fiore. *The Medium is the Massage: An Inventory of Effects*. New York: Random House, 1967.

McLuhan, Marshall, and Wilfred Watson. *From Cliché to Archetype*. New York: Viking, 1970.

Mercier, Hugo. *Not Born Yesterday: The Science of Who We Trust and What We Believe*. Princeton: Princeton University Press, 2020.

Mercier, Hugo, Pierre Bonnier, and Emmanuel Trouche. "Why Don't People Produce Better Arguments?" In *Cognitive Unconscious and Human Rationality*, edited by Laura Macchi, Maria Bagassi, and Ricardo Viale, 205–18. Cambridge, MA: MIT Press, 2016.

Mercier, Hugo, and Dan Sperber. *The Enigma of Reason: A New Theory of Human Understanding*. London: Penguin, 2018.

Mercier, Hugo, and Dan Sperber. "Why Do Humans Reason? Arguments for an Argumentative Theory." *Behavioral and Brain Sciences* 34, no. 2 (2011): 57–111.

Metzger, Meriam, and Andrew J. Flanagin. "Credibility and Trust of Information in Online Environments: The Use of Cognitive Heuristics." *Journal of Pragmatics* 59 (2013): 210–20.

Meyer, Jan, and Ray Land. "Threshold Concepts and Troublesome Knowledge: Linkages to Ways of Thinking and Practicing within the Disciplines." *Enhancing Teaching-Learning Environments in Undergraduate Courses* http://www.etl.tla.ed.ac.uk/docs/ETLreport4.pdf (13 Jan 2023).

Middendorf, Joan, and David Pace. "Decoding the Disciplines: A Model for Helping Students Learn Disciplinary Ways of Thinking." *New Directions for Teaching and Learning* 98 (2004): 1–12.

Miwa, Makiko. "Bandura's Social Cognition." In *Theories of Information Behavior*, edited by Karen E. Fisher, Sandra Erdelez, and Lynne (E. F.) McKechnie, 54–57. (Medford, NJ: Information Today, 2005).

Mon, Lorri. "Face Threat." In *Theories of Information Behavior*, edited by Karen E. Fisher, Sandra Erdelez, and Lynne (E. F.) McKechnie, 149–53. Medford, NJ: Information Today, 2005.

Nahl, Diane. "Affective Load." In *Theories of Information Behavior*, edited by Karen E. Fisher, Sandra Erdelez, and Lynne (E. F.) McKechnie, 39–43. Medford, NJ: Information Today, 2005.

———. "The Centrality of the Affective in Information Behavior." In *Information and Emotion: The Emergent Affective Paradigm in Information Behavior Research and Theory*, edited by Diane Nahl and Dania Bilal, 3–37. Medford, NJ: Information Today, 2007.

———. "A Conceptual Framework for Defining Information Behavior." *Studies in Multimedia Information Literacy Education* 1, no. 2 (2001): 1–16.

———. "Measuring the Affective Information Environment of Web Searchers." *Proceedings of the 67th Annual Meeting of the American Society for Information Science and Technology*, 41. Medford, NJ: Information Today, 2004.

Napier, Jaime L., and Jamie B. Luguri. "From Silos to Synergies: The Effects of Construal Level." In *Social Psychology of Political Polarization*, edited by Piercarlo Valdesolo and Jesse Graham, 143–62. New York: Routledge, Taylor and Francis Group, 2016.

Neiman, Astrida. "Natural Others? On Nature, Culture, and Knowledge." In *The SAGE Handbook of Feminist Theory*, edited by Mary Evans, Clare Hemings,

Marsha, Hazel Johnstone, Sami Machon, Ania Plomien, and Sadie Wearing, 26–44. Los Angeles: SAGE Reference, 2014.

Pace, David, and Peter Reigler. "Decoding the Disciplines: Improving Student Learning." http://decodingthedisciplines.org/ (13 Dec 2023).

Pagel, Mark D. *Wired for Culture: Origins of the Human Social Mind*. New York: Norton, 2013.

Pankle, Elisabeth, and Jason Coleman. "'There's Nothing on My Topic!' Using the Theories of Oscar Wilde and Henry Giruous to Develop Critical Pedagogy for Library Instruction." In *Critical Library Instruction: Theories & Methods*, edited by Maria T. Accardi, Emily Drabinski, Alana Kumbier, 3–12. Duluth, MN: Library Juice Press, 2009.

Parker, Nicola, and Jennifer Berryman. "The Role of Affect in Judging 'What is Enough.'" In *Information and Emotion: The Emergent Affective Paradigm in Information Behavior Research and Theory*, edited by Diane Nahl and Dania Bilal, 85–95. Medford, NJ: Information Today, 2007.

Pena, Michelle M., J. Zoe Klemfuss, Elizabeth F. Loftus, and Amelia Mindthoff. "The Effects of Exposure to Differing Amounts of Misinformation and Source Credibility Perception on Source Monitoring and Memory Accuracy." *Psychology of Consciousness: Theory, Research, and Practice* 4, no. 4 (2017): 337–47.

Pennycook, Gordon, Jonathan A. Fugelsang, and Derek J. Koehler. "What Makes Us Think? A Three-Stage Dual-Process Model of Analytic Engagement." *Cognitive Psychology* 80 (August 2015): 34–72.

Peters, M. "Metabolism." *British Medical Association A–Z Family Medical Encyclopedia*. London: Dorling Kindersley, 2004.

Pham, Michel Tuan. "Emotion and Rationality: A Critical Review and Interpretation of Empirical Evident." *Review of General Psychology* 11, no. 2 (2007): 155–78.

Pinker, Steven. *Rationality: What It Is, Why It Seems Scarce, Why It Matters*. London: Allen Lane, 2021.

Raoelison, Mattieu, Valerie A. Thompson, and Wim de Neys. "The Smart Intuitor: Cognitive Capacity Predicts Intuitive Rather Than Deliberate Thinking." *Cognition* 204 (June 2020). https://www.sciencedirect.com/science/article/pii/S0010027720302006 (14 Jan 2023).

Rieh, Soo Young. "Cognitive Authority." In *Theories of Information Behavior*, edited by Karen E. Fisher, Sandra Erdelez, and Lynne (E. F.) McKechnie, 83–87. Medford, NJ: Information Today, 2005.

———, "Judgment of Information Quality and Cognitive Authority in the Web." *Journal of the American Society for Information Science and Technology* 53, no. 2 (2002):145–61. https://doi.org/10.1002/asi.10017.abs.

Rippon, Gina. *Gender and Our Brains: How Neuroscience Explodes the Myths of the Male and Female Minds*. New York: Pantheon Books, 2019.

Russo, Alyssa, Amy Jankowski, Stephanie Beene, and Lori Townsend. "Strategic Source Evaluation: Addressing the Container Conundrum." *Reference Services Review* 47, no. 3 (2019): 294–313.

Ryles, Gilbert. *The Concept of Mind*. London: Hutchinson, 1949.

Sapolsky, Robert M. *Behave: The Biology of Humans at Our Best and Worst*. New York: Penguin Books, 2017.

Saunders, Laura, and John Budd. "Examining Authority and Reclaiming Expertise." *Journal of Academic Librarianship* 46, no. 1 (2020). https://doi.org/10.1016/j.acalib.2019.102077 (12 Jan 2023).

Saunders, Laura, and Melissa A. Wong. *Instruction in Libraries and Information Centers: An Introduction*. Champaign, IL: Windsor and Downs Press, 2020.

Savolainen, Reijo, "Emotions as Motivators for Information Seeking: A Conceptual Analysis. *Library and Information Science Research* 36, no. 1 (2010): 59–65.

———, "Everyday Life Information Seeking." In *Encyclopedia of Library and Information Sciences*, third edition, edited by Marcia J. Bates and Mary Niles Maack, 1780–89. Boca Raton, FL: CRC Press, 2010.

———, "Everyday Life Information Seeking." In *Theories of Information Behavior*, edited by Karen E. Fisher, Sandra Erdelez, and Lynne (E. F.) McKechnie, 143–48. Medford, NJ: Information Today, 2005.

———, "Expressing Emotions in Information Sharing: A Study of Online Discussion about Immigration." *Information Research* 20, no. 1 (2015). http://InformationR.net/ir/20-1/paper662.html (15 Jan 2023).

———, "Heuristics Elements of Information-Seeking Strategies and Tactics: A Conceptual Analysis." *Journal of Documentation* 73, no. 6 (2017): 1322–42.

———, "Information Behavior and Information Practice: Reviewing the 'Umbrella Concepts' of Information-Seeking Studies." *Library Quarterly* 77, no. 2 (2007): 109–32.

———, "The Interplay of Affective and Cognitive Factors in Information Seeking and Use." *Journal of Documentation* 71, no. 1 (12 January 2015): 175–97.

———, "Self-Determination and Expectancy-Value." *Aslib Journal of Information Management* 70, no. 1 (15 January 2018): 123–40.

Schmitt, Frederick F. "The Justification of Group Beliefs." In *Socializing Epistemology: The Social Dimensions of Knowledge*, edited by Frederick F. Schmitt, 257–87. Lanham, MD: Rowman & Littlefield, 1994.

———. "Socializing Epistemology: An Introduction Through Two Sample Issues." In *Socializing Epistemology: The Social Dimensions of Knowledge*, edited by Frederick F. Schmitt, 1–28. Lanham, MD: Rowman & Littlefield, 1994.

Schramm, Wilbur. *Men, Messages, and Media: A Look at Human Communication*. New York: Harper and Row, 1973.

Seale, Maura. "Critical Library Instruction, Causing Trouble, and Institutionalization." *Communications in Information Literacy* 14, no. 1 (2020): 75–85.

Shannon, Claude. "A Mathematical Theory of Communication." *Bell System Technical Journal* 27 (July and October 1948): 379–423, 623–56.

Shannon, Claude E., and Warren Weaver. *The Mathematical Theory of Communication*. Urbana: University of Illinois Press, 1949.

Sharpe, Kevin. *Reading Revolutions: The Politics of Reading in Early Modern England.* New Haven, CT: Yale University Press, 2000.

Shirky, Clay. "Clay Shirky: Institutions vs Collaboration," *TED* (2005), https://youtu.be/sPQViNNOAkw (14 Jan 2023).

Sigle-Ryshton, Wendy. "Essentially Quantified? Towards a More Feminist Modeling Strategy." In *The SAGE Handbook of Feminist Theory*, edited by Mary Evans, Clare Hemings, Marsha, Hazel Johnstone, Sami Machon, Ania Plomien, and Sadie Wearing, 431–45. Los Angeles: SAGE Reference, 2014.

Smith, Dolsy. "Iterable Ciphers for Insurrection." *Communications in Information Literacy* 14, no. 1 (2020): 28–45.

Soergel, Andrew. "24 U.S. States Will See a Minimum Wage Increase in 2020." *U.S. News—The Civic Report*, January 2020, C16–C19.

Solms, Mark. *The Hidden Spring: A Journey to the Source of Consciousness*. New York: Norton, 2021.

Stanovich, Keith E. *Rationality and the Reflective Mind.* (Oxford, UK: Oxford University Press, 2011).

"State Minimum Wages: Most States Have Raised Their Minimum Wage Above the Federal Level." *Supreme Court Debates* 24, no. 4 (2021): 14–15.

Steinberg, Laurence. "A Social Neuroscience Perspective on Adolescent Risk-Taking." *Developmental Review: DR* 28, no. 1 (2008): 78–106.

Steinbrenner, John D. *The Cybernetic Theory of Decision: New Dimensions of Political Analysis*. Princeton, NJ: Princeton University Press, 1974.

Stipling, Barbara. "Inquiry: Inquiring Minds Want to Know." *School Library Media Activities Monthly* 25, no. 1 (September 2008): 50–52.

Stonebreaker, Ileana, and Heather A. Howard. "Evidence-Based Decision-Making: Awareness, Process, and Practice in the Management Classroom." *Journal of Academic Librarianship* 44, no. 1 (2018): 113–17.

Sturges, Paul. "The Brain at the Centre of the Information Universe: Lessons from Popular Neuroscience." *Libellarium* 7, no. 1 (2014): 3–15.

Sunstein, Cass R. "Deliberating Groups versus Prediction Markets (or Hayek's Challenge to Habermas." In *Social Epistemology: Essential Readings*, edited by Alvin I. Goldman and Dennis Whitcomb, 314–37. Oxford, UK: Oxford University Press, 2011.

Surowiecki, James. *The Wisdom of Crowds: Why the Many are Smarter Than the Few*. London: Abacus, 2014.

Swanson, Troy A., and Heather Jagman, *Not Just Where to Click: Teaching Students How to Think About Information*. Chicago: Association of College and Research Libraries, American Library Association, 2015.

Taber, Charles, and Milton Lodge. "Motivated Skepticism in the Evaluation of Political Beliefs." *American Journal of Political Science* 50, no. 3 (2006): 755–69.

Tatum, Beverly Daniel. "The Complexity of Identity: 'Who Am I?'" In *Readings for Diversity and Social Justice*, edited by Maurianne Adams, Warren J. Blumenfeld, D. Chase J. Catalano, Keri "Safire" DeJong, Heather Hackman, Larissa E. Hopkins,

Barbara J. Love, Madeline L. Peters, Davey Shlasko, and Ximena Zúñiga, 7–9. New York: Routledge, 2018.

Thompson, Valerie A., Nicole H. Therriault, and Ian R. Newman. "Meta-Reasoning: Monitoring and Control of Reasoning, Decision Making, and Problem Solving." In *Cognitive Unconscious and Human Rationality*, edited by Laura Macchi, Maria Bagassi, and Ricardo Viale, 275–99. Cambridge, MA: MIT Press, 2016.

Tidline, Tonyia. "Dervin's Sense-Making." In *Theories of Information Behavior*, edited by Karen E. Fisher, Sandra Erdelez, and Lynne (E. F.) McKechnie, 113–14. Medford, NJ: Information Today, 2005.

Todd, Ross J. "Back to Our Beginnings: Information Utilization, Bertram Brookes, and the Fundamental Equation of Information Science." *Information Processing and Management* 35, no. 6 (1999): 851–70.

———. "Information Intents." In *Theories of Information Behavior*, edited by Karen E. Fisher, Sandra Erdelez, and Lynne (E. F.) McKechnie, 198–203. Medford, NJ: Information Today, 2005.

Tokuhama-Espinosa, Tracey. *The New Science of Teaching and Learning: Using the Best of Mind, Brain, and Education Science in the Classroom*. New York: Teachers College Press, 2010.

Torrell, Margaret Rose. "That Was Then, This Is Wow: A Case for Critical Information Literacy Across the Curriculum." *Communications in Information Literacy* 14, no. 1 (2020): 118–33.

Trippas, Dries, Simon J. Handley, and Michael F. Verde. "The SDT Model of Belief Bias: Complexity, Time, and Cognitive Ability Mediate the Effects of Believability." *Journal of Experimental Psychology* 39, no. 5 (2013): 1393–1402.

Tucker, Joshua A., Andrew Guess, Pablo Barberá, Cristian Vaccari, Alexandra Siegel, Sergey Sanovich, Denis Stuka, and Brendan Nyhan. "Social Media, Political Polarization, and Political Disinformation: A Review of the Scientific Literature." *William and Flora Hewlett Foundation*, March 2018, https://ssrn.com/abstract=3144139 or http://dx.doi.org/10.2139/ssrn.3144139 (17 Jan 2023).

Tversky, Amos, and Daniel Kahneman. "Rational Choice and the Framing of Decisions." *Journal of Business* 59, no. 4 (1986): 251–78.

Van der Kolk, Bessel A. *The Body Keeps the Score: The Brain, Mind, and Body in the Healing of Trauma*. New York: Viking, 2014.

Viael, Riccardo. "Brain-Based Bounded Creativity." In *Cognitive Unconscious and Human Rationality*, edited by Laura Macchi, Maria Bagassi, and Ricardo Viale, 315–44. Cambridge, MA: MIT Press, 2016.

von Hippel, William. *The Social Leap: The New Evolutionary Science of Who We Are, Where We Come from and What Makes Us Happy*. New York: Harper Wave, 2018.

Webb, Jennifer. *The Metacognition Handbook: A Practical Guide for Teachers and School Leaders*. Suffolk: John Catt Educational, 2021.

Whitmire, Ethelene. "Epistemological Beliefs and the Information-Seeking Behavior of Undergraduates." *Library and Information Science Research* 25, no. 2 (2003): 127–42.

Williamson, Kristy. "Discovered by Chance: The Role of Incidental Information Acquisition in an Ecological Model of Information Use." *Library and Information Science Research* 20, no. 1 (1998): 23–40.

———. "Ecological Theory of Human Information Behavior." In *Theories of Information Behavior*, edited by Karen E. Fisher, Sandra Erdelez, and Lynne (E. F.) McKechnie, 128–32. Medford, NJ: Information Today, 2005.

Wilson, E. O. *The Social Conquest of Earth*. New York: Liveright, 2012.

Wilson, Patrick. *Second-Hand Knowledge*. Westport, CT: Greenwood Press, 1983.

Wilson, Tom D. "Models in Information Behavior Research" *Journal of Documentation* 55, no. 3 (1999): 249–70.

———. "On User Studies and Information Needs." *Journal of Documentation* 62, no. 6 (2006): 658–70.

Wineburg, Sam, and Sarah McGrew. "Lateral Reading: Reading Less and Learning More When Evaluating Digital Information." *Stanford History Education Group* (September 2017). https://papers.ssrn.com/sol3/papers.cfm?abstract_id=3048994 (13 Jan 2023).

Wolf, Maryanne. *Reader, Come Home: The Reading Brain in a Digital World*. New York: HarperCollins, 2018.

Zakharov, Wei, Haiyan Life, and Michael Fosmire. "Undergraduates' News Consumption and Perceptions on Fake News in Science." *Portal: Libraries and the Academy* 19, no. 4 (2019): 653–65.

Zull, James E. *From Brain to Mind: Using Neuroscience to Guide Change in Education*. Sterling, VA: Stylus Publishing, 2011.

~

Index

About the Author

Troy Swanson is Library Department Chair and Teaching & Learning Librarian at Moraine Valley Community College, where he manages the faculty librarians, teaches information literacy, and coordinates the library's online presence. He is an adjunct faculty member at Dominican University's School of Information Studies. He is also the Legislative Chair for Cook County Teachers Union (IFT/AFT Local 1600) and has served as the president of the Moraine Valley Faculty Association.

Troy is the author or editor of several books and articles including coeditor of *Not Just Where to Click: Teaching Students How to Think About Information* which received the Ilene F. Rockman Publication of the Year Award from ACRL's Instruction Section. Starting in 2017, Troy has guest hosted a series on dis/misinformation for the *Circulating Ideas* podcast. He served on ACRL's Information Literacy Competency Standards for Higher Education Task Force, which drafted the *Framework for Information Literacy in Higher Education*. Over his tenure as a librarian and educator, Troy received his campus's Master Teacher and Innovation of the Year awards, as well as the ProQuest Innovation in College Librarianship award from ACRL.

www.ingramcontent.com/pod-product-compliance
Ingram Content Group UK Ltd.
Pitfield, Milton Keynes, MK11 3LW, UK
UKHW041450071026
15587UKWH00010B/724

9 781538 178928